Food Festival!

THE ULTIMATE GUIDEBOOK TO AMERICA'S BEST REGIONAL FOOD CELEBRATIONS

Alice M. Geffen
Carole Berglie

Grateful acknowledgment is made to the following for permission to reprint previously published material:

"Scampi in Butter Sauce" from *Garlic Lover's Cookbook*. Reprinted by permission of the Gilroy Garlic Festival Association, Inc.

"Deviled Crab" from *Crabbiest Recipes from the Annual Crab Cooking Contest*. Reprinted by permission of the National Hard Crab Derby Annual Crab Cooking Contest. Recipe submitted and prepared by Miss Nicki Dixon, Crisfield, Maryland.

"Wild Boar Sausage," "Venison Meat Loaf," and "Rabbit Pie" from *Annual Wild Game Supper Cookbook (From Beaver to Buffalo)*, published by the Annual Wild Game Supper, United Church of Christ, Bradford, Vermont.

"Hancock Dill Bread," "Sister Mary's Zesty Carrots," and "Rose Water Frozen Cream" from *The Best of Shaker Cooking* by Amy Bess Miller and Persis Fuller. Copyright © 1970 by Shaker Community, Inc. Reprinted by permission of Macmillan Publishing Company, Inc.

"Scallop Fritters," "Pickled Bluefish," and "Herring Roe and Eggs" from *Strange Seafood Recipes*, a cookbook compiled from the annual Strange Seafood Exhibition. Reprinted by permission of North Carolina Maritime Museum, Beaufort, North Carolina.

"Persimmon Upside-Down Cake" and "Brown County Persimmon Fudge" from *Old-Fashioned Persimmon Recipes*. Reprinted by permission of BEAR WALLOW PUBLICATIONS: The Old-Fashioned Recipes Series/& *Backroads Travel* Magazine and Guide.

Library of Congress Cataloging-in-Publication Data

Geffen, Alice M. Food festival!
Includes index.
1. Harvest festivals—United States—Directories. 2. Cookery, American.
3. Festivals—United States— 3. Festivals—United States—Directories.
I. Berglie, Carole. II. Title.
GT4403.G44 1986   394.2'6973   85-43461
ISBN 0-394-72966-8

Photographs throughout by Alice M. Geffen
Illustrations and calligraphy by Lilla Rogers
Design by Sara Reynolds
Manufactured in the United States of America

First Edition

Food Festival!

Pantheon Books

New York

To the memory of our mothers,
who made every meal festive

Contents

Contents

Acknowledgments

We would like to thank Barbara Kouts, Nan Graham, and Wendy Wolf for their help and encouragement. In addition, we are grateful to the many people connected with the various festivals who supplied us with information and made us welcome. Heartfelt thanks are also due to the relatives and friends with whom we stayed while traveling and to those closer to home who cheerfully sampled the recipes. Lastly, we are indebted to Raymond Sokolov, Jane and Michael Stern, and Calvin Trillin, whose books and articles on American food inspired us.

Introduction

SEVERAL YEARS AGO, while smacking our lips at our favorite annual chicken barbeque—given by the Cutchogue (New York) Fire Department—we began to think that there must be thousands of such local food celebrations and festivals all over the country. We decided to explore this premise. Our first stop was the Wild Game Supper in Bradford, Vermont, where we ate eight different kinds of game, prepared in a multitude of ways. And that was just the beginning. There followed the Hatch (New Mexico) Chile Festival, the McClure (Pennsylvania) Ninetieth Annual Bean Soup Festival, Michigan's Morel Hunt, the Indio (California) Date Festival, the Circleville (Ohio) Pumpkin Show, a Florida Mullet Festival, the Black-Eyed Pea Jamboree (Texas), and a Northwest Coast Indian-Style Salmon Bake, as we ate our way through the calendar and across America.

Many of these festivals have gained nationwide recognition, and, for some, tickets have to be ordered as much as a year in advance. Food festivals combine the excitement of a celebration with the fresh taste of local foods and the honesty of homemade preparations. In an era of potato flakes and imitation bacon bits, it's comforting to have the real thing.

This book is a chronicle of our adventures and a guidebook to outstanding festivals. It is also a cookbook, offering a tasting from festivals from all over the United States.

The book is arranged by seasons of the year, since many festivals center around seasonal foods. Not every festival could be included—strawberry festivals alone could fill a book—but we've attempted to give a sampling—those that stand out because they offer a little something special. We admit a certain bias toward festivals that have a small-town character, those that close down the town for the weekend or involve all the schoolchildren in painting the shop windows and making posters. We think that festivals are most fun when the music gets people moving, the parades bring cheers from the sidelines, and the cooking contests make local heroes of housewives.

The food, of course, is our major consideration. Most food festivals are stand-up affairs, where you go from booth to booth and sample different foods using the same ingredient (as at the Garlic Festival) or different preparations of the same food (as at the Boudin Festival). Some festivals have sit-down meals in addition to the booths (as at the Egg Festival), and a few are in themselves a meal (notably the dinner at the Shaker Kitchen Festival and the Bradford Wild Game Supper). Some are all-you-can-eat affairs (the Chincoteague Oyster Festival), but most are pay-as-you-go. Food varies from booth to booth, but somehow the crowd always knows: head for the booths with the longest lines or biggest crowds, for they will usually have the best food.

Festivals range in length from one day to two weeks. We have never spent more than two days at a festival, but there are families who come for the weekend or whole week. It's not unusual to see a section of the park or fairgrounds set aside for campers. Festivals are ideal entertainment for whole families. There's almost always something special going on for children, but there are also events and activities for retired people, locals, tourists, singles, and teenagers. Many festivals have a midway, often set off to the side. Almost all have at least one stage, for concerts, contests, and award ceremonies. Starting in the 1970s, many festivals added a foot race, some of which are officially sanctioned, but all of which attract an astonishing number of runners. Some festivals are agricultural fairs, so they have judgings for the best-looking livestock or produce. Often festivals include competitions that mean a great deal to the people in the region, like the ox pull at the Maine Egg Festival or the garlic topping in Gilroy, California. A great many have eating contests, races against time that are usually embarrassing but always a lot of fun. Other festivals have zany events like bed races or crazy costumes. We've also seen our share of tractor pulls, mud hops, and tugs-of-war. Most festivals have beauty pageants; after all, what kind of festival would it be without a queen to kiss the winners, award trophies, and generally assure that everyone has a good time?

Flea markets and crafts booths are a standard feature at festivals, and they vary in quality. Sometimes it's a chance to buy a unique country-made item, but more often than not the things for sale are from commercial kits or are so similar that they appear to be. We've also noticed that antique cars, old fire engines, and early farm equipment are big stuff. The parades are frequently a chance to sport these items, along with huge pieces of agricultural equipment, such as combines and tractors.

These are usually interspersed with high school marching bands, waving politicians, floats, and beauty queens in Corvette convertibles.

What you can expect in an hour or a day at a festival depends on your interests. Although we've enjoyed the carnival rides and games of chance, and attended the concerts and watched the races, our primary interest is the food. For that reason, we discuss only festivals whose emphasis is on a particular food. General street fairs, although fun, are not included in this book. Nor are the restaurant festivals (such as the famous "Taste of Chicago") nor broad ethnic fairs (like New York's Ninth Avenue International Food Festival) nor even specific ethnic fairs (such as the many Italian feasts in Boston).

Some festivals could not be included for lack of time. Often several festivals are held on the same weekend; we had to choose one. In all cases, we chose those that emphasized the food (over the arts and crafts) or were special in another way. With two exceptions (Lexington Barbeque Festival and International Zucchini Festival), all the festivals we've included have been going strong for at least five years—many for more than ten.

In this book we have focused on American foods and the celebrations surrounding them. Some festivals zero in on a local specialty, like the Maine Lobster Festival or the Windsor (Connecticut) Shad Derby. Some call attention to a food that remains unknown to most of the country, like the Persimmon Festival in Mitchell, Indiana, or La Belle's Swamp Cabbage Festival in Florida. Whereas many festivals celebrate a particular raw ingredient—like apples or rice or pecans—others involve a prepared item—like Louisiana boudin (a sausage), North Carolina's barbeque (chopped pork in a vinegar-based sauce), Rhode Island's johnnycake (a cornmeal pancake), and Illinois's burgoo (beef and vegetable stew). A number are also educational (the Strange Seafood Exhibition and the Indian Foods Dinner); a few are just plain funny (the Zucchini Festival and the Okra Strut); and one is a real extravaganza (the Bracebridge Dinner).

Food festivals are fun and joyous. They celebrate harvest and bounty. They are America letting loose for a party. We have tried to communicate some of that fun to you. We hope you'll go to all of them (as we have) and eat yourself silly and have a great time doing it.

Winter / Early Spring

Road Closed Festival Day!

Riverside County NATIONAL DATE FESTIVAL

FEB.12-21

Boudin Festival

Broussard, Louisiana

*B*OU-DIN! BOU-DIN! BOU-DIN!" The crowd cheers. It's the Boudin-Eating Contest at the annual Broussard Boudin Festival, held in Arceneaux Park, just south of town. The festival starts with the Boudin Marathon Run at 8:00 A.M. on Saturday and ends with a Greased Pig Contest on Sunday. In between are such lusty events as a boudin-making demonstration, a jambalaya tasting, some cracklin' making, and two boudin-eating contests—one for men, one for women. Throughout both days a variety of bands occupy the stage—Cajun, country-western, or French country-western, with names like Rockin' Dupsie, The Wheels, Atchafalaya, and Gurvin Matte and the Branch Playboys. There are also arts and crafts displays and a small section set aside for rides for children.

Boudin is a traditional Cajun food—a sausage consisting primarily of rice, pork, and seasonings. The pork mixture is simmered until soft, then piped into thick casings and tied in links. Depending upon how much cayenne is added, the boudin may be quite mild or blazing hot. The proportion of meat to rice determines to a large extent how juicy the sausage is: more pork, better boudin. Boudin is what you might call the hot dog of Acadiana.

Boudin booths are in the middle of the park, not far from the beer-wagon and the bandstand. Each booth sells its own version of the different types of boudin: mild white, white hot (the kind used in the eating contests), and the denser red boudin (made with pork blood). There's also a booth selling both mild and hot versions of a seafood boudin—not traditional, but still in the Cajun spirit. You can also buy some of the best cracklin' you'll ever get, plus barbecued pork chops, hot barbecued sausages, and po' boy sandwiches on fresh French bread loaves. The Knights of Columbus are selling jambalaya, made that morning in a huge caldron and stirred with a canoe paddle. And at one booth men are roasting a suckling pig in a "coon-ass microwave," a homemade oven with coals on top and the pig inside.

We sampled all the eats, then concentrated on the various types of boudin. The seafood hot we found the most interesting. It being our first, we ate the casings. Later, sampling the white, we did what most experienced boudin eaters do, we squeezed the sausage meat out of the casings with our teeth. This method allows you to focus on the boudin: more succulent stuffing, less tough casing. We found the red (sold only by LeBoeuf's, a local butcher and boudin maker) to be good but gamey; it's clearly an acquired taste. The white hot is the most popular, deservedly so. The cracklin's were crisp and salty and so popular they sold out early; and the pork chops had been smoked to a delicious turn.

Without doubt, the boudin-eating contests are the highlight of the festival. The crowd presses in eagerly to see who can consume the most the fastest. Every contestant is given three pounds of hot white boudin and three minutes in which to eat it. At the end of the time, whatever is left on the plate is weighed. The one with the least left is the winner and is crowned as such. The women's contest is the same, with the exception that the women don't have to eat the casings. Last year, the winner exclaimed, "I'm a small guy, but I can pack it in!" When it gets to the last thirty seconds or so, the crowds starts chanting, "Boo-DAHN! Boo-DAHN!" and cheering and clapping as the contestants stuff in as much as they can manage.

Amidst the beer, crowds, and spicy food, the alluring smells of various barbecues waft through the air. The music is nonstop, foot-stompin' Cajun and country; there is an atmosphere of joy, fun, and celebration. All kinds of people come—white, black, young, old, teenagers with their dates, parents with young children, middle-aged people with parents. And everyone has fun—*le boudin est fait du porc, c'est bon le boudin; c'est Cajun.*

Boudin Blanc

Here is a recipe for the standard type of boudin, most popular at the festival. This version is moderately hot, but if you prefer, adjust the quantity of red pepper up or down. Casings are available from butchers who make their own sausage, and in some supermarkets or specialty shops. Or you can order them by mail from Standard Casings, 121 Spring

Street, New York, New York 10012. If you don't have a sausage horn, you can improvise with a wide-nozzle funnel and the end of a wooden spoon.

3 pounds boneless pork shoulder
4 onions, chopped
10 scallions (both green and white parts), chopped
1 cup chopped celery leaves
½ cup chopped fresh parsley
2 teaspoons salt, or to taste
1 teaspoon black pepper, or to taste

6 cups cooked rice (preferably medium grain)
2 teaspoons cayenne pepper, or to taste
5 feet of sausage casing, soaked in warm water to soften for about 15 minutes

Place the meat in a large pot and cover with about ½ inch water. Bring to a boil and cook until tender, about 1 hour. Drain and set aside, reserving the cooking liquid.

Add the onions to the meat-cooking liquid and simmer over medium heat until soft. Add the scallions, celery leaves, and parsley and simmer until soft, then add the salt and black pepper. While the onions and scallions cook, break up the meat into small shreds or cubes. Add to the onions and scallions and cook until the water is almost evaporated, about 20 minutes. The meat will become very soft, and the mixture will take on a characteristic "gamey" aroma. When there is no more liquid in the pot, add the rice and mix well. Season with additional salt and pepper if desired, and add cayenne pepper to taste. Let the mixture cool to room temperature.

Rinse the casings by running water through them. This will also let you check for any breaks or tears in the skin. Fit the casing onto a sausage machine or onto the tip of a large-mouthed funnel. Stuff the casing with the rice-meat mixture, tying links about every 6 inches. Leave a slight (¼ inch) gap between the links so that you can cut them apart later should you wish. Fill all the casings, pricking the skin occasionally to release air that may have become trapped in the filling. Push the filling down into the casings so that they are tight, then tie the ends. The boudin are now ready to be boiled and served, or they can be frozen for later use.

When ready to eat, bring a large kettle of water to a boil and add the boudin. Heat until warmed through, about 10 minutes, then serve immediately. To eat, use your teeth and lips to pull the stuffing out of the casings, then discard casings.

Makes about 12 to 15 links, each about 6 inches long

Hot Seafood Boudin

We weren't able to get the actual recipe from the Crab House in Lafayette, which has a booth at the festival each year, but this recipe comes as close as any mortal can to their wonderful spicy boudin.

1 cup cooked long-grain rice
½ pound shelled raw shrimp,
    chopped fine
½ pound fresh or frozen crab
    meat, picked over and
    shredded
2 scallions (both white and
    green parts), minced
2 cloves garlic, minced
1 teaspoon salt
1 teaspoon cayenne pepper
1 tablespoon Tabasco sauce
¼ cup cracker meal
2 feet of sausage casings,
    soaked in warm water for
    15 minutes to soften

Mix the rice with the shrimp, crab meat, scallions, garlic, and seasonings. Add the cracker meal to bind the mixture so that you have a moist but compact stuffing.

Rinse the casings, then fit onto a sausage machine or onto the tip of a large-mouthed funnel. Stuff the mixture into the casings, occasionally pricking the casing to release any air that might have accumulated in the filling. Make links about 6 inches long, tying both ends and leaving a little room between the ties so that you can cut the links later if you wish.

When ready to eat, bring a large kettle of water to a boil and add the sausages. Boil for about 8 to 10 minutes, or until thoroughly heated. Serve immediately. Eat as you would boudin blanc, and wash them down with lots of beer.

Makes about 7 links, each about 6 inches long

THE LOUISIANA BOUDIN FESTIVAL is held the last weekend of February in Arceneaux Park, Broussard. Most events take place on Saturday between noon and 6, and Sunday between 10 and 6. There is no admission charge. Parking is wherever you can find a spot—either on the street or in a field behind the park. Individual booths sell food and drinks. There are about eight boudin booths; in addition, some booths sell jambalaya and barbecue; boudin runs about $2 a link.

Broussard is in southern Louisiana's Cajun country, about eleven miles south of Lafayette, off U.S. 90. For additional information, contact Martin Richard, Broussard, Louisiana 70518.

National Date Festival

Indio, California

WHAT A PERFECT BREAK from a cold winter! Actually it's more than just a date festival. Officially it's the Riverside County Fair, complete with midway, parade, pageant, cotton candy, and contests. Our favorite contest was the newspaper fold and toss, open to all newspaper deliverers. But wait—there's a newspaper fold and toss for *retired* (over sixty) deliverers as well! Other contests are the diaper derby, the dumbest-thing-I ever-saw olympics, a kitchen band contest, bearderino (a beard-growing) contest, and the "senior" olympics (lime golf, grapefruit shotput, and orange bowling for the young at heart). Scheduled events include daily camel and ostrich races, a parade with bands and elaborate floats, and live entertainment in the Shalimar Theatre.

Indio goes all out for this event—at the bank, tellers are dressed as Arabian princesses, and merchants conduct business in turbans. Everyone gets into the spirit, and that is what makes the National Date Festival much more than a county fair. Queen Scheherazade, crowned on the first night, holds court while visitors pay tribute to the exotic fruit of the desert.

You'll soon realize why dates are called the fruit of the desert. Forget those tough and tasteless packaged dates found in supermarkets. Here is the real thing, in over one hundred varieties—Medjhool, Black Beauty, Blonde, Brunette, Black Abada, Deglet Noor, Haziz, Thoory, Amirhaji, Saidy, Honey, Empress, to name a few. It's a bit of old Arabia in southern California.

The Coachella Valley of southern California is the only area in the Western Hemisphere where dates are grown commercially. Growers planted their first date trees around 1900—shoots from Algeria and Iraq that blossomed into a $3 million industry. The most widely grown dates are the Deglet Noors: 32 million pounds a year. The large Medjhools, soft and sensuous, are the most popular (and are often available nationally in natural foods stores). At the festival we discovered the Black

Abada—an excitingly different taste, capturing the mysteries of the East. Some of the local date growers have sales booths by the Shalimar Mall. There you can sample many of the varieties, buy a pound of dates to eat on the spot, or arrange to ship packages of dates home. If only there had been more booths and more samples.

Near the booths is the exhibit hall—the "Taj Mahal"—where the valley farmers display their cotton, potatoes, lettuce, and dairy products. But the most elaborate displays are for dates and citrus. One grower had a huge rotating table with a (papier-mâché) snake charmer, in the center, piping music. On the table were dishes, all carefully labeled, showing the many uses of dates: ice cream, cakes, cereals, candies, cookies, brownies, muffins, rolls, plus date granola, date sugar, date butter, date flakes, and date bits. Another exhibit featured a five-foot-high pyramid of dates surrounded by a "desert" of date calyxes (buds). The big citrus display was a "garden" with "porch pillars" made of oranges and grapefruits. Along the walls were box after box, row after row, of perfect dates— each variety clearly named. Date growing is also explained in a special exhibit. And a date orchard is located at the south entrance to the fair- grounds.

The fairgrounds are huge. Walkways are lined on both sides with booths selling all kinds of food—from Indian fry bread to tacos to hot dogs—and merchandise—from crazy hats to stuffed animals to belt buck- les. Inside the concession halls are yet more booths, these with people hawking floor cleaners, hand creams, furniture, chain saws, organs, books, games, even word processors. There is also a gems and minerals hall, a fine arts and photo gallery, a livestock exhibition, and a flower and garden show. The carnival area is off to one side, with games and rides for both children and adults. The camel races and other such events are held on the grandstand stage; many of these attractions cost extra.

An event that does not cost extra is the Arabian Nights Pageant, given nightly at 6:45. Don't miss this cast of one hundred as they assemble under the "Arabian sky" to present the story of Aladdin and the Magic Lamp. The show is described by the fair organizers as "an exciting Persian tale of romance and intrigue that ends in triumphant love."

We found all of the commercial offerings distracting at this festival, and we would have wished more emphasis on the dates, especially more opportunities to eat different kinds of dates. However, the festival draws over 175,000 visitors each year, and they come for everything that is offered. It really is more than a date festival; it's entertainment for the thousands of people who come seeking a warm, fun-filled break from winter. A date ice-cream cone under a sunny sky can be just that.

The following two recipes are from Hadley Date Gardens, one of the growers who exhibit and sell dates at the festival.

Date Waffles

These waffles are excellent with fig or rhubarb jam, or even maple syrup. If you wish, add more chopped dates for an even datier flavor.

2 cups all-purpose flour
½ teaspoon salt
2 teaspoons baking powder
2 large eggs, separated

4 tablespoons (½ stick) butter,
*   melted and cooled*
2 cups milk
1 cup finely chopped pitted dates

In a large bowl, sift together the flour, salt, and baking powder, then gradually add the egg yolks, melted butter, and milk, beating until the mixture is perfectly smooth. Add the chopped dates and stir to blend. In a separate bowl, beat the egg whites until stiff, then fold into the date mixture.

Heat a waffle iron until hot and add about ½ cup batter, or enough to fill your iron. Cook the waffles until done and serve immediately.

Serves 6

Moist Date-Nut Bread

This is a lighter bread than most date-nut loaves, with a marbled effect that results when the dates darken portions of the light-colored batter. It is also refreshingly not too sweet.

1 cup applesauce
3 tablespoons vegetable
*   shortening*
¾ cup chopped walnuts
1 cup chopped pitted dates
1½ teaspoons baking soda

½ teaspoon salt
2 large eggs
1 teaspoon vanilla extract
1 cup sugar
1½ cups sifted all-purpose
*   flour*

In a small saucepan, heat the applesauce until almost boiling, then add the shortening, allowing it to melt; stir to blend well and remove from the heat. In a medium mixing bowl, combine the walnuts, dates, baking soda, and salt and stir with a fork until the fruit and nut bits are dusted and separated. Add the hot applesauce mixture and let stand for 20 minutes.

Preheat the oven to 325°F. Grease a 9-by-5-inch loaf pan.

In a large mixing bowl, beat the eggs until foamy, then add the vanilla and sugar and mix again until blended. Add the applesauce-date mixture and stir until blended. Gradually add the flour until the mixture is smooth. Turn the batter into the loaf pan and bake for 1 hour, or until a cake tester comes out clean. Allow to cool in the pan for 10 minutes, then turn out onto a wire rack to finish cooling. Wrap in foil and let sit overnight at room temperature before slicing. This loaf also freezes well.

Makes 1 large loaf

The following two recipes are from Shields Date Gardens. Shields is the only grower that sells date crystals, which are dehydrated bits of dates. The crystals store for long periods and can be reconstituted easily, to be used in any recipe that calls for chopped dates. You can order date crystals—as well as a variety of other date products—from Shields Date Gardens, 80-225 Highway 111, Indio, California 92201.

Date-Fudge Cake

2 tablespoons boiling water
½ cup date crystals
¼ cup vegetable shortening
2 squares (2 ounces) semisweet
*   chocolate*
½ cup water
1 cup sugar

1 large egg
1 cup sifted all-purpose flour
½ teaspoon salt
½ teaspoon baking soda
¼ cup sour milk (see note)
1 teaspoon vanilla extract

Pour the boiling water over the date crystals in a small bowl. Allow to swell while you prepare the rest of the recipe. Preheat the oven to 350°F. Grease an 8-by-8-by-2-inch cake pan and dust with flour.

Over low heat, melt the shortening in a small saucepan and add the chocolate. When the chocolate has melted, add the ½ cup water and the sugar. Stir until well blended, then remove from the heat and allow to cool.

When the chocolate mixture has cooled, add the egg and mix well. Gradually add the flour and the salt. Dissolve the baking soda in the sour milk and add to the batter. Add the vanilla and the reconstituted date crystals and blend well. Pour the batter into the pan and bake for 30 minutes, or until a cake tester comes out clean. Allow to cool in the pan for 10 minutes, then turn out onto a wire rack to finish cooling.

NOTE: To make sour milk quickly, add a few drops of distilled white vinegar to the ¼ cup milk. Or substitute ¼ buttermilk if you have it on hand.

Indio Date Ice Cream

This creamy rich ice cream contains bits of dates. Use it to make a date shake or serve it with a dark chocolate sauce.

1 cup date crystals	*Pinch salt*
1 cup milk	*2 cups half and half*
2 large eggs	*1 vanilla bean, split in half, or 1*
½ cup sugar	*tablespoon vanilla extract*
1½ tablespoons all-purpose flour	*2 cups heavy cream (see note)*

Soak the date crystals in the milk for about 1 hour, or until plumped. Beat the eggs in a mixing bowl until light and foamy; set aside.

In a heavy saucepan over low heat, combine the sugar, flour, and salt. Gradually stir in the half and half and continue stirring until the mixture is smooth. Add the vanilla bean (if using) and cook the mixture over very low heat, stirring constantly until all the ingredients are thoroughly dissolved and the mixture thickens, about 15 minutes.

Scoop out a small ladleful of the hot mixture and stir it into the beaten eggs to warm them. Then pour the egg mixture into the saucepan and cook for a few minutes more, stirring gently. Remove the vanilla bean; it will have flavored the cream. (If you are using the extract, add it at this point.) Add the reconstituted date crystals (and any liquid that remains), then chill the mixture in the refrigerator for several hours.

When the mixture has cooled completely, stir in the cream and process in your ice-cream freezer according to the manufacturer's directions. Pour into containers and freeze. *Makes about 1 quart*

NOTE: For a lighter version of this ice cream, substitute 2 additional cups of half and half for the cream.

THE NATIONAL DATE FESTIVAL is held at Indio the middle of February, usually for ten days. All events take place at the fairgrounds, Route 111 and Arabia Street, Indio. Admission to the grounds ($4 adult, $2 children) includes all stage and arena attractions and the pageant, but extra fees are charged for many entertainment events. Dates and date products are for sale at the festival; a date ice-cream cone costs about $1.50. Other foods (hamburgers, tacos, and so forth) are sold at many stands; a taco runs $3 or so. Dates (in bulk) and date products are also for sale at local farm stands, off the fairgrounds; prices at the farm stands differ.

Indio is about 150 miles east of Los Angeles, off I-10. For further information, contact Riverside County National Date Festival, P.O. Drawer NNNN, Indio, California 92202; phone (714) 342-8247.

Swamp Cabbage Festival

La Belle, Florida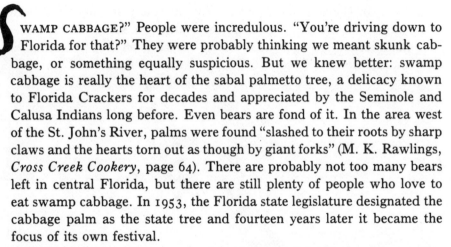

"SWAMP CABBAGE?" People were incredulous. "You're driving down to Florida for that?" They were probably thinking we meant skunk cabbage, or something equally suspicious. But we knew better: swamp cabbage is really the heart of the sabal palmetto tree, a delicacy known to Florida Crackers for decades and appreciated by the Seminole and Calusa Indians long before. Even bears are fond of it. In the area west of the St. John's River, palms were found "slashed to their roots by sharp claws and the hearts torn out as though by giant forks" (M. K. Rawlings, *Cross Creek Cookery*, page 64). There are probably not too many bears left in central Florida, but there are still plenty of people who love to eat swamp cabbage. In 1953, the Florida state legislature designated the cabbage palm as the state tree and fourteen years later it became the focus of its own festival.

In times past, cabbage palm logs were used for dock pilings or log cabin walls. Hats, mats, and baskets are still made from the leaves. The sabal palmetto is also a favorite landscape plant of Florida. In fact, cabbage palms are so much a part of everyday life all over the state that schools and churches, crossroads and cemeteries often bear the cabbage prefix: Cabbage Grove School, or Cabbage Palm Church. The palms are found in hammocks, pinelands, and savannahs, in swamp forests and wet prairies.

There is some controversy as to whether or not it is legal to cut down the trees—for the entire tree must be cut in order to get the "heart," leading one writer to call hearts of palm "millionaire's salad." What we were able to discover is that the trees are protected by law, but you can cut swamp cabbage on private property if you have the written permission of the landowner. In La Belle, during the last weekend of February, there must have been a lot of written permissions: about eight hundred trees were cut to feed the crowds. Luckily the sabal palmetto is plentiful. Some harvesters claim that the tree reseeds itself and that, under natural growing conditions, three trees will replace each one that is cut during a five-year period.

Once the palmetto is cut, the heart is removed and prepared in one of many ways: raw in a salad, braised and served like a vegetable, used in baking cakes and cookies, baked in casseroles, deep-fried as fritters (a special treat at the festival), or steam-fried with white bacon. Stewed with bacon is the way it is served at the festival, as a vegetable to accompany the barbecued steak or barbecued ribs.

The Swamp Cabbage Festival is held beneath gracefully arching live oaks that grow along the Caloosahatchee River. Spanish moss and air plants hang from the spreading limbs and give you the feeling of being inside a spider's web. Among the palmettos and low-growing shrubs, booths decorated with palm fronds are set up to sell crafts, cook food, and offer information (some political campaigning goes on here, as it does at most festivals). Many of the booths are run by Seminole Indians, who sell their colorful shirts and jackets, as well as make pumpkin bread, hamburgers and tacos, and wonderful fruit-filled fry breads. Most people buy a platter of barbecue, served with stewed swamp cabbage, or try the fritters, which are served crisp and very hot. The cabbage itself has a mild taste, delicate and slightly reminiscent of artichoke hearts. Its texture varies, with some pieces very firm and others quite soft. The difference depends on where on the bud the pieces are cut; ones from closest to the center are the softest.

It is possible to buy a bud at the festival and take it home. We did so, and hefted our three-foot long, twenty-pound stump into the trunk of the car. When trimmed and peeled it would yield a heart weighing about three pounds. Once home, we had to boot it out, which is to say, peel the many layers of waxy leaves off to get at the tender (the heart). The end is called the turnip, and the outside cover, the boot. Layer by layer we removed the tough outer leaves until we had a cream-colored tip. It was almost ivory, so pure and smooth. But the tip discolors quickly, so we sliced it for our pot and quickly covered the cut pieces with cold water until we were ready to stew it. An average bud, such as we had, would serve eight people.

A demonstration of booting out a cabbage is held each year at the festival to acquaint the newcomers with this technique. But it is a lot easier to come to the festival; enjoy the entertainment, parade, and beauty queens; and eat the swamp cabbage already prepared.

Stewed Swamp Cabbage

This is the way the cabbage is served at the festival, and the way that most Floridians prefer it. Once you've booted it out, the cooking is easy. This recipe uses half of an average heart, so you can chop the remainder for salad.

½ heart swamp cabbage
½ pound streaky salt pork
½ cup water

Using a stainless-steel knife to avoid discoloration, chop the cabbage into about 1-inch pieces. You should have about 5 cups chopped cabbage. Cover with cold water and set aside.

Chop the salt pork into 4 or 5 large pieces and render in a large pot or Dutch oven. If possible, use a stainless-steel pot. Once you've got a goodly amount of fat rendered out (about half the salt pork), drain and add the cabbage along with the additional ½ cup water. Bring to a boil, cover, and reduce the heat to a simmer. Cook the cabbage for 1½ hours, or until nicely softened and the flavors have blended. Serve hot, with barbecue or roasted meats.   *Serves 4*

THE SWAMP CABBAGE FESTIVAL is held in La Belle on the last full weekend in February. Most activities take place on Saturday, including the parade, although there are plenty of goings-on on Sunday, too. Swamp cabbage is served with dinners on both days. The steak and swamp cabbage platter costs about $7. The "bud" we bought was $5. There are no admission charges; parking is in a field nearby, about a three-minute walk from Barron Park. Most events take place at the park, except the dances and the quilt show. The parade comes right by the park.

La Belle is at the intersection of Routes 29 and 80, about 35 miles east of Fort Myers. For information and a schedule of events, write Greater La Belle Chamber of Commerce, P.O. Box 456, La Belle, Florida 33935; or phone (813) 675-0125.

Vermont Maple Festival

St. Albans, Vermont

WHEN THE DAFFODILS were blooming and the forsythias full, we headed north to Vermont, where the only sign of spring was the steam rising from the maple sugarhouses. Snow was still on the ground (and there was a forecast for more that night), but the sap was running and sugarhouses were in full operation. It was mid-April and time for the Vermont Maple Festival, held each year (since 1967) in St. Albans, Franklin County.

Franklin County, population 35,000, is the largest producer of maple syrup in the United States—several million gallons annually. But hard times have hit Franklin County, as they have the entire industry, for maple syrup coming from Canada in recent years has been providing stiff competition for this old American standby.

The festival kicked off on Friday with the assembling of the world's largest sundae: As the festival brochure claimed, "A recession is like an ice-cream sundae—You have to learn how to lick it." Into it went 18,225 pounds of ice cream; 300 pounds of whipped cream; 1,000 pounds of maple syrup; 1,000 pounds of chocolate chips; a truckload of peaches from Alabama, a planeload of pineapples from Hawaii, plus strawberries, cherries, walnuts, and pistachios. Construction started at 8:30 in the morning and wasn't completed till noon, when the eating began.

Saturday opened with a pancake breakfast—with maple syrup, of course. Then the various exhibits opened up: arts and crafts, antiques, and the maple exhibition. Sugar makers competed for the highest quality products in eight categories (maple cream, maple fudge, maple syrup, and Indian sugar, to name a few). There were over fifty samples of syrup, which led one of the judges to quip, "There isn't a sweeter job in St. Albans." There was also a demonstration of maple-candy making, and you could stroll past the other educational exhibits while enjoying a cup of maple coffee with a maple-glazed doughnut. Free samples of maple syrup helped us learn about the different grades—fancy, grade A medium amber, and grade A dark amber. Although fancy was light and delicate, and A medium was mild and syrupy, we preferred A dark for its more robust, intense maple flavor. The grade depends on the sugar content of the sap and the holding time in the evaporator. The lighter syrups are the earlier ones in the season and those that come out of the evaporator first. Grade A dark is enhanced by a sweet caramel taste and, though recommended for use in baking and cooking, is no slouch on pancakes either.

At the festival you can buy just about everything maple: maple fudge, cupcakes, cheesecakes, dumplings (hot), bars, sundaes, taffy, popcorn, cream. But perhaps the biggest novelty for us was the maple cake, a small square of freshly boiled-down syrup. It's pure maple—intense and sugary, not creamy as are maple cream candies. And there was also an old favorite, "sugar on the snow," which is hot maple syrup poured onto crushed ice. The syrup stiffens instantly, and you eat the taffylike candy with a pickle on the side to cut the sweetness. It's fun and reminded one of us of her childhood in upstate New York, where she poured maple syrup on real snow and ate it.

The whole town is involved in the Maple Festival, and many shop windows have maple-related displays. The main street is blocked off, and in the middle are the booths as well as the contests, including a pancake-flipping contest, a maple syrup and pillow event (like a tar and feathering, only using maple syrup), a maple can throw, and the lumberjack events (cross-cut sawing, log chopping, chain-saw cutting, log rolling, and skidding logs with horses through an obstacle course). A cooking contest is also a feature of the festival, and the restaurant in the department store on the main street features samples of the winning recipes from the morning's judging.

Saturday night brought the maple banquet, highlighted by maple-cured baked ham and a maple cake. Three hundred people sat at long tables and listened for their name, or the names of friends and neighbors, as the winners of various contests were announced. A statewide maple essay contest had been held; the Maple Queen was crowned; and "Mrs. Maple," the winner of the cooking contest, was named. The agricultural awards were also made, and we learned that most of the sugar making is still in family businesses, passed down from generation to generation.

After dinner, most people drove over to the nearby Bellows Free Academy auditorium for the fiddlers' contest. Others, we are sure, kicked up their heels at the Maple Dance. We opted for the fiddling, really more of a fun country music and dance show, complete with clogging, joke telling, harmonica playing, and singing—songs like "Pork 'n Beans,"

"Buckwheat Batter," and the "Green Mountain Waltz." The dynamic ten-member Julie Beaudoin family played the piano, accordion, guitar, recorder, fiddle, and spoons while they tap-danced and sang. Most festivals are daytime events, and very few have any real evening entertainment, so this show was a treat.

We didn't want to leave Vermont without visiting a sugarhouse. On the outskirts of town we saw steam rising into the sky, and we pulled over to an unprepossessing wooden building. Inside were the long, wide tubs—the evaporators—bubbling wildly atop a large firebox. Sap is collected from mid-February through April, traditionally in buckets attached to taps in the trees, though nowadays a sugar maker often just hooks up plastic tubing from the tree tap directly into the sugarhouse. The gathered sap is stored in large tanks and flows into the evaporators as needed. Depending on the sugar content of the sap, from twenty-five to sixty gallons of sap are boiled down to make one gallon of maple syrup. We bought a couple of taps to take home and try on our maple tree . . . and a gallon of syrup in case the taps didn't work.

Maple recipes are distributed freely at the festival, and the ones that follow are adaptations courtesy of the Vermont Department of Agriculture.

Maple Baked Ham

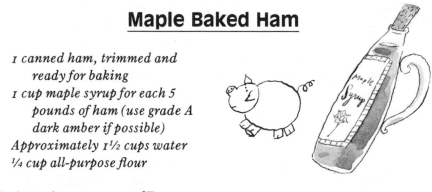

1 canned ham, trimmed and
*   ready for baking*
1 cup maple syrup for each 5
*   pounds of ham (use grade A*
*   dark amber if possible)*
Approximately 1½ cups water
¼ cup all-purpose flour

Preheat the oven to 350°F.

Place the ham in a heatproof baking dish and bake, uncovered, until half done (allow about 15 to 20 minutes per pound). As the ham bakes, remove some of the drippings from the pan and set them aside.

Pour the maple syrup over the ham, letting it drip down into the pan. Continue baking the ham until done; if the top begins to brown too much, cover lightly with foil, removing it just before serving in order to crisp the top. As the ham cooks, the syrup will caramelize in the pan. If desired, baste the ham with the pan juices.

When the ham is done, remove it from the pan and set aside. With the baking pan set over high heat, add about ½ cup water to the pan and stir to loosen the caramelized maple syrup; it will soften and blend with the water. Mix the flour with the reserved ham drippings, making a smooth paste, then add about 1 cup water and mix well; add the mixture to the baking pan. Bring to a boil, stirring constantly. A thickened, dark brown sauce will form. Serve the sauce hot in a bowl or pitcher and pour over the slices of ham.

Vermont Maple Baked Beans

1 quart (2 pounds) dried yellow-
  eye or navy beans
½ teaspoon baking soda
2 teaspoons salt
1 medium onion, peeled

¼ cup molasses
3 tablespoons maple syrup (pref-
  erably grade A dark amber)
½ teaspoon dry mustard
½ pound salt pork

Wash and pick over the beans, then cover with cold water. Add the baking soda and soak overnight. In the morning, rinse the beans and cover with fresh water. Parboil until the skins wrinkle, about 10 minutes, then drain off the bean water and set both beans and cooking water aside.

Place the whole onion in the bottom of a bean pot or casserole with a tight-fitting lid. Add the beans, molasses, maple syrup, and mustard. Stir to blend. Score the salt pork and place it on top of the beans, then slowly pour the reserved bean-cooking water down the sides of the pot until the beans are covered with liquid. Cover the pot and bake in a slow oven (about 325°F) for about 8 hours. Check periodically, adding more water as needed to keep the beans moist while they bake.

When the beans are firm but done, uncover the pot and bake for an additional hour to crisp the salt pork. *Serves about 8*

Maple-Bread Pudding

This is our favorite maple dessert. The custard and bread pudding cook on top while the maple syrup and raisins are below. When served, the maple sauce at the bottom is poured over the top.

¾ cup maple syrup (preferably grade A dark amber)
3 slices white bread, with crusts removed
1 tablespoon butter or margarine
½ cup chopped nuts or raisins
1 teaspoon lemon juice
2 large eggs
2 cups milk
¼ teaspoon salt
¼ teaspoon vanilla extract

Pour the maple syrup into the top of a double boiler and heat over hot water. Butter each slice of bread, then cube the slices and add to the syrup. Stir in the nuts or raisins and the lemon juice.

Beat the eggs, milk, salt, and vanilla together and pour over the bread mixture. Do not stir. Cover and set over gently boiling water to cook for 1 hour. Check the level of the water in the bottom of the double boiler and refill with hot water if it drops too low.

Scoop out servings of pudding and place them in individual bowls. Pour the maple sauce over and serve at once.   *Serves 6*

Maple-Walnut Fudge

Every Vermont cook seems to have a recipe for maple fudge. This version is our adaptation of the best of them—but it makes only a small quantity, for those who prefer just a taste.

1 cup maple syrup (preferably grade A, medium or dark)
⅓ cup half and half
Dash vanilla extract
¼ cup chopped walnuts

Heat the maple syrup and the half and half in a saucepan over medium heat until the temperature rises to 325°F on a candy thermometer, or until the mixture reaches the soft ball stage. Do not stir the mixture while it heats.

Remove the saucepan from the heat and let it cool slightly—to about 150°. Add the vanilla and beat the mixture until it turns from glassy to slightly dull. Add the nuts and stir quickly; the nuts will soon reduce the temperature even more, and the mixture will stiffen rapidly. Pour the fudge into a lightly greased 8-inch pan and let cool. Cut into squares and eat. *Makes sixteen 2-inch squares*

THE VERMONT MAPLE FESTIVAL is held in St. Albans on a weekend in mid-April. Most events—including the lumberjack competitions, maple banquet ($6), fiddlers' contest ($2.50), and dance ($4.50)—take place on Saturday; the parade is on Sunday. Arts and crafts, the maple exhibits, and maple-pancake breakfast ($2.50) are on both days. Tickets for the banquet can be purchased by mail in advance; other tickets are available at the door. All exhibits, contests, and food booths are located in the center of town; the dance, banquet, breakfast, and fiddlers' contest are in nearby buildings, but on a cold spring night you would want to drive rather than walk (it snowed the night we were there). If you plan to stay overnight, make advance reservations at one of the two motels in town; they fill up at festival time.

St. Albans is in the northwest corner of Vermont, just 30 miles north of Burlington, off I-89. For information about the festival and accommodations, contact the Vermont Maple Festival Council, Inc., Box 255, St. Albans, Vermont 05478; phone (802) 524-5800.

World Catfish Festival

Belzoni, Mississippi

*B*ARKING FISH, mud puppies, bullheads, whisker faces—regardless of their local names, catfish are caught and eaten in many parts of the United States. In Mississippi and other delta states, they are also farmed. And in Humphreys County, Mississippi—the self-proclaimed catfish capital of the world—over 22,000 acres of ponds produce millions of pounds of fish each year. The governor of Mississippi, in his annual proclamation, declares, "There is no greater delicacy than Mississippi farm-raised catfish . . . ," and goes on to proclaim the first week in April as Mississippi Farm-Raised Catfish Week. The highlight of this week is the annual catfish festival hosted by the town of Belzoni, the county seat.

It was a sunny April day when we drove the seventy-five miles north from Jackson across flat, often flooded, countryside. Small houses and farms were set back off the road, flowering trees graced side yards. We drove through towns named Yazoo City, Craig, Louise, Midnight, and Silver City, heading for a celebration of the fish that Craig Claiborne has described as "the finest freshwater fish in America, including pike and carp." Over twenty thousand people come to Belzoni for the festival, and though many are involved in the catfish-farming industry, others come because they like catfish, especially this farm-raised variety.

The courthouse lawn was the focal point for the festival. In the pond in front, kids angled for wooden toy catfish. The streets were turned into a bazaar. The 10,000-meter Catfish Classic had been run at 8:30 that morning, and runners were still milling around with their numbers pinned to their chests. Crowds were gathering all morning—bus tours from Jackson, families in station wagons and pickups. A school bus stopped near the festival center to take passengers on a tour of the catfish ponds and factories. While the runners received their awards, others were buying their tickets for the catfish dinner. On the side lawn, a crowd gathered around a man playing the glass harp, and in front of the court house Minnie Simpson's School of Dance was presenting the "Catfish Follies."

Behind the courthouse, we marveled at the quantity of food being prepared for the dinner. Catfish fillets by what seemed like the ton were being dusted with cornmeal and dipped into hot fat until they were crispy deep-fried curls. Balls of cornmeal dough were also deep-fried into crunchy, almost greaseless hush puppies. The midday catfish dinner was being served, and people passed along the food route to pick up their platter of catfish, hush puppies, cole slaw, and Coke. They ate at long, stand-up tables and as they dispensed the obligatory ketchup onto their catfish fillets, they discussed the festival, the catfish, and the weather.

Is farm-raised catfish better than river catfish? There's no question that raising catfish in manmade ponds and feeding them grain removes some of the uncertainty of eating them. Many kinds of catfish are scavengers, and they eat whatever is along the bottom. Nicknames such as mud puppies and mud cats tell the story: oftentimes, caught catfish is tough, fishy, and gritty- or muddy-tasting. The catfish at Belzoni are developed from a variety of channel catfish—a predator, not a scavenger—and are fed a steady diet of grains to develop a sweet flavor. They are harvested at optimum sizes and quick-processed, often frozen, then shipped to over thirty-five states. The people with whom we shared our table at lunch mentioned that they felt the farm-raised fish were fresher and had a more pleasant taste. They are also easier to cook, since they come to market already skinned. (Catfish are difficult to skin because of the barbs along their sides and also because the skin adheres very tightly to the flesh.)

We'd hate to lose the sight of people in the South spending a rainy day out catching catfish, especially since river catfish have a gutsiness that the farm-raised variety lack. But the tamer fish is just as good to eat. The flesh is moist and delicate, and the fish lends itself to a variety of preparations. For many people, especially those in Belzoni that day, farm-raised catfish represent the food of the future: tasty, versatile, and inexpensive. It is a food worthy of celebration, and Belzoni comes through with a first-rate toast to the county's newest and most profitable industry.

Preparing catfish the way it is served at the festival is simple, but to be authentically southern, use only white cornmeal.

Fried Catfish Fillets

3 pounds catfish fillets
1½ cups white cornmeal

Vegetable shortening or oil for
deep frying

Wash and dry the fillets. Place the cornmeal on a sheet of waxed paper and coat each fillet with the meal; set aside.

Add shortening or oil to a deep fryer or deep pot until it is at least 4 inches deep. Heat until the temperature reaches 375°F. Add 2 or 3 fillets at a time and deep fry until golden on both sides, about 3 to 5 minutes. Remove and drain the fish on paper towels while you continue to fry the remaining fillets. If the oil temperature drops below 375°F, allow it to reheat before adding the next batch of fish, and don't add more than a few fillets at a time or the temperature will drop too much and the fish will be greasy. Serve hot, with freshly made hush puppies.

Serves 6

Mississippi Hush Puppies

1½ cups white cornmeal
½ cup all-purpose flour
½ medium onion, minced
Pinch salt
1 tablespoon cayenne pepper

1 large egg
1 cup buttermilk
Dash vinegar
Vegetable oil or shortening
for deep frying

Combine all the ingredients except the oil in a large bowl and stir well; set aside.

Add the oil or shortening to a depth of at least 4 inches in a deep fryer or deep saucepan and heat. When it reaches 375°F, drop the batter into the oil, a tablespoonful at a time, cooking no more than about 6 at any one time. Allow the hush puppies to get crisp on the bottom, then turn and fry on the other side; the entire frying process takes about 5 minutes. Remove the hush puppies as they are done and drain on paper towels for a minute, then serve while still very hot. *Serves 6*

THE WORLD CATFISH FESTIVAL is held in Belzoni, Mississippi, every April. All events take place on Saturday, on or near the courthouse lawn, except for the tours to the catfish farms. If you want to take the free tour (and we recommend it), sign up early in the morning—the first bus leaves at 10. The catfish-and-hush-puppy lunch is served from 11 to 2; tickets ($4.50) are available at the festival. Otherwise there are no admission charges. Parking is on side streets or in local lots.

Belzoni is about 80 miles north of Jackson, on U.S. 49W. For information, write to the Belzoni Chamber of Commerce, P.O. Box 268, Belzoni, Mississippi 39038; or phone (601) 247-2616.

Spring

Cosby Ramp Festival

Cosby, Tennessee

OME SAVOR THE MYSTERIES of the ramp—the vilest-smelling, sweetest-tasting weed in East Tennessee. The ramp is a member of the onion tribe of the lily family, commonly called a wild leek. It tastes like a strong onion crossed with a garlic and a leek, and it thrives in the higher elevations of the Appalachian Mountains. For generations, mountain people have considered ramps to possess medicinal properties and to be an essential spring tonic for overcoming winter's sluggishness. The approved accompanying beverage is sassafras tea, but other more powerful ones are sometimes substituted.

Ramps can be dished up in a variety of ways: raw, parboiled, fried in fatback grease, or scrambled with eggs. And they are at their best for eating the end of April and the beginning of May.

The Cosby Ramp Festival has been held the first Sunday in May since 1954. The state resolution establishing the festival cites that, ". . . this legendary root, the mountain ramp, is purported to supply unyielding powers believed to have furthered the chivalrous and intrepid deeds of those who have chosen the mountains for their home."

Whether the ramp is responsible for all that valor may be questionable, but it's a good reason for coming to East Tennessee. Here, on the western edge of Great Smoky Mountain National Park, people gather every year to eat ramps and have fun. And there's plenty of both.

The most popular dish at the festival is the ramp plate. The ramps—bulbs, stems, and leaves—are chopped coarsely, then placed in a large cast-iron skillet with melted fatback. They are stirred and gently sautéed (nearly stewed) until quite limp—about thirty minutes or so—then some raw eggs are scrambled in—just enough to temper the wild taste of the ramps. The mixture is stirred and sautéed some more, until the greens and eggs blend completely. While it cooks, more fatback grease is spooned in. Sounds greasy, but miraculously it is not.

The ramps are served up on a plate along with thick slices of fatback bacon, which has been fried till it's cracklin' crisp. You also get a piece of fried cornbread—a light cornmeal patty that is crusty outside with solid corn flavor inside. The ramps are slightly sweet, with an onion-garlic flavor that contrasts with the salty fatback and the mild cornbread.

Other dishes for sale are the bean plate (beans in sauce, fatback bacon, and fried cornbread) and the barbecued chicken plate (half a chicken, chips, and a couple of raw ramps). Coffee, tea, and sodas are also sold, as are T-shirts, hats, posters, and programs. There is a ramp table, too, where you can buy a bunch to take home.

While the food is being fixed, a succession of bands play bluegrass, gospel, and country music. In the recent past, entertainers such as Crystal Gayle, Earl Thomas Conley, Lester Flatt, and the Knoxville Blue Grass came here; earlier ramp festivals featured Eddie Arnold (the "Tennessee Plowboy"), Roy Acuff, Tennessee Ernie Ford, Kitty Wells, Dorothy Collins, and Brenda Lee.

Of course politicians turn out for an event packed with so many potential votes. Most years the governor comes as well as some local members of Congress. One year Harry Truman was the keynote speaker.

At noon, no less than fifteen beauties line up on stage, each hopeful that she will be crowned "Maid of Ramps." Competition is stiff, and people cheer for their hometown favorites. The winner is kissed by the politicians, photographed for the newspaper, and presented with flowers. After the beauty pageant, the emcee reminds the crowd: "This is a day for you, for you to have a good time. Eat a lot of ramps."

Ramps are only very rarely available in supermarkets, but you may be fortunate enough to find them on a walk in the country. They grow in shady, open woodlands in the eastern half of the United States, and seem to prefer slopes; we located a large cluster on Long Island's North Shore and found that they transplant well to a shady backyard garden.

Mountain Ramps with Scrambled Eggs

15 medium ramps   *3 eggs, lightly beaten*
4 ounces fatback or bacon

Peel away the outer dark layer from each ramp and trim off the roots. Chop the tops and bottoms together in a bowl until all the pieces are small, about ½ inch in size.

Render the fat in a large skillet over medium heat, then add the chopped ramps and cook until the greens turn a dull olive color, about 10 minutes. Add the eggs and scramble with the ramps until the eggs are cooked but still soft. Serve with Tennessee Fried Cornbread and strips of crisp bacon. *Serves 2*

Tennessee Fried Cornbread

These are crispy cornmeal patties, good for scraping up the last bit of ramps and eggs on your plate.

¼ cup white cornmeal   *¼ cup milk*
Dash baking powder   *1 tablespoon bacon fat, melted*
Pinch salt

Heat a griddle or skillet until very hot.

In a mixing bowl, combine the cornmeal with the baking powder and salt. Stir in the milk and add the bacon fat. Mix only until blended, then drop the mixture by large tablespoonfuls onto the hot griddle. Brown the patties on one side, about 3 minutes, then turn and brown on the other side, another 2 minutes. *Serves 2*

THE COSBY RAMP FESTIVAL is held the first Sunday in May. The program begins around 10 and goes on till about 6. There is a $5 admission charge (per person); food costs extra: The ramp plate is $3, bean plate $3, chicken $4, and sodas are 50¢. All events take place on the festival grounds, Kineauvista Hill.

Cosby is located off I-40, near Newport, Tennessee, on the western border of Great Smoky Mountain National Park. Additional information about the festival can be obtained by writing to the Cosby Ruritan Club, Cosby, Tennessee 37722.

Also in early May there are ramp festivals in Waynesville and Franklin, North Carolina. Both towns are on the eastern side of Great Smoky Mountain National Park. For information about these festivals, contact the North Carolina Department of Tourism, Raleigh, North Carolina 27611; phone 1-800-438-4404 (out-of-state); 1-800-334-1051 (in-state).

Breaux Bridge
Crawfish Festival

Breaux Bridge, Louisiana

CRAWFISH, CRAYFISH, CRAWDADS. Or maybe you call 'em creekcrabs or mudbugs. No matter what you name them, these miniature freshwater lobsters are a cause for celebration in southern Louisiana's Cajun country. In Breaux Bridge, this celebration takes the form of a twenty-four-hour party in the streets. Some celebrating probably begins on Friday evening, but the real affair begins Saturday morning and lasts into Sunday morning. The heaviest action is at the intersection of Main and Bridge streets, with food booths neck and neck with one another and spirited bands performing where the streets spoke out from the center of town.

The action starts early Saturday morning. By 9:30, people are already eating crawfish and drinking beer everywhere you look. By noon, the streets are deeply littered with crawfish shells and beer cans. Music— jazz, country Cajun, and rock— is incessant. The crowds are thick. There's dancing in the street and eating on the curbs. It's a hell of a good time, and there's a lot of crawfish to eat.

We got there early (9:00 A.M.—and recommend you do the same) and walked to downtown while it was still possible to see from one side of the street to the other. Banners were hung in front of the homes of past festival queens. Some residents had marked off desirable parking spots. Others, especially those closest to the action, roped off their front yards to keep the crowds from trampling their lawns. Downtown, in wooden commercial buildings with corrugated-tin overhangs and ironwork balconies, the shopkeepers sold T-shirts, posters, insulated beer-can holders (including a model that you can wear around your neck, thereby leaving your hands free for peeling), and other festival paraphernalia. The food stands were already selling crawfish, and 10:00 A.M. wasn't too early to begin sampling the crawfish pies. A woman with a crawfish corsage and another with small plastic crawfish pins on her bonnet stood nearby as we admired a booth's small bread loaves in the shape of crawfish.

Crawfish throws—little plastic toys—were the gifts tossed out by the royalty who rode on their floats as the parade entered the center of town. Queen Crustacea looked regal as she glided by, while the bands from the regional high schools played Cajun tunes and marches. It was all very lively; in fact, it was one of the best festival parades we've seen.

With the Louisiana rhythms in our heads, we swayed down Bridge Street to a booth with tables and chairs. It was time to try the "boiled." Our hefty serving of crawfish was boiled in cayenne pepper and seawater, then piled high on a Styrofoam plate. The pepper clinging to the shells got on our fingers as we peeled the tails and it singed our lips as we popped the crawfish into our mouths. We peeled some more, sucked the fat from the heads, and licked the pepper off our fingers. On to the étouffé. Etouffé is smothered crawfish tails—a very gently stewed crawfish dish with scallions, onions, and spices served with white rice. Crawfish dogs are étouffé on a hot dog roll, and crawfish pie is étouffé in a pastry turnover. The best étouffé is made with the fat from the heads of the crawfish; light yellow and soft, it has a rich flavor that gives the étouffé its character. The tails are firm and sweet. All the étouffé at the festival is good, although it varies in intensity.

By noon, the streets of Breaux Bridge were shoulder-to-shoulder people. Walking down the street was difficult, but passing by the jazz band or rock stage had become nearly impossible. Off to the side, we located the Cajun band (Acadiana Breakdown), and sat on the grass under a tree listening to old favorites on the accordion and fiddle. People were waltzing, as they so often do at Louisiana festivals.

In the afternoon, excitement mounted for the crawfish peeling and eating contest and the crawfish races. For the eating contest, up to a dozen trenchermen (and women) sat at a large table atop a flatbed truck, and each was given five pounds of boiled crawfish. Whoever ate the most in one hour would be the winner. (If any of the contestants finished their five pounds, they would get another five pounds.) The entire tail had to be eaten, but they could forgo the head fat. Contestants could drink whatever they wished to help them along, though beer was the favorite. As the crowd cheered them on, the contestants tried to break the record of thirty-six pounds. They peeled and ate, peeled and ate, until either their time was up or they gave up. The year we came to Breaux Bridge, no records were broken, but a heap of crawfish was eaten.

The races gave us a new insight into thoroughbreds. Crawfish were put under a bucket, and a circle was drawn a set distance from it. When the bucket was lifted, the crawfish were off and running. The first to cross the circle won the heat, and then the winners of the ten heats raced for the championship title. There are favorite racers, and some owners breed training teams, but often it is the feisty "black horse" crawfish who is first to cross the circle and achieve a fame it never dreamed of in its mud hole.

Crawfish are a symbol of Louisiana, but especially of Acadiana. These lobsterlike crustaceans live in the bayous, in freshwater canals and marshes, where they burrow in the mud. Crawfish can be found inhabiting streams all across the United States, but only here do people eat so many of them. There is another crawfish festival—in Pequot Lake, Minnesota—but the Breaux Bridge event is much more famous. Most of the people we spoke to there said that they ate crawfish at least twice a week, and many caught their own. One man confided, "I don't catch 'em; those things have claws and they bite."

There are two kinds of crawfish: deepwater and pond- (or farm-) raised. It appears that there is some controversy about the relative merits of the two. Some people say there's a difference; others hold that the harder-shelled deepwater is best for boiled, whereas pond-raised is best for étouffé. Diehards and purists will tell you that there's a world of difference—just as there is between brewed and instant coffee—but they'll also admit that the untrained palate probably can't tell the difference. Pond-raised are becoming the dominant type, however, particularly for those shipped to other parts of the country. At the festival both kinds were served, and we sure couldn't tell the difference. All the crawfish was wonderful, as étouffé, in pies, or simply boiled.

Crawfish Étouffé

Allow at least 1 hour to clean the crawfish, especially if you're new at it.

4 pounds live crawfish　　　　*1 onion, chopped*
2 tablespoons roux (see note)　*Salt to taste*
1 ¼ cups water　　　　　　　 *Cayenne pepper to taste*
8 scallions, chopped

Fill a large pot half full with water and bring to a boil. Add the crawfish all at once, then cover and steam over medium-high heat for 5 minutes. The crawfish will have turned red, and all should be killed. Let cool or rinse with cold running water.

When the crawfish have cooled, separate the tail pieces from the bodies and remove the meat from the tails. Set the tail meat aside; you should have about 1½ cups, and it should resemble curled-up shrimp. From the heads, pull out the yellowish fat, located high in the body near the eyes; set aside. You should have about ⅓ cup fat.

In a small, heavy saucepan with a tight-fitting lid, add the roux and ¾ cup of the water. Bring to a boil over high heat, then reduce the heat and simmer for 30 minutes. As the roux mixture cooks, you'll be able to stir it and blend the roux with the water. Continue to stir until the mixture is smooth.

Add the scallions and onion to the roux and simmer an additional 5 minutes. Add the reserved crawfish fat, stir to blend, then add the tails, the remaining ½ cup water, and the seasonings. Cover and simmer gently for 10 to 15 minutes, or until the flavors blend. Check the seasonings and adjust if necessary. Serve over medium-grain white rice.

Serves 4

NOTE: Roux is available in jars, in a concentrated form. You can also make roux by browning equal parts flour and vegetable oil until the mixture is a milk-chocolate brown.

Crawfish Pie

The pies at the festival are modifications of the regular crawfish pie, shaped instead like a turnover so that you can buy your pie and walk away eating it in your hand. This recipe is for the type sold at the festival.

½ cup (1 stick) butter or
margarine, chilled
1½ cups plus 1 tablespoon all-
purpose flour

2 to 4 tablespoons water
2 cups étouffé (see previous
recipe)
1 egg white, lightly beaten

First make the pastry. In a large bowl, cut the butter or margarine into 1½ cups of the flour with a fork or 2 knives until the mixture resembles coarse meal. Add water to the mixture until it holds together in a ball. Knead for about 1 minute, then wrap the dough in waxed paper and chill in the refrigerator for at least 30 minutes.

Roll out the dough to a thickness of about ⅛ inch. Cut 5-inch circles; you should be able to cut out 8 circles by combining the scraps and rolling them out again. Preheat the oven to 350°F.

Drain off about 1 cup of the liquid from the étouffé and mix with the remaining 1 tablespoon flour. This will thicken the mixture slightly, enough to hold it together as a filling for the pie. Blend the thickened liquid with the remaining étouffé, then spoon some of it onto each circle, slightly off-center and not quite to the edges. Brush the edges of the circles with the beaten egg white, then fold over and pinch closed to form a semicircular turnover. Place the turnovers on a baking sheet, brush the tops with the remaining egg white, and bake for 30 minutes, or until the tops are lightly browned. Serve immediately.   *Makes 8 pies*

THE BREAUX BRIDGE CRAWFISH FESTIVAL is held the first Saturday in May on even-numbered years only. All events take place in the center of town. There are no admission fees; parking is on side streets, and if you don't come early, you'll have trouble finding a spot. Things begin to get under way about 10:00 A.M. and the music and partying go on well into the night. By noon there are already large crowds. There is no place to sit down, except on the ground under a tree. Some of the food booths have tables and chairs for patrons. A plate of "boiled" costs $5 and is a good-sized serving. Crawfish pies are $1.25 each and are small.

Breaux Bridge is on Route 31 (off I-10), about 7 miles east of Lafayette. For information write the Breaux Bridge Crawfish Festival Merchants Association, Inc., 117 North Main Street, Breaux Bridge, Louisiana 70517; or phone (318) 332-2345.

Eastern Shore
Seafood Festival

Chincoteague, Virginia

*T*HE LINE OF CARS, vans, pickups, and motorcycles starts forming about 11:00 A.M. on the road leading to Tom's Cove Park, site of the Eastern Shore Seafood Festival. Drivers shut off their motors, open windows, and let the salty bay breezes blow in. Oyster shells line the shore, and gulls and terns glide past the docks and marshes. People step out of their cars to chat with each other; and country music from a van down the line keeps everyone in an upbeat mood. By noon the line is at least a couple of miles long.

The gates open at 1:00 P.M., when the people and cars charge into the park. An hour is not too long a wait for this seafood celebration par excellence, where the clams are sweet and tender, the oysters cold and briny. Most reassuring is the sign as you enter: EAT ALL YOU WANT, BUT EAT IT HERE, PLEASE. Our only worry was would we get to try everything before the festival ended at 4:00 P.M.? With separate booths for each seafood preparation, the festival is a rambling smorgasbord of saltwater delights.

If clams are your favorite, you'll sample some fritters that are creamy-soft inside a dark and crispy crust. Or fried clams that are large and firm—a far cry from those tasteless and tough clam strips you're served in most roadside restaurants. The steamed clams are the most popular. These littlenecks are chewy and dry, hot from the steam of the huge caldron in which they are cooked ever so gently. Dip them in the clarified butter served alongside and you'll be tempted to spend the rest of your time eating only steamed clams.

If it's oysters you crave, you can begin with the oyster fritters: crisp, lacy nets that barely contain the plump oysters within. Frying up the fritters are rows of gray-haired ladies. They all look like your grandmother, and they care as much as she probably did about the food they serve you. Or try the briny Chincoteague salt oysters, shucked before your eyes and shimmering in their shells.

All told, you can sample the freshest seafood you'll ever get: raw littleneck clams and Chincoteague salt oysters, clam and oyster fritters, steamed clams, fried clams, and fried fish (sea trout). There's also cole slaw, hush puppies, and French-fried sweet potatoes. The sweet potatoes are terrific. Deep-fried as white potatoes would be, these turn a golden brown. The potato strips are then sprinkled with cinnamon and sugar and handed to you while still burning hot. That's the problem with this festival. Each individual food is so fresh, so simply and finely prepared, that you almost hate to move on to the next booth.

This is a true food festival. There's no entertainment, no distraction. People come in and head for their favorites, then carry their plates to the nearby picnic tables. There's lots of talk about the year they ran out of steamed clams and whether that might happen again. It's a congenial crowd; not the usual mixture of people that attend most festivals, but rather more of a white-collar group taking the afternoon off from work for some good eats.

As the afternoon goes by, the lines at the booths get longer while people wait for the next batch of fried fish or hush puppies. But the wait gives you a chance to make room for the food to come, to clear your palate before the next taste. If you want to avoid the crowds, then come early and head immediately for the foods you want the most.

Steamed Clams Chesapeake

This recipe is courtesy of the Office of Seafood Marketing, Department of Economic and Community Development, Annapolis, Maryland.

3 dozen littleneck or small cherrystone clams
Salt and pepper to taste

½ cup water
Butter, melted, to taste

Wash the clams thoroughly. Place in a large pot. Sprinkle lightly with the salt and pepper, and then add the water. Cover tightly and bring to a boil. Reduce the heat and steam for 5 minutes, or until the shells open wide.

Drain the clams and serve with the hot melted butter. If desired, you can reserve the cooking liquid and strain it, then serve it along with the clams. *Serves 2*

French-Fried Sweet Potatoes

This recipe is from the Virginia Sweet Potato Association.

2 large sweet potatoes   *Sugar to taste*
Vegetable shortening for deep   *Ground cinnamon to taste*
  frying

Peel the potatoes and cut each into ¼- to ½-inch strips.

Heat the shortening to 350°F and add about half the potato slices. Fry until golden brown, about 10 minutes, then drain on paper towels. Sprinkle while still hot with sugar and cinnamon and continue to fry the remaining potatoes. Serve while warm.   *Serves 2*

THE EASTERN SHORE SEAFOOD FESTIVAL is held in Chincoteague on the first Wednesday in May from 1:00 to 4:00 P.M. Tickets are $15 per person, all you can eat. Beer is 50¢ a glass; soda is included in the ticket price. To get tickets by mail, write: Eastern Shore of Virginia Chamber of Commerce, Accomac, Virginia 23301. Ticket requests are filled in early October for the following May's event. A limited number of tickets are available, so write early.

The festival is held at Tom's Cove Park. You will have no trouble finding it, as Chincoteague is a small town, and on festival day the line winds through town. Chincoteague is on the Eastern Shore of Virginia, about 180 miles southeast of Washington, D.C. For further information, call the Chamber of Commerce at (804) 787-2460.

National Mushroom Hunting Championship

Boyne City, Michigan

Harrison Mushroom Festival

Harrison, Michigan

MAY IS MOREL month in Michigan. There is a morel hunt in Lewiston; a festival in Harrison; and another in Mesick; as well as the National Mushroom Hunting Championship in Boyne City. The flier for the Boyne City hunt invited us to "enjoy the company of hundreds of mushroom-loving enthusiasts; breathe cool, clean, clear air; experience the beauty of the north woods in the springtime; and pick and eat fresh mushrooms (no experience necessary)." We decided to concentrate our mycological efforts on the championship, held on Mother's Day weekend. (The Harrison festival is held the same weekend, so we'd be able to collect our fresh morels, then go down to Harrison and eat some ready-cooked.)

The highlight of the Boyne City weekend is, of course, the hunt itself, although the north woods are indeed beautiful this time of year. It almost always rains. Some people say that's better for morel hunting, while others prefer sunshine. Everyone, we were to learn soon, has his or her own theory. We gathered up these theories—look at the ground at an angle, check under elm and ash trees, watch for brown tips sticking up through the leaves—and collected maps of forest roads and state lands. It seemed simple; just watch the ground around you, and you'd fill your bag with these dark, curly-topped beauties.

Alas, after several hours of scouring the ground with no luck, it was obvious that we had to seek out the experts. Back at the school parking lot, the entrants in the hunt were lined up in their cars awaiting the start of the championship. Dana Shaller and Paul Whipple (two past winners) were heading off together with a colorful sign tacked to the cab of their truck. Excitement was building until, at the stroke of 11, the fire engine led off, its siren wailing. It was followed by the ambulance, a police car, and the participants. We tagged along at the end of the line and followed everyone else as they were led to a "secret spot" (the spot changes every year).

The parade of cars turned down a one-lane forest service road and suddenly stopped. Participants got out of their cars and gathered at the front of the line to hear the rules read aloud. Then a gun was fired and people were off, running through the woods with their sacks and shopping bags. For the next ninety minutes these hunters dispersed in the woods, putting their theories to work. At the sound of the siren, all contestants had to stop collecting and return to the lead car. While we waited for them to return, we located and dug up a mess of ramps (see page 29). At this time of year, the woodlands have a variety of wild flowers and plants emerging, and indeed the air is cool, clean, and clear. The Michigan north woods can yield up quite a good living if someone knows where to find things and what to eat: ramps, morels, fiddleheads, chanterelles, and wild asparagus. One picker told us that he collects and sells these foods to restaurants and gourmet shops so that he can buy steak. "If I don't find anything one day, well, at least I've had a nice day in the woods."

One by one, the morel hunters emptied their sacks onto the hood of the official car. The most morels, the winner. At present the record is held by Stan Boris of nearby Petoskey. In 1977 Mr. Boris collected 915 morels, or about 1 morel every six seconds. Whatever theory Boris has, it works. The day we joined them, the hunt was poor, and few people returned with more than a handful of morels. Morels start popping up through the leafy groundcover in spring when the oak leaves are the size of a mouse's ear, but this spring the weather was cold, and both the oak leaves and the morels were a bit shy.

Many people from these parts have been hunting morels since childhood, and their parents hunted before them. Morels do grow in other parts of the country, but in this area of Michigan there is much relatively undisturbed state land and also a population whose ethnic backgrounds include an appreciation of wild mushrooms. The most popular way to enjoy them is to dust them lightly with flour, sauté them, and serve them on toast. Sometimes a little wine is added to the pan, but mostly the fixings are simple.

In contrast, down at the Harrison Mushroom Festival, Betty Ivanovich was busy demonstrating ways to make other mushroom dishes. Betty, a mycologist and editor of the Michigan Mushroom Hunters Club newsletter, was serving a hearty mushroom soup, as well as mushroom turnovers and stuffed mushrooms hot from the oven.

The Harrison festival is a sharp contrast with Boyne City's activities. Many of these events are indoors, including an arts and crafts show, where the theme was to have been mushrooms (we couldn't detect it through the exhibits). Maps of local hunting spots were being given out, and there was other information available on hunting wild mushrooms and morels in particular. We picked up the morel maps with the hope of finding some specimens in this more southern region of the state, but again we had no luck. Morel hunting is a skill that takes some time to hone.

Morels grow in many parts of the United States, and once you know them, you can't mistake them for any other mushroom. Fresh morels are available in spring only, from large gourmet and department stores (Macy's, Bloomingdale's, Dean & DeLuca, and so on). Dried morels are available year-round from gourmet stores or by mail order from Betty Ivanovich, 7626 Auburn Road, Utica, Michigan 48087.

Sautéed Fresh Morels

The simplest of preparations, this is the way most of the mushroom hunters in Michigan like their morels.

1 pound fresh morels	*3 tablespoons butter*
Flour for dusting	*1 cup dry white wine*

Separate the stems from the morel caps and discard the stems. Place the caps in a bowl of water and swoosh the morels around a little to loosen any sand particles from the grooves. Let the morels sit in the water for about 30 minutes; the dirt will drop down to the bottom of the bowl. Remove the morels and dry them thoroughly. If possible, let sit out for about 1 hour so that all the crevices dry thoroughly.

Lightly dust the morel caps with flour. Heat the butter in a skillet until it just begins to turn light brown, then add the morels and sauté over high heat very briefly—about 1 to 2 minutes. Add the wine, stir briefly, and remove from the heat to serve. *Serves 4*

Creamed Morel Soup

This is a creamy soup speckled with bits of morels. It is adapted from Berry Ivanovich's *Morel Mushroom Cookbook,* and although the original recipe calls for fresh morels, you could also make the soup with dried.

4 tablespoons (½ stick) butter or margarine

½ pound fresh morels, chopped (see note)

1 medium onion, chopped

½ cup chopped fresh parsley

1 tablespoon flour

1 can (14 ounces) beef broth (see note)

1 cup heavy cream

1 tablespoon buttermilk or yogurt

Salt to taste

Melt the butter or margarine in a large skillet over high heat. Add the morels, onion, and parsley. Sauté, uncovered, until all the juices evaporate.

Stir in the flour, then remove the pan from the heat and blend in the beef broth until the mixture is smooth. Return to medium heat; bring to a boil, stirring constantly.

Pour the mixture into a blender and whirl at high speed. Add the cream and buttermilk or yogurt, then place the mixture in a saucepan. Reheat (but do not allow to boil) and serve. *Serves 4*

NOTE: To use dried morels, substitute 1½ ounces for the pound of fresh. Soak in 2 cups hot water for about 30 minutes, or until the mushrooms have swelled to their original size. Drain and pat dry, then set aside to use in the recipe. Strain the soaking liquid and use in place of the beef broth.

Batter-Fried Morels

This is not our preferred way to eat morels, but it is a favorite among the mushroom hunters.

1 pound fresh morels or 3 ounces dried

1 cup all-purpose flour

1 teaspoon baking powder

Salt to taste

1 large egg

1 cup milk

Vegetable oil for deep frying

If you are using fresh morels, soak them in salt water for 30 minutes to loosen all bits of sand or soil. Drain and dry, then trim the stems. If using dried, cover with boiling water and set to soak for 30 minutes, or until completely swelled. Drain and dry, then trim the stems.

In a bowl, mix the flour with the baking powder and a pinch of the salt. Make a well in the center and add the egg and milk. Gradually incorporate the flour into the well and stir until the batter is smooth.

Heat the oil in a deep pot or deep fryer until it reaches 375°F. Dip individual morels into the batter and lift out, tip up. (You don't want to get the batter into the center of the morel.) Drop the morels into the hot oil and deep fry for about 2 minutes. Turn and fry on the other side. Both sides should turn a rich golden brown. Drain on paper towels and sprinkle with salt. Serve at once.   *Serves 4*

THE NATIONAL MUSHROOM HUNTING CHAMPIONSHIP is held on Mother's Day weekend in Boyne City, Michigan. The main events are the morel hunt (Saturday) and the finals (Sunday). There are entry fees for contestants, but there is no other admission charge. Local restaurants feature morels in various preparations, and some people might sell morels privately. The mushroom seminar is free.

Boyne City is off Route 75, about 200 miles north of Lansing. For additional information, contact the Boyne City Chamber of Commerce, 28 South Lake Street, Boyne City, Michigan 49712; phone (616) 582-6222.

The Harrison Mushroom Festival is also held in early May. Contact the Harrison Chamber of Commerce, P.O. Box 682, Harrison, Michigan 48625; phone (517) 539-6011. The Mesick Mushroom Festival takes place the second week in May. For information contact the Mesick Area Chamber of Commerce, P.O. Box 253, Mesick, Michigan; phone (616) 885-1280.

Windsor Shad Derby

Windsor, Connecticut

AT CERTAIN SPOTS along the Connecticut River each May, the shad fishermen are nearly elbow to elbow, casting their willow-leaf lures across the water only to pull them back and cast again until they snag their catch. Others, less sporting or less patient, go after the fish with a gill net. But to enter the shad derby, the most prestigious event of the annual Windsor Shad Festival, the fish must be caught with a line.

May is the time when the shad leave the salty waters of the Atlantic and move upstream to spawn. They've spent the past weeks feeding heavily to prepare for the journey, and when they reach the Connecticut, and its tributaries such as the Farmington, fishermen pluck out roe and buck shad that reach six to eight pounds. The run is so heavy, we were told, that a ton of shad is taken out of the river each day of this thirty-day derby.

By the time we arrived at the derby—for the shad festival dinner—the catch had dwindled, but evidence of the shoreline crush remained. Last-minute fishermen stood on the banks of the Farmington still making a stab for the big one, but they talked enviously of the posted records of past days. The shad dinner is the conclusion of the derby, both the end of the shad run and the close of the competition. Though earlier events of the festival include an opening gala, the naming of a Shad Festival Queen, a road race, a tennis tournament, an art festival, and a senior citizens' ball, the final weekend is the highlight with the Derby Day on the Green (shad dinner, flea market, games, and parade) and the fishing awards at Bart's, a store specializing in fishing tackle.

This festival was begun in 1954 under the auspices of the Windsor Rod and Gun Club. Members of the club became concerned about cleaning up the Connecticut River and, to draw attention to their project, they staged a one-day fishing contest. Since then, thousands of anglers have participated in the Shad Derby. The former one-day event has grown to a month-long celebration involving civic groups and sponsoring many activities, but never losing sight of the importance of a clean river for a good shad run.

Shad is the largest member of the herring family. It is an anadromous fish, meaning that, like the salmon, it is hatched in fresh water, lives most of its life in salt water, then returns to its birthplace to spawn. At one time, the rivers all along the East Coast were clogged each spring with shad fighting their way upstream. But as early as the 1780s, dams were constructed on some of these rivers; later on, pollution from factories spoiled the water. Shad like clean, free-flowing rivers, so by the end of the last century they had, along with some other fish, become almost a memory. But work by environmentalists, shifts in economy, and construction of fish ladders eased the shad back into the rivers of the Northeast. The Connecticut is especially good for shad; some say that the fish from here is the best.

Shad is a sleek, elegant fish. The flesh is tawny and fine grained. When cooked, it has a distinctive flavor—assertive but not strong. The roe is a gastronomic treasure, but the fish has been less valued at times and in some parts of the country because of its intricate bone structure. With over 1,500 bones, all very fine and curved, it is not a meal for the timid. Older recipes call for lengthy cooking times (a couple of hours) to dissolve the bones, but that would seem to sacrifice the delicate quality of the flesh. Shad can be boned, but it is almost a lost art. Luckily, John Cordillo, a member of the Windsor Rod and Gun Club, demonstrates the boning technique at the festival—should you want to learn.

Even though the derby is the focus of the festival, you also get a good opportunity to enjoy the catch itself. The easiest way is to buy a ticket for the festival's shad dinner. Here you get half a shad fillet (deftly boned), along with cole slaw and a roll. The fish is served plain, baked with the merest touch of paprika and a slice of lemon. It is fresh and good, and the delicate flavor of the shad comes through. The dinner is prepared by the Lions Club, and the Rod and Gun Club manages the beer booth nearby. There's no dessert, so as you leave the dinner, pass by the Windsor Senior Citizens' booth for some of their cookies "made by grandmother." Restaurants in town also feature shad during the month.

The motto of the derby is The Shad Always Return. Let us hope they will.

Shad Baked in Cream

This recipe is a past winner in the Shad Derby cooking contest, reprinted by permission of Edward J. Kernan & Co.

3 pounds boned shad fillet
Salt and freshly ground pepper
to taste
2 tablespoons butter
1 cup heavy cream
¼ cup chopped fresh parsley

Preheat the oven to 400°F. Butter a baking dish and place the fish in, then sprinkle with salt and pepper and dot with butter. Bake, uncovered, for 20 minutes, then add the cream and bake an additional 10 minutes, basting the fish with the cream a few times. Sprinkle with the chopped parsley and serve immediately.   *Serves 6*

Hot-Smoked Shad

Some of the fishermen we talked to at the festival described how they smoke the shad they catch. Here's a method of hot smoking that seems to work best, but you'll need a regular smoker to prepare the fish this way.

Approximately 1 pound boned
shad fillet
1 cup coarse salt
2 cups water

Hickory sawdust and twigs
Salt and pepper to taste
2 tablespoons brown sugar

Rinse the fish in cold water. Dissolve the salt in the 2 cups water and place in a shallow pan. Add the fillet and soak for 10 minutes to leach the fluids. Rinse the fish carefully, then let air-dry completely. (If you are eager to start smoking the fish, you can dry it by gently wafting a hair dryer over it until it is completely dry.) The fish *must* be dry before you begin to smoke it.

Preheat the smoker to 150°F, using hickory sawdust and twigs. Have enought sawdust on hand to maintain a steady temperature for several hours.

Sprinkle the fish with salt and pepper, then sprinkle over the brown sugar. Place the fish in the hot smoker and smoke for about 4 hours, or until the fish is firm throughout and slick on top.

Allow to cool, then refrigerate until ready to eat. The smoked fish will keep for approximately 2 weeks in the refrigerator.

Serves 4 as appetizer

THE WINDSOR SHAD DERBY is held each year through the month of May, with activities culminating near the end of the month. Unless you're entering the derby itself, the day to go is Shad Derby Day, when the shad dinner is served and most activities (including a parade) take place. The fishing-awards ceremony is the following day. Parking is at the high school, and free buses transport festival-goers to the green, where the arts and crafts booths and food booths are set up. A short walk from the green is the Farmington River, where last-minute derby entrants are still casting their lines. There is no admission charge to the festival. Dinner tickets ($4) are purchased when you go in to eat; the dinner is served outdoors on the green, from 11 to 3. Other booths sell foods ranging from hamburgers to home-baked cookies; beer, coffee and tea, and sodas are also for sale. Most booths are run by civic groups, and proceeds go to benefit various charitable causes, such as scholarship funds and civic projects.

Windsor is located about 8 miles north of Hartford, Connecticut, off Route 159. For additional information, contact the Windsor Shad Derby Festival, P.O. Box 502, Windsor, Connecticut 06095.

Delmarva Chicken Festival

Delmarva Peninsula
Delaware/Maryland/Virginia

W HEN FRANK PERDUE'S chickenlike face comes on television to tell about his juicy fresh birds, you might think he has a nice little farm someplace in the country, where the chickens run around pecking as they please. But chickens are big business nowadays, and a goodly number—including Frank Perdue's—come from the Delmarva Peninsula, where "chicken is king."

The Delmarva Peninsula is a two-hundred-mile stretch of Delaware, Maryland, and Virginia, with the Atlantic Ocean on one side and Chesapeake Bay on the other. The land is flat, fertile, and sunny, so both chickens and the feed for them grow well. Each year the Delmarva poultry industry toasts its chicken-growing fortunes at a huge poultry extravaganza that features industry exhibits, chick-hatching before your very eyes, a chicken cook-off, a parade, rides and games, plus fried chicken made in a ten-foot-wide frying pan.

Delmarva calls itself the birthplace of the commercial broiler industry and credits its beginnings to Mrs. Wilmer Steele of Ocean View, Delaware. For several years, Mrs. Steele maintained a small laying flock, but in 1932 she started a brood of five hundred chicks. At sixteen weeks, when the birds were about two pounds, she sold them to a local buyer. The following year she started a flock of one thousand birds, and by 1936 Mrs. Steele was producing approximately ten thousand broilers. Chickens were now being grown for their meat rather than their laying ability.

These young, tender chickens could be prepared in many ways that had been unsuitable for the older and larger chickens of the past. Hatcheries quickly sprang up to supply baby chicks. Mills moved into the area to provide ready-mixed feed for the poultry dealers, who also developed into a business as a result of this new industry. Soon the farm kitchens and home dressing plants were replaced by large processing units. It was the beginning of big business for the peninsula.

By 1948 (the year of the first festival), American consumers wanted a chicken with more meat on it, so after experiments with crossbreeding and feeding, the Delmarva chickens gained weight, grew longer drumsticks, and developed broader breasts. By 1957, Delmarva was turning out 150 million plump birds a year, and there was a chicken in everyone's pot. Today the poultry industry on Delmarva consists of nine companies that operate twelve feed mills, sixteen hatcheries, and fourteen processing plants. The chickens are shipped nightly in refrigerated trucks to metropolitan areas throughout the Northeast. Chances are, if you live in New York or Philadelphia or Boston and you ate chicken last night for dinner, it came from Delmarva.

The culinary heart of the Delmarva Chicken Festival is the all-American fried chicken. For the festival, hundreds of chickens are cut up, lightly dusted with flour and seasoning, and deep-fried to a crunchy crispness in the giant frying pan. At any one time, about four hundred pieces of chicken sizzle in the 150 gallons of oil; the men at the pan tenderly stir the chickens every two minutes with a garden rake, while the propane gas heaters keep the oil at an even temperature of 300 degrees. Although a commercial seasoning (English's) is used to coat the chicken, it is done with a light hand, and the breasts, drumsticks, and wings emerge from the pan with juicy flesh and a thin golden crust, occasionally dry at the edges. The fried chicken platter (a quarter chicken, applesauce, and roll) is the favorite, but you can have an almost equally good barbecued chicken instead, cooked over the customary portable barbecue; it is served with chips, pickles, and a roll.

The dramatic event of the festival is the cook-off. Winners of this contest go on to the finals for the National Chicken Cook-off in Dallas, Texas; the prizes are good, so the competition is stiff. Contestants prepare their dishes in small individual working areas equipped with a stove and a table, while visitors stroll from booth to booth, asking questions and chatting with the entrants about their recipes. Many of the cooks sauced or seasoned cut-up chickens, but the majority of recipes were uninspired assemblages of canned soups and packaged seasonings with novelty decorations that the contestants hoped would catch the judges' eyes.

But even if the results are questionable, it is fun to speak with the contestants and to share their hopes for winning. Ernestine Edwards, from Lewes, Delaware, stood in front of her stove and commented, "I've been workin' and workin' to make a chicken that was edible." The name of her recipe—Honey-Almond Chicken—was also emblazoned on her

T-shirt. According to Mary Smith, from Port Deposit, Maryland, her recipe was for chicken wings because "I have five children so we have to use every part of the chicken and make it interesting. If nothing else, I've enjoyed myself."

Crowds also gather for the chicken-plucking contest, an event where the locals really show their stuff. The chickens are pinned up on hooks, and the contestants dress in protective plastic. At the sound of the gun, they pull every which way at the feathers until the bird is denuded or until their time is up. Feathers fly—into the air, all over the ground, and onto the eyebrows and noses of the competitors. Usually the race is among the employees of the different processing plants, but politicians and festival organizers occasionally compete. The men's race one year was a pick-off between two state secretaries of agriculture; Wayne Cawley of Maryland won over Don Lynch of Delaware.

Perhaps the most unexpected element of the festival is the industry exhibit, which documents the festival from 1948 through 1974. The news clippings that form the exhibit chronicle the times by tracing America's eating habits, dress fashions, and social values. In 1948, food writer Clementine Paddleford noted that "fried chicken is better than in the old days." Until 1953, noted another story, the fried chicken was given away. One clever journalist headed his story "they beat the drumsticks on the Eastern Shore." Also in the industry exhibit one can listen to a recording of the fast-paced chicken auction; compare the barred rock male of the '20s with the modern-day white broiler crossbreed; or watch the agonizingly slow hatching of the chicks as they emerge wet, scrawny, and tired. And for the kids there's the chance to hold a soft and fuzzy chick in their hands.

Delmarva is probably one of the more commercial festivals, but that shouldn't dissuade you from attending this fun event. The location changes each year—always a town along the peninsula—and the elaborateness of the event depends on the people of the host town. But though other things about the festival may change, the chicken is always good—in fact, it's delmarvelous!

The following two recipes were entries in the 1982 recipe contest, and the Chicken Korma was a winner. The third recipe was the first-place winner in the 1981 National Chicken Cooking Contest.

Gail Tierney's Deviled Chicken

½ cup (1 stick) butter
1 broiler-fryer (about 3 pounds),
    cut up
1 tablespoon paprika

1½ teaspoons salt
1½ teaspoons dry mustard
½ teaspoon chili powder
Dash cayenne pepper

Place the butter in a medium saucepan and melt over low heat. Remove from the heat. Dip the chicken pieces in the melted butter, one piece at a time, turning to coat. Place the chicken, skin side up, in a single layer in a large, shallow baking pan.

Preheat the oven to 350°F.

To the remaining butter, add the paprika, salt, mustard, chili powder, and cayenne pepper; stir to mix, then spread the mixture over the chicken. Bake, uncovered, turning and basting every 15 minutes for about 1 hour, or until a fork can be inserted into the chicken with ease. Serve immediately. *Serves 4*

Harjit Bhatti's Chicken Korma

8 ounces plain yogurt
2 teaspoons curry powder
1 teaspoon salt
1 teaspoon ground coriander
1 teaspoon minced fresh ginger
4 cloves garlic, minced
½ teaspoon cayenne pepper
½ teaspoon lemon juice

8 chicken thighs, skin removed
2 tablespoons vegetable
    shortening
1 medium onion, chopped
1 large tomato, peeled and
    chopped
2 bay leaves

In a deep bowl, make the marinade by mixing together the yogurt, curry powder, salt, coriander, ginger, garlic, cayenne pepper, and lemon juice. Add the chicken thighs, turning to coat. Cover and let stand at room temperature for 30 minutes.

Place the shortening in a large skillet over medium heat. Melt completely, then add the onion and cook, stirring, for about 5 minutes or until light brown. Stir in the tomato and bay leaves; cook for 5 minutes. Add the chicken and marinade mixture to the skillet and mix well. Cover and simmer over medium heat, stirring frequently, for about 30 minutes, or until a fork can be inserted into the chicken with ease. Remove bay leaves. Serve over hot white rice. *Serves 4*

Impossible Chicken Pie

1 small chicken (about 2¾
  pounds), cut up
2 cups water
2 teaspoons salt
1 cup shredded mozzarella
  cheese
1 can (6 ounces) tomato paste
1 teaspoon dried oregano leaves
½ teaspoon dried basil leaves or
  1 teaspoon fresh
½ cup small-curd cottage cheese
⅔ cup biscuit mix

1 cup milk
2 eggs
¼ teaspoon pepper

Place the chicken in a deep saucepan. Add the water and 1 teaspoon of the salt. Cover and simmer for about 45 minutes, or until a fork can be inserted into the chicken with ease. Let cool.

Separate the chicken meat from the bones. Discard the bones and skin. Cut the chicken into bite-sized pieces and place in a large bowl; add ½ cup of the mozzarella cheese, the tomato paste, oregano, and basil. Stir to mix; set aside.

Preheat the oven to 350°F. Place the cottage cheese in a lightly greased 10-inch quiche pan or deep-dish pie pan and spread evenly. Place the chicken mixture evenly over the cottage cheese.

In a bowl, place the biscuit mix, milk, eggs, pepper, and the remaining salt. Beat for 1 minute with a hand mixer, then pour over the chicken mixture. Bake for about 30 minutes, or until brown and a knife inserted in the middle comes out clean. Remove from the oven and sprinkle with the remaining mozzarella cheese. Let set for 5 minutes before serving.

Serves 4

THE DELMARVA CHICKEN FESTIVAL is held at a different place on the Delmarva peninsula each year in early June. It's a two-day event; the exhibits, giant fry pan, chicken barbecue, and food concessions operate on both days. The Poultry Princess pageant is on Friday night and the cooking contest is on Saturday morning. In general, more goes on on Saturday. The chicken dinners cost $5; other foods and drinks are also for sale. There is no admission charge to the festival grounds.

The Delmarva Peninsula is made up of Delaware, the eastern shore of Maryland, and the eastern shore of Virginia. The location for the festival is decided the summer before. For information about the dates and location, contact the Delmarva Poultry Industry, Inc., R.D. #2, Box 47, Georgetown, Delaware 19947; phone (312) 856–2971.

Pink Tomato Festival

Warren, Arkansas

*B*RADLEY COUNTY, Arkansas, is the "Land of Tall Pines and Pink Tomatoes." It is also a land of hot sun, rich soil, and abundant moisture—all favorable conditions for growing large, juicy tomatoes. The tomatoes from Bradley County are pink; that is, they are picked when the blush of ripeness begins on them, spreading in a faint star from the blossom end of the fruit. The tomatoes are weighed, graded by hand, and shipped to areas of the Midwest. By the time the refrigerated trucks reach Ohio, Illinois, and other points north, the tomatoes are fully ripe and ready to be eaten.

The people in Warren—the Bradley County seat—are proud enough of their tomatoes to celebrate them every year at harvest time. Upward of seventy thousand people come annually (since 1956) to buy large quantities of tomatoes—bushels of them, in fact—so that they will have enough to can for the coming year. They also come to Warren to eat fresh, vine-ripened tomatoes, to tour the tomato fields, to watch the tomato-eating contest, perhaps even to enter the tomato toss, and certainly to enjoy the All-Tomato Luncheon. This is the time each June when Warren paints the town "pink."

Tomatoes have been grown commercially in Arkansas since the 1920s, and today they represent a $7.5 million crop, half of which is totaled up annually in Bradley County. There are about four hundred tomato farms in the county, utilizing about 48,000 acres. Visitors to the festival get the opportunity to take a free tour of some typical tomato fields, to see how these fleshy vines are coaxed to grow between networks of cord, in rows spaced about six feet apart. Their roots are heavily mulched with soil, and the mulch covered with black plastic, so that they appear to be sprouting from long, dark pillows. The irrigation lines run below the plastic mulch, and thus these pampered plants receive a steady trickle of moisture, allowing them to form plump and juicy tomatoes while their roots stay warm under a soil blanket. The harvesting is done by hand each year and usually takes from five to six weeks.

The year we attended the festival the organizers of the event were in a bind. The harvest was late because of a cool spring, so there would not be enough tomatoes to sell at the festival. To make matters worse, they had to use tomatoes from Florida for the tomato-eating contest and also for the tomato toss and the tomato bobbing. During the eating contest, the participants—especially the perky Miss Arkansas, Mary Stewart—grimaced at the thought of eating non-Arkansas tomatoes, and perhaps that is why even the winner only managed to eat two of the required four pounds in the given four minutes.

The cooks of the All-Tomato Luncheon did manage to find some cherry tomatoes for the salad, and although they were a little more green than pink, they had that distinctive Arkansas flavor. The rest of the luncheon consisted of their pink-gold juice, a somewhat typical fresh tomato juice in welcome contrast to the canned variety; ham with Bradley County sauce, a thick sweet-and-sour tomato-based sauce; green tomato beans with toasted almonds, which consisted of chopped green tomatoes cooked up with tender green beans (unfortunately from a can); "tomarinated" carrots, cooked carrots in a zesty tomato vinaigrette; and tomato finger rolls, light dinner rolls with a hint of pink. For dessert, there was "heavenly tomato cake," a brownielike chocolate sheet cake with a tomato-based chocolate icing. The cake was very good, even though someone from the outside would be hard-pressed to guess there were tomatoes in it.

During the luncheon there is a lot of talk about how wonderful Bradley County tomatoes are and how good tomatoes are for the county's economy. There are even some small jabs at inferior Florida or California tomatoes, which are picked green and gassed until they turn red (but remain unripe, as any supermarket shopper knows). The speeches are all by local officials and county ag agents, but they are brief and entertaining. Then the luncheon comes to a close with the auction of the boxes of tomatoes. Since this is a fund-raising event, the bids are usually high, and if the buyer is a man, he often gets a bonus kiss from Miss Arkansas. It is all good fun, as is the rest of the festival.

The following are dishes served at the All-Tomato Luncheon.

Bradley County Sauce
for Baked Ham

1 pint prepared chili sauce
¼ cup cider vinegar
½ cup dark brown sugar
1 tablespoon prepared mustard
*1 cup crushed pineapple, with
    juice*

1 teaspoon ground ginger
1 tablespoon soy sauce
2 tablespoon cornstarch
*1 pound baked ham,
    sliced*

Mix the chili sauce, vinegar, brown sugar, mustard, pineapple and juice, ginger, and soy sauce, then add the cornstarch and blend well. Cook over medium heat until slightly thick, stirring occasionally. Serve either hot or cold over slices of baked ham.   *Serves 6*

Green Tomato Beans
with Toasted Almonds

¼ cup slivered almonds
*4 tablespoons (½ stick) butter or
    margarine*

½ teaspoon salt
¼ cup chopped green tomatoes
4 cups hot cooked green beans

In a saucepan, sauté the almonds in the butter or margarine over low heat until golden brown, stirring occasionally. Remove from the heat and add the salt and tomatoes. Pour the tomato mixture over the beans in a saucepan and mix well. Serve at once.   *Serves 6*

Tomarinated Carrots

3 pounds carrots, peeled and
   sliced
Salt to taste
1 can condensed tomato soup
⅓ cup vegetable oil

½ cup vinegar
½ cup sugar
1 teaspoon dry mustard
1 teaspoon Worcestershire
   sauce

Cook the carrots until tender in a small amount of salted water. Drain well and let cool.

Combine the remaining ingredients for the dressing. In a large mixing bowl, layer the carrots and pour the dressing over. Refrigerate overnight and serve cold the next day. *Serves 6 to 8*

Tomato Finger Rolls

2 cakes yeast or 2 packages (¼
   ounce each) active dry yeast
¼ cup sugar
1 cup skim milk, warmed to
   105–115°F
½ cup tomato juice, warmed to
   105–115°F

½ cup vegetable shortening,
   melted
Approximately 5 cups sifted
   bread flour
1 teaspoon salt
1 egg white, lightly beaten

Crumble the yeast into a mixing bowl. Add the sugar, milk, and tomato juice and stir until the yeast is dissolved. Stir in the shortening, then sift in 4 cups of the flour and the salt, stirring it into the liquid mixture a little at a time until a soft dough forms. Turn the dough out onto a floured board and add the remaining 1 cup flour as you begin to knead the dough. Knead for 5 minutes, or until the dough is elastic. Set the dough in a greased bowl and allow to rise in a warm place for about 30 to 45 minutes, or until doubled in bulk.

Punch down the dough and let it rest for 10 minutes, then shape into 12 dinner rolls. Brush the tops of the rolls with additional melted shortening and allow to rise again until doubled in bulk, about 30 minutes.

Preheat the oven to 400°F. Brush the rolls with the beaten egg white and bake for 15 to 20 minutes. Let cool on racks.

Makes 1 dozen rolls

Heavenly Tomato Cake
with Tomato Icing

CAKE

½ cup (1 stick) butter or margarine
½ cup vegetable shortening
2 cups sugar
2 large eggs
¼ cup cocoa powder
2 cups all-purpose flour

1 teaspoon baking soda
½ cup tomato juice
1 cup hot water
1 ½ cups miniature marshmallows
1 teaspoon vanilla extract

ICING

12 cup (1 stick) butter or margarine
¼ cup tomato juice
2 tablespoons water

¼ cup cocoa powder
¼ teaspoon salt
1 pound confectioners' sugar
1 cup chopped toasted pecans

Preheat the oven to 350°F. Generously grease a 15½-by-10½-by-1-inch sheet cake pan.

For the cake, cream together the butter or margarine, shortening, and sugar. Add the eggs, one at a time, beating well after each. Sift together the cocoa, flour, and baking soda. Add the sifted mixture to the creamed mixture, mixing thoroughly.

In a separate bowl, combine the tomato juice, hot water, and marshmallows, then add this mixture to the batter. Add the vanilla and stir. The batter will be thin, and the marshmallows will come to the top; don't worry—they blend in while the cake bakes. Pour the batter into the prepared pan and bake for 35 minutes, or until the center springs back when pressed with a finger.

While the cake bakes, prepare the icing. Combine the butter or margarine, tomato juice, water, cocoa, and salt in a saucepan. Heat until boiling, then remove from the heat and add the confectioners' sugar; beat well, then stir in the nuts. When the cake is done, spread with the icing while still hot. Allow the cake to cool, then cut slices and serve as you would brownies. *Serves 8 to 10*

THE PINK TOMATO FESTIVAL in Warren is held to coincide with the pink tomato crop in early June. Festivities take place from Thursday to Saturday, with most events on Friday afternoon and all day Saturday. There are no admission charges; parking is on a side street, wherever you can find a spot. The All-Tomato Luncheon is held at noon on Saturday; tickets are $5.50 and may be purchased in the morning at the municipal building, across the street from the courthouse. Free tours of the tomato fields are run by the County Extension Service. Buses pick riders up right after the luncheon; otherwise, all events are held in the middle of town, mostly at the Courtsquare (in front of the courthouse). Local farmers sell tomatoes there, too.

Warren is in south-central Arkansas, about 90 miles south of Little Rock, at the intersection of Routes 4, 15, 8, and 189. For a schedule of events, write the Bradley County Chamber of Commerce, Municipal Building, Warren, Arkansas 71671; or phone (501) 226-5225.

Jambalaya Festival

Gonzales, Louisiana

WHEN WE WROTE TO GONZALES, Louisiana, for information about the Jambalaya Festival, we hardly expected the enthusiastic invitation we received: "At the outset I will guarantee that you will enjoy the Jambalaya Festival and add real spice to your book by watching this unique method of cooking, and that you will enjoy eating this great dish.
. . . If you have never been this way before, be prepared to meet the friendliest and most hospitable people in the world." And so we did. We enjoyed the festival, loved the jambalaya, and were warmly received.

Gonzales, known since 1967 as the Jambalaya Capital of the World, is about fifteen miles south of Baton Rouge, east of the Mississippi. The area originally belonged to the Houmas Indians and in 1773 was settled by the Acadians, exiled from Canada. Early commercial activity consisted of a cotton gin and a sugarhouse, established in the second half of the nineteenth century. In 1887 Joseph "Tee Joe" Gonzales operated a general store, and later that year a post office under the name of Gonzales was established.

Jambalaya (pronounced *JAM-bah-lie-ah*), the word for which some say derives from the Spanish word for ham (*jamón*), found its way into Creole-Cajun cookery in the late eighteenth century. It can be made with ham, chicken, sausage, fresh pork, shrimp, and oysters (all together or separately), to which shortening, rice, onions, garlic, pepper, and other seasonings, and sometimes tomatoes, are added. And, as anyone from East Ascension Parish will tell you, it's best made in Gonzales.

The atmosphere at Gonzales harks back to old-fashioned church fairs. In the nineteenth century, such fairs in southern Louisiana towns were large public gatherings. People would bring their black iron pots from home, parishioners would donate the ingredients, open wood fires were built, and jambalaya was made and served to the crowd. Later, politicians took over the custom and served jambalaya at rallies—it was an easy and inexpensive way to feed a lot of people while making themselves look good to their constituents. Though the festival is now held to draw attention to Gonzales, the politicians are still in evidence, as they are at most festivals.

But people don't come to the Jambalaya Festival for politics. They come to listen and dance to Cajun music, to watch the cooking contest, and to eat the prizewinning jambalaya. For most people in this part of Louisiana, the preparation of food is not a dull domestic chore; it is an obsession. So when the contest comes along, it's a chance to give this obsession full reign, and cooks vie for the jambalaya championship. The year we came to Gonzales, there were thirty entrants, from whom six finalists were selected. The contestants must supply their own thirty-gallon cast-iron cooking pot (at one time, these pots were used for laundry), into which they must put a three-to-one mixture of chicken to rice (no sausage). The amount and type of seasonings are also regulated, and the contestants must prepare their jambalaya over a wood fire behind a fenced-in area that is monitored by officials. When the cooking is finished, usually in about three or four hours, the contents of the pot must be within four inches of the top. A sample is taken from each pot, then the large pots are removed to the cafeteria, where the jambalaya is served up to the crowds who attend the festival.

Just about all the contestants are men, mostly two-man teams sponsored by local companies or organizations. They take turns tending the pot and the fire below it, and when it is time to give their jambalaya a stir, they use a long-handled spatula to lift and sift the ingredients, being careful not to break or mash the rice kernels. The jambalaya is judged for appearance, overall flavor, flavor of the rice, and flavor of the chicken, which must dominate. Five judges, one of which is a former winner, taste the samples and pick the best, noting that it is the combination of seasonings that makes for the greatest difference among the samples. But what's the secret of a winning jambalaya? We asked a contestant who had won for several years consecutively, and he noted that it took experience and a touch of luck; but, in addition, it helped to have a seasoned old pot, to measure the water for the rice accurately, and to brown the chicken with the onions for more flavor. We also observed that the longer the chicken is browned and the darker it gets, the more flavorful the resulting jambalaya.

In contrast to the main cooking contest, the mini-jambalaya contest calls for somewhat different cooking skills. These cooks have to put a mighty effort into producing a zesty half cup of jambalaya, using a one-quart cast-iron pot and cooking it over a fire of kindling. The small fire gets very hot, and the contestants must make their brew along the curb of the main street as the crowds hang over them. Though originally begun as a novelty, this contest is also difficult to win, and competition is mighty stiff.

Inside the school cafeteria, when we were there, crowds of visitors collected their helpings of jambalaya (from the pots of the semifinalists of the main contest), then moved over to the dining tables and adjusted the seasonings to their own liking with hot Cajun sauce—sprinkled or sometimes poured on! To us, the jambalaya was just fine as it was—fluffy rice permeated with rich chicken flavor, with bits of onion, green pepper, and scallions, and with a heavy spiking of black and cayenne pepper.

As we downed forkfuls, the joyous sounds of Cajun music came in through the wide doors of the cafeteria. At this end of the street the stage was set up for small Cajun bands, while at the other end, rock groups performed. But the action here was more fun, as the happy, slightly discordant Cajun waltzes got people's feet tapping and hips swaying. Soon couples made a dance floor of the town's main street and shouted the names of favorite songs they wanted to hear. As the group responded, we realized why it is that we love Louisiana's food festivals the most: They represent the traditional French love of good food, the Spanish love of good drink, and the Cajun love of their slogan, *"Laissez les bon temps rouler!"*

Chicken Jambalaya

The secret of a flavorful jambalaya is in the initial browning of the chicken. Keep turning and cooking the pieces until they turn a very dark brown.

1 large chicken (about 3½ pounds), cut up
4 large onions, chopped
3 cloves garlic, chopped fine
3 cups water

2 cups long-grain rice, rinsed
½ cup chopped scallion greens
Salt and pepper to taste
½ teaspoon cayenne pepper, or to taste

In a large cast-iron pot, brown the chicken over high heat in its own fat until it turns dark, dark brown—about 1 hour. Add the onions and garlic and fry until they turn brown, too—about 10 minutes more. Add the water and simmer the chicken until tender, about 30 minutes. Add the rice along with the scallion greens, salt and pepper, and cayenne. Stir lightly. Bring the liquid to a boil and cook over medium heat until most of the water is gone and the rice starts to puff. Stir the mixture carefully, lower the heat, and cover to cook slowly until done, about 30 minutes more. When done, season with more cayenne pepper if desired.

Serves 6

THE GONZALES JAMBALAYA FESTIVAL is held the second weekend in June every year, sponsored by the Jambalaya Festival Association. The cooking contest begins on Saturday at 7:00 A.M.; the booths and carnival rides open at 10:00. On Sunday, the cook-off finals are held (judging is at 11:30); and the mini-jambalaya-cooking contest is that same afternoon. Jambalaya is served in the school cafeteria both days from 11:15 until 8:30. Music is ongoing, ranging from Cajun waltzes at one end of town to country rock at the other. Parking is first-come, first-find-a-spot-nearby, so it's a good idea to arrive by at least 11 the day you wish to come. There is no admission charge. Food booths sell everything except jambalaya, which can only be had in the cafeteria. A plate (servings are very large) costs $3.50.

Gonzales is located about 15 miles south of Baton Rouge, off U.S. 61. For further information, contact the Jambalaya Festival Association, P.O. Box 1243, Gonzales, Louisiana 70737.

National Asparagus Festival

Shelby/Hart, Michigan

E VERY INCH EDIBLE," not something you can say about most eats. But that's the slogan for the National Asparagus Festival, held jointly each year in Shelby and Hart, Michigan. If you're used to buying asparagus from California, you'll probably wonder what they're talking about—don't you have to snap off all the tough white ends of asparagus so that all you're left with is the tender green part? That tough bottom is white because it was growing underground. When asparagus is harvested by machine, the cut is made below the soil line. But when it's harvested by hand, it is snapped off at the soil line. Thus, every inch is tender and delicious.

The organizers of the festival want to call attention to the greater appeal of their Michigan asparagus, and they do that by putting on a fun-filled event that includes airplane rides, a horseshoe tournament, an art fair, square and round dances, a cook-off, a fireman's water competition, a talent show, a fishing contest, and a bed race. (We'll explain!) There is also an extensive parade of asparagus floats, school bands, fire engines, farm machinery, horses and riders, clowns, and antique cars. To get the parade started, a skydiver plummets into the center of town wearing a red suit and trailing a red-and-orange parachute.

Shelby is a small town near the eastern shore of Lake Michigan, on the lower peninsula. Main Street is a few blocks long, with a variety store, florist, grocery, bakery, bank, drugstore, bar, and post office. On festival weekend, the stores have sidewalk sales. There's no shopping mall, so people come to Main Street to shop, just like they used to in small towns all over America.

On Saturday morning, before the festival really gets under way, the action is at the bakery. A sign in the window announces ASPARAGUS BREAD TOASTED 50¢. Inside, people greet one another as they order their eggs or pancakes. Today's special is a sweet loaf made with flour, shortening, soda, asparagus, walnuts, cinnamon, and sugar. It's served by waitresses wearing Asparagus Festival aprons. Lots of the customers are wearing green today, too.

On the morning we were there, a shop down the street announced GREEN STALK SALE DAYS. A local bar, the Brown Bear, had posted a menu in their window that offered fried asparagus, asparagus soup, and asparagus gravy with biscuits. We succumbed to the fried asparagus and crunched on whole stalks that had been dipped in batter and deep fried— finger food with an edible handle.

For a more substantial taste of asparagus, we headed down a side street to the Shelby Congregational Church. In the basement, the asparagus luncheon was under way, organized by the Women's Fellowship. Lunch was an asparagus casserole, with ham, hard-cooked eggs, and lots and lots of asparagus chunks in a creamy cheese sauce. The casserole was served with cole slaw, a roll, coffee, and a piece of cake. The cakes were homemade: chocolate, maple, German chocolate, and devil's food, among others. The luncheon is held on alternating years, and we considered ourselves fortunate to have been at the festival that year.

Some of the festival activities take place in nearby Hart, a town slightly larger than Shelby. We decided to drive up to Hart and watch the bed race. This is a peculiar American pastime that would be difficult to explain to a foreigner. They're wacky, just a touch insane, and a whole lot of fun. Contestants decorate an old brass bed, put it on wheels, and race it down the main street of town. There's a passenger—usually a young woman dressed in costume or bedclothes—who gets a bumpy, often swerving ride. After all, beds aren't the easiest to steer. In Hart the streets are lined with spectators cheering on their favorites. The races are swift, the beds colorful. After a tight race, we learn who's the winner and get a chance to take a closer look at the winning design.

By late afternoon people start to gather for the asparagus smorgasbord, held at the Shelby High School cafeteria and sponsored by the Chamber of Commerce. The year we attended, dinner consisted of a tossed salad with raw asparagus chunks, lime gelatin salad with grated raw asparagus, a creamy asparagus soup, baked stuffing with asparagus and flavored with thyme, boiled asparagus with a Cheddar cheese sauce, roast beef with scalloped potatoes, meatballs in a sweet-and-sour asparagus sauce, and a bowl of garnishes (apple rings, pickles, and olives). Dessert was an asparagus cake; that is, a white cake with flecks of asparagus and a sugar icing that was colored green. Our preference among this assortment was for the plain asparagus with cheese sauce. Somehow the flavor of those green stalks is just too good to cover up.

Why does Michigan asparagus taste so good? The soil here in Oceana County is light and sandy, giving the asparagus crown, or root, an abundant supply of oxygen. About twelve thousand acres of plants are growing in this part of the state. In spring, the rising soil temperature triggers fresh growth from the crowns below, and the spears start shooting up. The harvest generally lasts about six weeks, and the festival is planned for the peak of that harvest. Dykstra Farm Market, from nearby New Era, sells tender young asparagus in quantity, both at their farm stand and on the street in Shelby during the festival. As well as eating your fill of aparagus right on the spot, you can buy pounds of it to take home.

Asparagus Quiche

In Michigan, asparagus quiche is a popular item. This recipe is enough for two quiches, each 9 inches in diameter. The recipe is based on one developed by the Michigan Asparagus Advisory Board.

2 cups grated cheese (Swiss, Cheddar, or a combination)
Two 9-inch pie shells, baked
¾ pound asparagus, broken into pieces and cooked until tender (or a 10-ounce package frozen asparagus pieces, cooked)
3 large eggs
1 can (13 ounces) evaporated milk

Approximately ¼ cup whole milk
½ teaspoon salt
¼ teaspoon pepper
Dash nutmeg

Preheat the oven to 375°F.

Sprinkle the cheese over the bottoms of the pie shells. Arrange the asparagus over the cheese.

Beat the eggs lightly. Add enough milk to the evaporated milk to make 2 cups. Combine the milk mixture with the eggs and add the seasonings. Pour the mixture over the asparagus in the shells.

Bake the quiches for about 45 minutes, or until a knife inserted in the center comes out clean. Let the quiches sit for at least 10 minutes before cutting them into wedges. *Each quiche serves 4 to 6*

Creamy Asparagus Soup

Many cream soups are thickened too much. This version makes a lighter soup that is creamy but is thickened with a puree of asparagus for a stronger asparagus flavor.

1 pound asparagus
1 medium onion, chopped
2 tablespoons vegetable oil

1 can (14 ounces) chicken broth
1 can (13 ounces) evaporated
skim milk

Cut the stems of the asparagus into small pieces; reserve the tips.

Sauté the onion in the oil in a heavy saucepan until the onion is wilted. Add the chopped asparagus stems and sauté for about 3 minutes more, or until the stems glisten and are slightly wilted. Add the chicken broth, then measure an additional canful of water into the saucepan. Cover and bring to a boil, then reduce to a simmer and cook until the asparagus is very tender, about 20 minutes

Whirl the soup mixture in a blender until smooth, then stir in the evaporated milk. Blend with a spoon and add the asparagus tips. Heat gently over a low heat until the tips are tender, about 5 minutes, then serve. *Serves 4*

The best asparagus is often the plainest—just gently and lightly boiled or steamed, graced with a simple sauce. Here are two such sauces, which are a change of pace from the usual and more time-consuming hollandaise. These are reprinted from *A Festival of Good Eating*—recipes from former National Asparagus Festival cooking contests.

Bacon and Bread Crumb Sauce

4 strips bacon

¼ cup bread crumbs

Fry the bacon until very crisp. Remove the bacon, then add the bread crumbs to the fat and sauté until browned, stirring constantly. Crumble the bacon and add to the crumb mixture. Sprinkle over a platter of hot asparagus. *Serves 4*

Mustard Sauce

½ cup (1 stick) butter or
    margarine
1 tablespoon lemon juice
¼ teaspoon salt

3 egg yolks
2 teaspoons Dijon-style
    mustard

Heat the butter or margarine over low heat until it begins to bubble. Blend the remaining four ingredients together in the jar of a blender. With the blender set on high, remove the inner portion of the lid and slowly add the bubbly butter. Blend until smooth, then pour at once over the cooked asparagus.

Serves 6

Asparagus Surprise

This was the grand-prize winner from the cooking contest the year we attended the festival. Developed by Sharon Dykstra, this recipe encases asparagus stalks in rolls of cheese, ham, and chicken breast. The surprises are the tender stalks inside each delicious bundle.

4 chicken breast halves
4 thin slices boiled ham
4 slices Swiss cheese
16 spears asparagus, cooked un-
    til tender-crisp and trimmed
    to about 4 inches long

4 tablespoons (½ stick) butter,
    melted
⅓ cup dry bread crumbs
2 tablespoons grated Parmesan
    cheese

Preheat the oven to 350°F.

Skin and bone the chicken breast halves. Lightly pound with a meat mallet. Place 1 slice ham and 1 slice cheese on each breast, then add the asparagus spears, 4 spears to each roll. Carefully roll up and press in the sides. Tie with a string or secure with toothpicks. Dip the rolls in the melted butter, then in the bread crumbs and Parmesan cheese.

Bake in a greased baking dish for 40 minutes. Remove from the pan and stir the remaining drippings until smooth, then spoon over the chicken rolls.

Serves 4

THE NATIONAL ASPARAGUS FESTIVAL is held in Shelby and Hart on the second weekend in June. The site of the parade alternates from year to year, but some events take place in each town. Most events are on Saturday, including the parade, the asparagus luncheon ($3.25), the asparagus smorgasbord dinner ($6.50 for adults, $4 for children), and the dances. No advance tickets are needed for any event. Nearly everything takes place in downtown Shelby/Hart, though you may want to drive to the high school for the dinner. There is no admission fee to the festival, and parking is on side streets. Asparagus is sold at local farm stands and at stands in town.

Shelby and Hart (8 miles apart) are located near Lake Michigan, off U.S. 31, about 70 miles northwest of Grand Rapids. For information, write the National Asparagus Festival, Box 153, Shelby, Michigan 49455.

Ipswich Strawberry Festival

Ipswich, Massachusetts

NYTHING YOU CAN MAKE from a strawberry." That's how the strawberry festival at the Ipswich United Methodist Church was billed. The festival is a church fundraiser, going strong annually since 1935, and all the foods served are old family recipes, mostly those of Mrs. Althea Mathews and her mother, who started the festival. As Mrs. Mathews explained to us, she keeps after the cooks in the kitchen preparing the shortcakes, pies, jams, and other berry desserts so they do exactly as the recipes say and don't take shortcuts just to save a little time. It sounded like our kind of festival.

Strawberry festivals are almost as plentiful as strawberries in June, and although each one might be fun for local people, few are worth a trip of more than five miles. We'd been to lots, searching for one that celebrated the strawberry as it deserved. No shipped-in fruit for us; we wanted small local berries, which have the truest flavor. No supermarket sponge cakes, either; we wanted the real thing: honest-to-goodness biscuit shortbread with real whipped cream. And it wouldn't bother us at all if we had to eat some creamy strawberry ice cream or have a couple of pieces of strawberry pie as well.

Ipswich is a picturesque New England town north of Boston, near Cape Ann. Among other things, it's famous for its clams. But come June, the town turns out for strawberries. Here, in the community room of the white clapboard church, women wearing strawberry aprons dish out strawberry shortcake, strawberry pie, strawberry ice cream and sundaes, strawberry jams, strawberry tarts, strawberry punch, strawberry turnovers, strawberry frappés (milkshakes), and strawberry-banana supremes. About a thousand people stream in and out of the church, some eating their treats at the long tables set up in the basement, others taking home whole pies to enjoy later. Outside the church, on the lawn in front and along the side, strawberry fanciers stroll amidst tables with old lamps, books, games, dishes, and other items that usually grace white-elephant tables.

The strawberries used to prepare the many festival dishes come from a local farm. They are small, sweet, and intense with flavor—something that has been all but lost in the proliferation of the large, cottony berries that are more commerically viable. When hulled and left to mascerate, they yield a clean and pure strawberry taste that dominates the pie, sundaes, and other desserts here. The shortcake, to our way of thinking, is the star of the festival. A real baking-powder biscuit, light and fluffy with a slightly toasted top, is split in half, covered with berries and drizzled with their own juices, then topped with light-as-air real whipped cream. Not too sweet and oh-so-strawberry, it spoke summer to our palates.

Nowadays strawberries are grown in every state of the union, with California supplying about 55 percent of the commercial crop. It's interesting to note that before 1880—in essence, before the railroads crossed the country and linked farm with city—strawberries were a luxury grown only locally or by people in their own gardens. This is because strawberries are highly perishable if they are any good, and must be eaten very soon after harvest. Yet as far back as the 1850s, there were strawberry festivals not to sell T-shirts or give platforms to politicians, but purely in appreciation of this magnificent fruit. The Ipswich Strawberry Festival follows in the grand tradition.

The following are adapted from family recipes given to us by Althea (Hebb) Mathews, the organizer of the festival.

Old-Fashioned Strawberry Shortcake

BISCUITS

2 cups all-purpose flour
4 teaspoons baking powder
½ teaspoon salt

1½ tablespoons sugar
⅓ cup butter or margarine
¾ cup milk

SHORTCAKE

1 pint fresh strawberries,
washed and hulled

Sugar to taste
1 cup heavy cream, whipped

Make the biscuits first. Preheat the oven to 450°F. Sift the dry ingredients together twice; work in the butter or margarine with a pastry mixer, fork, or your fingertips, then add the milk gradually until the mixture is of a consistency to handle easily. (Dust your hands with a little flour to keep them from getting sticky.) Turn the dough out onto a floured board and pat gently, then gently roll out to a ¾-inch thickness. Handle the dough as little as possible. Cut the biscuits with a 3-inch cutter or use the top of an inverted glass or cup; you should have 12. Arrange half the biscuits on a greased cookie sheet, butter each, then place the remaining circles on top of the other biscuits (in other words, double thickness). Bake for 12 minutes, or until the tops are lightly speckled with brown. Makes 6 double biscuits.

Slice the larger strawberries so that they are all about the same size. Toss with sugar until they are the desired sweetness. Split open the warm biscuits and place some strawberries on the bottom half. Layer with a couple of spoonfuls of whipped cream. Place a biscuit half on top and serve.   *Serves 6*

Strawberry Turnovers

CRUST

> 4 *cups all-purpose flour*
> ½ *cup sugar (optional)*
> 1½ *teaspoons salt*
> 1 *cup vegetable shortening*
> ½ *cup (1 stick) butter or*
>   *margarine*

> 1 *large egg, lightly beaten*
> ½ *cup water*
> 1 *tablespoon white vinegar*
> 1 *egg yolk, lightly beaten, or*
>   ¼ *cup milk*

FILLING

> 1½ *quarts fresh strawberries,*
>   *washed and hulled*
> ½ *cup water*
> ½ *cup sugar*

> 2½ *tablespoons cornstarch*
> 1 *tablespoon butter or*
>   *margarine*

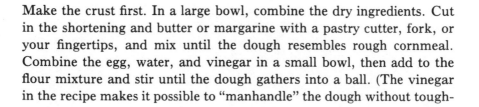

Make the crust first. In a large bowl, combine the dry ingredients. Cut in the shortening and butter or margarine with a pastry cutter, fork, or your fingertips, and mix until the dough resembles rough cornmeal. Combine the egg, water, and vinegar in a small bowl, then add to the flour mixture and stir until the dough gathers into a ball. (The vinegar in the recipe makes it possible to "manhandle" the dough without tough-ening it.) Wrap the dough in waxed paper and chill for at least 30 minutes.

Place 1 quart of the berries aside. Take the remaining pint and crush to a puree in a saucepan. Stir in the water, sugar, and cornstarch and place over medium heat. Bring to a boil and boil for 2 minutes, or until clear. Add the butter or margarine and allow to cool to room temperature. Meanwhile, cut the remaining quart of strawberries into large dice. When the sauce has cooled, mix with the reserved strawberries.

Preheat the oven to 425°F. Divide the dough in half and roll out one half to a ⅛-inch thickness. Cut 8 rounds each 6 inches wide, then place about 3 tablespoons of the strawberry mixture on each and fold over. Wipe the edges with a pastry brush dipped in water and seal with the tines of a fork. Brush the tops with egg yolk or milk and prick the tops. Bake for 20 minutes. While the first batch is baking, roll and fill the remaining batch. Bake and allow to cool before serving.

Makes 16 turnovers

THE UNITED METHODIST CHURCH in Ipswich, Massachusetts, holds its annual strawberry festival on a Saturday in mid-June—the time when strawberries are at their most luscious. The festival is from noon to 4:00 P.M., but it is unlikely that you could spend more than an hour gorging on strawberry delights. There is no admission charge; each strawberry dish is priced individually, with shortcake running about $1.25 per serving.

Ipswich is a town about 30 miles north of Boston. The festival is held in the basement of the United Methodist Church, 20 North Main Street, Ipswich. For additional information, contact them at (617) 356–2307. Parking is on the street.

Summer

National Cherry Festival

Traverse City, Michigan

IMAGINE WALKING through an orchard on a sunny day, picking sweet cherries and popping them in your mouth. Sounds wonderful, doesn't it? On Michigan's Old Mission Peninsula, where there's an especially large concentration of cherry trees, you can make this dream come true. We did—first at an old abandoned orchard near Omena, then the following year as part of the National Cherry Festival in Traverse City.

The National Cherry Festival is cherry-filled fun in spite of itself. It's a good example of what happens when a tourist town holds a festival in honor of the local product: a confused mixture of good intentions and commercial intervention. We came for the cherries—Michigan produces 70 percent of the world's supply—and we did get to eat them, but we had to fight our way through a maze of wacky contests (frog races, bicycle rodeo, moto-cross, a pet show, and a bed race) and games (bingo every day). We expected to gorge ourselves on different versions of cherry pie, but all we found were prepacked individual slices from a local baking concern. In the Cherry Tent, we had good chilled cherry juice, a novelty called cherry nuggets (sugar-coated dried cherries), and a gooey cherry sundae, but where—oh where—were grandmother's cherry pies?

The real cherries, we soon found out, were either still in the orchard or part of the Very Cherry Luncheon. The luncheon is held on the Friday of this week-long festival. Here a visitor can enjoy a cherry-filled meal beginning with a cold cherry soup, followed by a variety of main courses, salads, and breads that contain cherries, and topped off with a selection or two from the three-tiered dessert table. This buffet table is the highlight of the luncheon, and with good reason. Heaped high from one end to the other, it is a cornucopia of old-fashioned cakes, pies, puddings, and cookies prepared by the growers' families—a cherry-lover's fantasy come true.

Another big hit of the Cherry Festival is the pie-eating contest, open to children of all ages. The kids lie on their stomachs onstage, with their hands behind their backs and a paper plate containing a pie slice in front. At the whistle, they eat the pie, mouths only. It's a bit gruesome to watch, but the crowd cheers on its star eaters, and the winner is selected as soon as one of the children finishes the pie. One little boy shrieked, "I don't like cherries!" but others relished the chance to get right into it. Other contests (for adults) included pit-spitting, won recently by Rick "Pellet Gun" Krause, who sent a cherry stone flying 53 feet 7½ inches.

The cherry orchard tour is another feature of the festival, and this will get you among the trees so that you can start eating. The buses take you to a farm (a family operation) high on a hill overlooking both Grand and Little Traverse bays. We were given a tractor ride between rows of sweet cherry trees and were told that both tart and sweet cherries were grown in Michigan and that in fact the state leads the nation in the production of tart cherries. The orchard we were in was mostly sweet cherries, a mixture of dark red varieties like the bing, which is shipped to most supermarkets, and a pale yellow variety (Queen Anne), which is mostly bleached in brine and then dyed to become maraschino cherries. They are also canned in a light sugar syrup and sold as Royal Anne cherries.

As we heard about the life expectancies of the cherry trees, or why the bases of their trunks are painted white (to reflect the heat of the snow and keep the bark from burning), or how the cherries are harvested ("shaken") by machine, we decided to "harvest" some ourselves by hand. The wine-dark bing cherries were perfect, warm from the midday sun. The surprise, however, was in the less sweet Queen Annes; with their yellow skins faintly flushed with rose, these had a flesh that was juicy and fragrant, not syrupy sweet. The Queen Annes don't make it to most markets—certainly not to those outside of the area—but you can often buy them at the end of the tour when the tractor brings you conveniently back to the grower's fruit stand.

We found touring the cherry orchard the most fun of this festival. And we were wild about the new dried tart cherries that the cherry growers had introduced that year. They fueled us as afternoon snacks as we drove across the country. The National Cherry Festival does not give cherries the celebration we think they deserve, but the orchard tour and the Very Cherry Luncheon make a trip to the peninsula worth a cherry fancier's time.

The following are cherry treats you are likely to find among the several hundred homemade desserts at the Very Cherry Luncheon.

Tart Cherry Torte with Cherry Sauce

Though made with tart cherries, this cake is still a bit sweet, and you might prefer to serve it with vanilla ice cream in place of the cherry sauce.

TORTE

2 cups (one 16-ounce can) tart
    cherries
¾ cup sugar
1 teaspoon baking soda
1 cup all-purpose flour
⅛ teaspoon salt

1 teaspoon ground cinnamon
1 large egg, lightly beaten
1 tablespoon margarine or
    butter, melted
½ cup broken walnuts

CHERRY SAUCE

½ cup sugar
½ teaspoon salt
1 tablespoon cornstarch

1 tablespoon margarine or
    butter

Preheat the over to 350°F.

Drain the cherries, reserving the juice for the sauce. Sift together the sugar, baking soda, flour, salt, and cinnamon. Add the egg and the margarine or butter, then fold in the drained cherries and walnut pieces. Pat the batter into a greased 8-inch square pan and bake for 35 to 40 minutes, or until the center bounces back when depressed with a finger.

While the cake is baking, combine the sugar, salt, and cornstarch for the sauce in a saucepan. Add enough water to the reserved cherry juice to make 1 cup liquid. Gradually add the cherry liquid to the dry ingredients and cook, stirring, until thick and clear, about 5 minutes. Remove from the heat and add the margarine or butter to glaze. Serve over slices of the cake.

Makes 1 square cake

Cherry Chip Bundt Cake

Make this recipe in a fancy Bundt form or use a standard tube pan.

2 cups all-purpose flour
¾ cup sugar
¾ cup vegetable oil
2 large eggs
2 teaspoons vanilla extract
1 teaspoon baking soda
1 teaspoon ground cinnamon

⅛ teaspoon salt
1 can (21 ounces) cherry pie
  filling
1 cup (6 ounces) chocolate chips
½ cup chopped almonds
Confectioners' sugar

Preheat the oven to 350°F. Grease and flour a Bundt pan or 10-inch tube pan.

In a large mixing bowl, combine the flour, sugar, oil, eggs, vanilla, baking soda, cinnamon, and salt. Mix well, then stir in the cherry pie filling. Add the chocolate chips and the nuts. Pour the batter into the prepared pan and bake for 1 hour, or until a toothpick inserted in the thickest part comes out clean. Take the cake from the oven and let cool on a rack for 10 minutes. Remove the cake from the pan and let cool completely. Dust with confectioners' sugar.   *Makes 1 large cake*

Fresh Cherry-Berry Pie

The tartness of the cherries blends well with the delicate sweetness of the raspberries. This is a marriage made in fruit country.

Pastry for a two-crust 9-inch pie
½ egg white, lightly beaten
2 cups pitted fresh tart red
  cherries
1½ cups fresh raspberries

3 tablespoons tapioca
1 cup sugar
1 tablespoon butter or
  margarine

Preheat the oven to 400°F.

Roll out the bottom crust and lay it in the pie pan. Brush with a light coating of beaten egg white to keep it from getting soggy as the pie bakes.

In a mixing bowl, combine the cherries and raspberries. Add

the tapioca and sugar and blend well. Let stand for 15 minutes, or until the tapioca softens and the sugar begins to draw off the liquid from the fruit and slowly dissolve.

Pour the mixture into the lined pan and dot with butter or margarine. Roll out the top crust and lay it over the filling, then flute the edges and prick steam holes in the top. Bake the pie for 10 minutes at 400°, then lower the temperature to 350° and bake for 30 minutes more, or until the filling starts to bubble up through the steam holes. Allow to cool, then serve. *Makes 1 pie*

THE NATIONAL CHERRY FESTIVAL is held in Traverse City the week following July 4. There are events and contests on each day. Cherry orchard tours ($1) are offered daily. The Very Cherry Luncheon is usually held on Friday. There are several parades, each with a theme. Most events take place at the twin tents area; the luncheon is at a local hotel ($6 for adults/$4 for children). Parades take place downtown, about two blocks from the twin tents. A carnival with rides is set up across the street from the tents. Many families come prepared to spend several days at the festival, so Traverse City tends to get booked up, especially the campground in town. If you plan to come on the weekend, it would be a good idea to have reservations.

Traverse City is located on Grand Traverse Bay, about 185 miles north of Lansing, off U.S. 31. Sleeping Bear Dunes National Lakeshore is nearby (25 miles) and is definitely worth a visit. For more information about Traverse City and the festival (including a schedule of events), write National Cherry Festival, P.O. Box 141, Traverse City, Michigan 49684. Tickets to the luncheon (and other ticketed events such as the high school band competition, the queen's coronation ball, and the chicken barbecue on the beach) may be purchased by mail.

Minnesota Wild Rice Festival

Kelliher/Waskish, Minnesota

*B*ACK IN THE EARLY 1900s, the boggy soil in northern Minnesota was drained and opened up for homesteading. Settlers moved in and tried growing a variety of crops, but the naturally high water level made it backbreaking work. The farms were soon abandoned, and the land reverted to the state. For years it remained a remote area populated mostly by herons, geese, and ducks, who fed on the seeds of the wild grasses that grew in abundance.

Among those wild grasses and boggy lands were lakes that sprouted wild rice each year. The rice had been harvested and marketed for decades, but it wasn't until about twenty-five years ago that local people took another look at these sodden areas. They built dikes to create rice paddies, channeled more water from neighboring peat bogs, and planted seeds from the rice growing in the wild. Their experiment worked, and today there are about twenty growers, producing over 3 million pounds of rice annually. It is basically the same rice as grows in the wild, but its conditions for growth are controlled, robbing nature of its fickleness while ensuring larger, better-quality wild rice.

As a cultivated crop, wild rice is relatively new. So is the Wild Rice Festival, held each July since 1972. The festivities are shared by two northern Minnesota towns—Kelliher and Waskish—although the people who participate come from other towns in the vicinity as well. This two-day event includes softball and volleyball championships, country craft fair and flea market, bicycle and tricycle races, a demolition derby, horseshoe pitching, a kiddie parade, and a full-fledged parade of beauty queens, local merchants, and charity groups. But, though all these diversions are fun, the stress at this festival remains on the local product. Adults and youngsters compete in demonstrations on cooking and serving wild rice, with samples for tasting. Local groups have booths selling wild rice baked goods and wild rice cookbooks. There are educational displays about the cultivation of wild rice. Even the beauty pageant contestants must give a short talk on an aspect of growing or cooking wild rice.

You'll learn a lot about wild rice here. You'll find out that it is not a grain but a grass, and that it requires a water level of six to eight inches in the spring to germinate and send up its first leaf. This sliver of a leaf grows higher as the water level gradually lowers until it forms a segmented stalk and sends up a cornlike tassel with lovely chartreuse flowers. The flowers go to seed as the water drains away completely during the summer, and in September of each year the growers hop up onto their big combines fitted with gigantic balloon tires. These large combines bend the stalks over, cut them free, and then separate the rice from the chaff—a mechanized version of ancient Indian methods. The grain is washed and processed, then graded by length and width. Broken grains are sold at a lower cost, often to be ground into wild rice flour, while the long, dark beauties are packaged for shipment to gourmet stores throughout the country and around the world. The rice being produced in these man-made paddies is still called wild rice. Although it has been cultivated, it has not been domesticated, and it is every bit as nutty in flavor and crunchy in texture as its uncultivated counterpart.

On Saturday of the festival, in front of Kelliher High School, big chunks of beef brisket turn slowly on portable rotisserie barbecues. The meat is basted hourly as it gently cooks over a mixture of briquets and wood chips, acquiring a lusty, smoked flavor. The barbecue is served up Saturday night to over five hundred people. Along with the meat are two baked wild rice dishes—one with carrots, one with mushrooms—a crisp wild rice salad, and moist wild rice fruit bars. Dinner is served cafeteria style, and you can go back for seconds should you wish. We thought the barbecue a tasty accompaniment to the rice dishes.

The next morning the scene shifts to Waskish, where the pancake breakfast is held outdoors, near the recreation center. Don't miss the pancakes, especially if you have some mistaken notion about what a pancake is. You're in Minnesota, where Scandinavian Americans make their pancakes thin and light as mountain air. In this case, they have mixed up some cooked wild rice into their batter, so the cakes take on a nutty taste.

At the festival you'll also have the opportunity to buy wild rice bread—a soft, slightly sweet loaf studded with rice kernels. Perhaps you'll be lucky enough to sample some popped wild rice—kernels that have been heated in hot oil until they expand and pop, much as popcorn does. Popped wild rice kernels resemble Chinese rice sticks and are delicious. Lastly you'll have the chance to buy, at bargain prices, a year or two's worth of wild rice to take home.

Two-Way Wild Rice Bread

There are two types of wild rice bread baked in Minnesota: the first is a simple white bread into which is kneaded some cooked wild rice; the other is a nutty-tasting loaf that contains some wild rice flour. The following recipe combines the two, for a loaf made with both wild rice flour and wild rice kernels.

1 package (¼ ounce) active dry
   yeast
¼ cup water, warmed to 105–
   115°F
2 cups milk, scalded, then
   cooled to lukewarm (105–
   115°F)
¼ cup sugar
1 tablespoon salt
3 tablespoons vegetable oil

4 cups bread or all-purpose flour
1 cup wild rice flour (see note)
1 cup cooked wild rice

In a large mixing bowl, dissolve the yeast in the warm water. Add the milk, sugar, salt, and oil, then gradually stir in 3 cups of the bread or all-purpose flour and all the wild rice flour. Knead the dough until soft, adding the additional 1 cup flour to keep the dough from getting sticky. Knead for about 10 minutes, or until the dough is smooth and elastic. Form into a ball and place in a greased bowl. Cover and let rise for 1 hour, or until doubled in bulk.

When the dough has doubled, punch down and let rest for 10 minutes. Roll out on a floured surface to an even ½-inch thickness and spread the cooked wild rice over it. Roll up and shape into 2 loaves. Place in greased 8½-by-4½-inch loaf pans and let rise again until doubled, about 40 minutes.

Preheat the oven to 400°F. Bake the loaves for 25 to 30 minutes, then set on a rack to cool. This bread is excellent accompanying a main course and is also good toasted. *Makes 2 loaves*

NOTE: You can make wild rice flour by grinding uncooked kernels in a blender or food processor until they resemble coarse black pepper. In the rice-growing area, you can purchase grade 4 rice, which is mostly broken bits of grains and is best suited for such grinding. One pound of broken rice will yield 2½ cups flour.

Wild Rice Pancakes

1 cup cooked wild rice
½ cup (1 stick) butter, melted
3 large eggs, lightly beaten
1½ cups milk

2 tablespoons sugar
1 cup all-purpose flour
2 teaspoons baking powder
½ teaspoon salt

Place the wild rice in a bowl; add the butter, eggs, milk, and sugar and mix until smooth. Add the flour gradually to form a smooth batter. Stir in the baking powder and salt and set aside.

Heat a griddle until very hot, then spoon the batter by small ladlefuls onto the griddle. Let the pancakes brown on one side, then turn and cook on the other side briefly until browned. Serve with maple syrup and butter.   *Serves 4*

Wild Rice Salad

1 cup uncooked wild rice
2 cups water
2 eggs, hard-cooked and chopped
2 scallions, chopped
1 stalk celery, chopped

¼ cup fresh or thawed frozen peas
3 to 4 Spanish olives, chopped
1 tablespoon capers

DRESSING

1 tablespoon Dijon-style mustard
¼ cup wine vinegar

¾ cup salad oil
Salt and pepper to taste

It is not necessary to rinse the wild rice unless it seems gritty. Place the rice in a saucepan with the water and bring to a boil. Cover and let cook for 20 to 45 minutes, or until done. (The cooking time varies greatly, depending on the nature of the rice.) Drain the rice and let dry.

In a large salad bowl, place the cooked rice, chopped eggs, scallions, celery, peas, olives, and capers. Combine the ingredients for the dressing in a small jar and shake well. Add the dressing to the salad and toss well. Chill for about 30 minutes, then serve.   *Serves 2 to 4*

Popped Wild Rice

Try this instead of popcorn the next time you want a quick snack. It won't look like popcorn, but you'll hear the familiar "pop" as the kernels burst open.

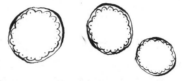

Vegetable oil for frying
½ cup uncooked wild rice
Salt

Pour the oil into a skillet until it reaches a 1-inch depth. Heat until quite hot, about 350°F. Test to see if it is ready by dropping a single rice kernel in; if the kernel immediately swells up, then the oil is ready.

Place 1 tablespoon of the rice in a strainer, then lower the strainer into the oil. Shake the strainer as the kernels puff and pop—about 1 minute. Then lift the strainer out of the oil and drain the rice on a paper towel. Continue to fry the remaining kernels, 1 tablespoonful at a time. Salt the popped rice and serve while still warm.   *Serves about 6*

THE MINNESOTA STATE WILD RICE FESTIVAL is held on a weekend in early July. On Saturday, the events are in Kelliher; on Sunday in Waskish. The Wild Rice Food Show takes place Saturday morning; the wild rice and barbecue beef supper is Saturday evening. On Sunday is the wild rice pancake breakfast. Contests and games take place both days. There is no admission charge to festival events; the supper costs $5 (tickets are bought at the door), and the pancake breakfast is $2. No reservations are needed.

Kelliher is located about 50 miles north of Bemidji; Waskish is 17 miles farther north along Route 72. There is camping in Kelliher, but the nearest motels are in Bemidji. For additional information, write to the Wild Rice Festival Committee, Kelliher, Minnesota 56650.

Black-Eyed Pea Jamboree

Athens, Texas

*T*HE GRAND PRIZE WINNER of the 1983 black-eyed reci-pea contest was a wedding cake made with—you guessed it: black-eyed peas. It was presented on a small table, under an arch decorated with flowers. Alongside the cake stood the cook (and inventor), dressed as a bride. Clearly it was the most elaborate, spectacular—and different—dish of the contest.

The cook-off is big stuff, with lots of prize money, but it's not easy. There are four categories and four semifinalists in each category, with only one winner for each category. To enter the contest you must come up with an unusual way of preparing black-eyed peas; that's the first problem. Then, if you are the winner, you must prepare the dish again the following day for four hundred people, so that festival-goers can sample your winning reci-pea. Black-eyed peas, also called cowpeas, are usually prepared in a small variety of ways: boiled up plain or maybe with a little hambone; as part of hoppin' John, a mixture of rice, peas, and ham; or, on rare occasions, in a salad or soup. They are a leguminous lentil with a black center, popular in the South and parts of the West, especially East Texas. Most people just like 'em straight, and coming up with a new and appealing use for them can be quite a challenge. Certainly a wedding cake is something no one ever thought of before.

Growing and processing black-eyed peas are a large part of life in Athens, Texas. So it naturally became the black-eyed pea capital of the world, and the site for the annual (since 1971) jamboree, where each July there are lots of pea events—from pea poppin' and pea shelling to a pea pickers' square dance and a black-eyed pea dinner.

With booths selling barbecue of all kinds, plus their own versions of black-eyed peas, this jamboree is a fun-filled event for food lovers who are partial to a smoky flavor. The barbecue here is East Texas style; that is, mostly beef, because you are in Texas, with a vinegary tomato sauce, because you are in East Texas. If you are blessed with a big appetite, you can saunter down the row of booths and sample each one.

The Sweet Adelines, a barbershop quartet, sing while they slice and serve their brisket. But if your capacity isn't as great as you'd like it to be, just head straight for Po' Melvin's, where a Louisiana cook has taken his hand to the local specialty.

Mel LeMane is a Cajun, now living in Irving, Texas, who makes a mighty fine brew. His peas are simmered with ham, scallions, and bacon, but the secret, says Mel, is to use fresh peas. He serves his with jalapeño cornbread—a combination born in heaven. Mel was a winner at the Texas state fairs in 1980, '81, and '82. He also entered the cooking contest the year we attended the jamboree, and came in second. Mel presented his reci-pea in a tureen that looked like a giant black-eyed pea, but we guessed the judges didn't think black-eyed peas and ham unusual enough to win the grand prize. We asked Mel how a Cajun feels about cooking Texas style. He replied that he likes to eat and that "only a coon-ass would have two kitchens and one bathroom."

There are lots of other activities at the jamboree, including a swim meet, a parade, a carnival, an arts and crafts show, a bicycle race, and a beauty pageant. The highlight of this three-day celebration, however, is the National Terrapin Races. These races are for children, who pit their pet terrapins against one another on a track about six feet long. The children carry their racers in an assortment of containers. We saw one very young boy holding his turtle in a basket carefully lined with tissue. Nearby, the winners of the pea-shelling contest were finishing up, with groans of "toughest peas I've ever had to shell." As the hulls from the peas flew to the ground near the terrapin track, the children readied their pets for the next heat. The little boy looked worried. Should he give his little pet a warm-up run on the track? Did the terrapin with the racing stripes really seem that fast?

Round about four on Saturday afternoon, the line starts to form for the black-eyed pea dinner. This is a buffet line, and dinner consists of chicken-fried steak (a thin Salisbury steak that is breaded and fried) with cream gravy, cole slaw, green beans, black-eyed peas, and cornbread. On the side a condiments table had pickles, onion rings, and three kinds of wonderful hot peppers. This is a Texas-style country dinner, and the food is simple but good. After dinner most people headed over to nearby Bruce Field to hear the Charlie Daniels Band.

Black-eyed peas are supposed to bring good luck, especially if eaten on New Year's Day. They certainly bring that and a whole lot of fun to East Texas. Y'all come back real soon.

Black-eyed Peas and Ham

This is Po' Melvin's recipe, as he serves it at the festival.

½ pound bacon, chopped
2 cups scallions, chopped
1 quart fresh black-eyed peas
(see note)

2 cups cubed boiled ham
Salt and pepper to taste

Fry the bacon until crisp, then add the scallions to the bacon and drippings. Sauté the scallions until soft, then add the black-eyed peas and the ham. Cover with water and add 1 additional cup water. Cover and cook until the black-eyed peas are tender, about 10 minutes. Serve with jalapeño cornbread.   *Serves 4 to 6*

NOTE: Fresh black-eyed peas are so far superior in this recipe that it has been difficult to come up with a substitute for those not fortunate enough to have them in their markets. You could make the dish with canned black-eyed peas, but don't use dried.

Jalapeño Cornbread

This is a crumbly cornbread, almost a large biscuit. The hotness here is moderate; increase the amount of chopped peppers if you want more fire.

1 cup yellow cornmeal
½ cup all-purpose flour
1 tablespoon baking powder
1 teaspoon salt
¼ cup lard or shortening

2 large eggs, lightly beaten
½ cup milk
1 pickled jalapeño, trimmed,
seeded, and minced

Preheat the oven to 350°F. Grease a 9-inch square baking pan.
   In a bowl, combine the cornmeal, flour, baking powder, and salt. Cut in the lard or shortening until the mixture resembles coarse meal. Add the eggs and milk and stir until the mixture is smooth. Add the minced

pepper and stir to blend in. Pour the mixture into the prepared pan and bake for 20 to 25 minutes, or until the cornbread has risen and is firm in the center. Push the center down; it should bounce back. Allow to cool slightly before cutting and serving. *Serves 6*

"Eyes of Texas" Salad

This recipe won Linda Martin of Athens, Texas, the Grand Championship in the 1982 Black-eyed Pea Jamboree cooking contest.

1½ cups canned black-eyed peas, drained
1 cup chopped cooked chicken
¼ cup chopped celery
½ teaspoon salt

1 cup cooked white rice
¼ cup chopped onions
¼ cup mayonnaise
1 teaspoon black pepper
Dash hot sauce

DRESSING

1 avocado, seeded, peeled, and mashed
½ cup sour cream
1 teaspoon garlic salt
½ cup mayonnaise

½ teaspoon Worcestershire sauce
¼ teaspoon salt
1 teaspoon lemon juice

In a bowl, mix the ingredients for the salad and pack them into a greased 1-quart ring mold. Chill in the refrigerator for 30 minutes.

While the salad sets, mix the ingredients for the dressing. "Ice" the salad with the dressing or mound the dressing in the center, with the salad forming a ring around it. *Serves 6*

THE BLACK-EYED PEA JAMBOREE is held in mid-July in Athens, Texas. Food and souvenir booths and the carnival rides are open Friday, Saturday, and Sunday, but most contests and events take place on Saturday and Sunday. The cook-off finalists are judged on Saturday at 1:00 P.M. (open to the public); the country dinner (featuring black-eyed peas, of course) is served at 5:30. The dinner is cafeteria-style; tickets are $3.95 and are available at the door or in advance from the festival booth.

On Sunday, festival-goers have an opportunity to sample the cook-off winners' "reci-peas." And there are also pea-shelling and pea-popping contests. All events (except Saturday night's concert) are held on the festival grounds at Henderson County Junior College. There is parking on local streets; plan to arrive by 9:30 A.M. on Saturday if you want to see the parade. There is no admission charge to the festival; all events except the concert and dinner are free. Tickets for the concert and dinner can be purchased by mail from the Athens Chamber of Commerce (or at the door).

Athens is located about 75 miles southeast of Dallas, off U.S. 175. For a schedule of events and additional information, write the Chamber, P.O. Box 608J, Athens, Texas 75751; or phone (214) 675–5181.

Central Maine Egg Festival

Pittsfield, Maine

W E SAT DOWN TO BREAKFAST one July morning up in Pittsfield, and asked the farmer next to us just what the difference was between a brown egg and a white egg. His answer? "Brown eggs are fresh eggs; white eggs are imported." We smiled, then he gave us the reasoning behind his retort. Ninety-five percent of New England's eggs are brown. They come from Harco, Plymouth Rock, Warren, Comet, and Rhode Island Red hens. Had we been eating a white egg just then, chances are it would have been imported from some state like New Jersey—and therefore not as fresh.

We *were* eating brown eggs, and they were fresh and hot. It was a chilly morning, but we had headed for the open tent in Manson Park, where breakfast was being served at the Central Maine Egg Festival. There, working in an efficient, assembly-line fashion, were women from the local Arts Club standing around the rim of a ten-foot-wide frying pan. They were tossing in slices of buttered bread and slabs of ham, then flipping them with long-handled spatulas. To one side, other women were cooking up smaller pans of eggs—individually prepared and any way you wanted them.

As we watched our eggs being scrambled, the cook explained that in years past they also used to make the eggs in the giant pan. The skillet was donated in 1973 by Alcoa Aluminum. Dupont Company gave it a Teflon coating, and the Maingas Company installed the burners for heating it. Over the years, however, the pan began to warp, and now its use is limited to toast and ham. We took our plate of scrambled eggs and ham down the line, picked up toast and jelly, scooped up our helpings of molasses-baked yellow-eye beans (people in Maine seem to eat beans at every meal), and chose our cups of coffee and tea. It was a hearty way to start a festival day.

A short walk from the park took us back to the center of town for the parade. Store windows showed the results of a highly competitive window-decorating competition. All the windows had paintings based on an egg theme: WE BREAK FOR THE EGG FESTIVAL was the winner in the fourteen-to-seventeen age group, with a picture of eggs being scrambled in a skillet. The cleverest was the adult winner: EGGSTRA, EGGSTRA, read the headline of the *National Eggquirer*, with lead stories such as WHOLE FAMILY SCRAMBLED IN BIZARRE INCIDENT and EGG BAND HATCHES NEW CRAZE—CRACKIN'.

By 9:00 A.M. the parade was under way. Flags lined both sides of Main Street, and balloons were tied to the street corners. As with most festival parades, here was the usual procession of beauty queens, high school bands, and politicians. This parade also featured the high-stepping Sharpies, a drill team from Augusta, Maine, who put on a dazzling display, sending their plastic rifles crisscrossing their formation, then under and over their arms. The Boy Scout float showed scouting in action: tents, trees, a canoe, and an actual campfire with a chicken cooking.

Other floats came by, including the Eggshop Quartet singing, "Egg MacDonald had a farm . . . with a yolk, yolk here . . ." Farm machinery crawled by us, followed by a manure spreader full of manure and manned by a candidate running for local office. His sign read, POLITICS IS A LOT LIKE FARMING. The parade ended with an extensive collection of antique fire engines, including a demonstration of an 1836 hand pump owned by the Dexter Fire Department.

At the conclusion of the parade, everyone walked back to Manson Park to visit the food and crafts booths, play the games (darts, bingo, games of chance), and take a spin on some of the rides. On a field adjacent to the booths, kids were taking part in the Egglympics. These races were like an old-fashioned field day: not too formal and a lot of fun. The children, ranging from one to eleven years old, had to carry an egg from one point to another, balancing it atop a cardboard roll. They also had to push an egg with their nose, carry an egg in a spoon, and balance an egg on a plate. The festival organizers used to use raw eggs, we were told, but it got too messy.

This festival has a prestige event as well. It is the World's Largest Egg Contest, with the winning egg gilded and put on display in succeeding years. The judging is by water. That is, to determine the size (its volume), the egg is measured by the amount of water it displaces. The contest is always close. At the time we were there only seventeen cubic centimeters separated the tenth place from the first place. The winner, from Detroit, Maine, selected her giant egg from among the twenty thousand she collects on her farm each day.

We went over to take a look at the past winners. The eggs were all big—a lot bigger than what most shoppers in supermarkets are used to. These gilded eggs seemed graceful and elegant. The gilding highlights the perfect shape of this food on which we all very much depend.

There's another example of that dependence at lunch on Saturday. The omelet luncheon is an Egg Festival tradition, sponsored by the Hospital Auxiliary. It's an omelet of your choice, made with any or all of the following: onions, green peppers, mushrooms, ham, cheese. Each omelet is prepared individually and served with coffee or tea, roll and butter, and a fruit salad. And the question of whether the chicken or the egg came first is settled here, because the chicken barbecue is served in the late afternoon of the festival, followed by two band concerts and a display of fireworks. All told, this festival is a lot of fun in celebration of the incredible, edible egg.

Festival Omelet

The ingredients below are for 1 serving. Multiply the recipe for as many servings as you need, and use ½ to ⅔ cup of the egg mixture for each 2-egg omelet.

2 large eggs
2 to 3 tablespoons water
⅛ to ¼ teaspoon salt
Dash pepper
1 tablespoon butter

¼ cup filling (chopped onions,
green peppers, cooked
mushrooms, boiled ham, or
Cheddar cheese)

Mix the eggs, water, salt, and pepper until blended.

Heat the butter in a 9- or 10-inch omelet pan or skillet over medium-high heat until just hot enough to sizzle a drop of water. Pour in the egg mixture; the mixture should immediately set at the edges. With an inverted pancake turner, carefully push the cooked portions at the edges toward the center so that the uncooked portions can reach the hot pan surface, tilting the pan and moving the cooked portions as necessary. While the top is still moist and creamy-looking, sprinkle on the filling. With the pancake turner turned upright, fold the omelet in half or roll, and either invert the omelet onto a plate with a quick flip of the wrist or slide it onto the plate.   *Serves 1*

THE CENTRAL MAINE EGG FESTIVAL is held in Pittsfield on the fourth weekend in July. All events (except the children's parade and the egg queen pageant) take place on Saturday. The festival begins with breakfast—eggs, of course—from 6:00 to 8:30 A.M. ($3) and goes on till the fireworks display at 9:30 P.M. An omelet lunch is served ($3.50); and in addition there are other food stands selling the usual hot dogs, pizza, and so forth. You buy your breakfast and/or lunch tickets at the door. The chicken barbecue is on Saturday from 4:00 to 8:00 P.M. and costs about $3.50; tickets are available at the dinner.

The festival takes place at Manson Park, except for the parade, which ends at the park. There is no admission fee, but a $2 parking charge is levied. The food tents are well supplied with tables and chairs, and there are chairs out in front of the stage, too.

Pittsfield is on Route 11/100, off I-95, about 30 miles west of Bangor. For information, write the Central Maine Egg Festival Corporation, Pittsfield, Maine 04967.

Pork, Peanut, and Pine Festival

Surry, Virginia

HEN WE TOOK OFF for the Pork, Peanut, and Pine Festival, we didn't know very much about it, but our craving for barbecue was becoming uncontrollable, and, besides, who could resist that name? It was a sure bet that pork meant pork barbecue—pit-roasted hunks of pork "pulled" off the bone and simmered for hours in a sweet-spicy sauce. And peanut was understandable too, since Virginia was the site of the first commercial crop of "goober peas." The pine part had us stumped, so we headed south to find out.

Our anticipation as we near any festival is often unbearable, and for this summertime Virginia event it started to build as we boarded the ferry to cross the James River. Many other people on the boat were also headed for the Chippokes Plantation Farm, site of the festival. We caught glimpses of fliers on the backseats of cars and heard squeals of excitement from children. A man on the ferry handed us a flier, commenting, "It's lots of good, clean fun." The flier listed the treats in store: barbecue sandwiches, pit-cooked barbecue, chitterlings, crackling, cornbread and biscuits, ham biscuits, pigs' feet, salted peanuts, peanut brittle, peanut cookies, peanut pie, peanut soup, spiced and sugared peanuts, grilled pork chops, candy, and fudge. Sounded like enough to keep us busy.

Fish jumped in the water, gulls circled overhead, and, as the ferry moved slowly across the James River, we were transported to a gentler world and an era we'd thought had long passed. Chippokes Plantation is a model working farm that displays and re-creates day-to-day activities of Virginia farm life from the past three centuries, but back in the 1700s it was one of the James River plantations. The river served as a water link bringing cotton from the plantations between Richmond and Williamsburg downriver to Norfolk and the Chesapeake. As you approach the grounds of Chippokes, you'll see demonstration plantings of Virginia's leading crops: corn, wheat, soybeans, tobacco, cotton, and—of course—peanuts.

The festival exhibits are set up in clusters, so the food booths are all together, while a few yards away, grouped around elegant, flowering crape myrtle trees, are the crafts booths. There are other attractions as well, including a display of antique farm equipment such as a two-man peanut cleaner from the 1700s and a peanut sheller from 1904. The two stages provide almost constant country music, and there are puppet shows for children, contests, and other entertainments. In the center are the industry booths—the explanation behind the festival itself. Pork (hog production), peanuts (mostly large podded types used for salted or roasted nuts), and pine (loblolly for lumber and paper) are the three major industries of Surry County. Each year, about seventy thousand people attend this celebration of local industries.

Now that the meaning of the festival was made clear, we headed immediately for the food booths. They were small, temporary stands, elaborately decorated with pine boughs, peanut shells, and deer antlers. The names of the sponsors—local churches, hunting clubs, and civic groups—were overhead: Runnymede Young Adult Choir, Mount Moriah A.M.E. Church, Jerusalem Baptist Church, Oak Grove Baptist Church, Mercy Seat Church, True Apostolic Church, Moonlight Hunt Club, Popular Lawn Baptist Church, First Assembly of God, Pastor's Lebanon Baptist Church, Cypress Baptist Church, Salisbury Hunt Club, Surry Volunteer Rescue Squad.

Working our way around the circle of booths, we sampled many varieties of barbecue, comparing their flavors and judging the spiciness of their sauces. We waited on line for the smoky and tender barbecued pork chops, a platter dish that comes with slaw and beans. Then we moved on to the vinegary chitterlings served with a flat and dense cornbread. When we heard that one booth had potato jacks, we rushed there to enjoy these pastry-covered purees of sweet potato, deep-fried to a golden crispness. Unfortunately the peanut soup we sampled was not good, too much like liquid peanut butter with nuts on top, and the ham biscuits, disappointingly, were not homemade, nor was the ham one of Virginia's wonderful cured masterpieces. But we happily concluded the feast with several varieties of peanut and peanut-raisin pie—the latter truly a concoction made in a peanut-lover's heaven.

Barbecued Virginia Pork Chops with Red Honey Sauce

This recipe is courtesy of the Virginia Pork Industry Commission.

1 cup catsup
¾ cup prepared chili sauce
½ cup honey (preferably from Virginia)
¼ cup dark brown sugar

4 tablespoons (½ stick) butter
1 teaspoon dry mustard
¼ cup water
6 pork loin chops (1 to 1¼ inches thick)

In a saucepan, combine all the ingredients except the chops. Bring to a boil, then remove from the heat. Place the chops on a grill over low to medium coals. Grill the chops for 10 minutes per side. Brush with the hot sauce. Continue cooking for 5 minutes more per side, or until done. *Serves 6*

Peanut-Raisin Pie

A wonderful change from pecan pie, this recipe is courtesy of the Virginia Peanut Growers Association.

3 large eggs
1 cup sugar
1 cup dark corn syrup
4 tablespoons (½ stick) butter, melted
½ cup raisins
1 cup chopped unsalted dry-roasted peanuts

1 tablespoon white vinegar
1 teaspoon vanilla extract
⅛ teaspoon ground cloves
One 9-inch deep-dish pie shell, unbaked

Preheat the oven to 350°F.

In a large bowl, beat the eggs. Add the sugar, corn syrup, and melted butter. Mix well. Stir in the remaining ingredients, and pour the mixture into the pie shell. Bake for 1 hour, or until set. Serve warm, with whipped cream or vanilla ice cream. *Serves 6 to 8*

Spiced Virginia Peanuts

These spiced peanuts are adapted from a recipe of the Growers' Peanut Food Promotions. They are best when made from freshly roasted large Virginia peanuts, available in some natural foods stores and occasionally in supermarkets. Hancock Peanut Company, Courtland, Virginia 23837, also ships fresh Virginia peanuts. To avoid spoilage, however, store all raw peanuts in the freezer until ready to use.

1 cup sugar
½ cup water
1 teaspoon ground cinnamon
½ teaspoon ground nutmeg

½ teaspoon ground cloves
2 cups shelled fresh-roasted
peanuts, skins removed
(see note)

In a saucepan, boil the sugar with the water and spices until the mixture is syrupy and threadlike, about 225°F on a candy thermometer. Drop in the nuts all at once and stir to coat, then pour the nut mixture onto waxed paper. Try to get the nuts into a single layer, smoothing the batter out as best you can. Allow to cool, then break up into clusters and pass among your guests or family as a snack.

NOTE: To roast raw peanuts in the shell, heat the oven to 350°F and spread the nuts on a large tray or baking sheet. The peanuts should only be in one layer, with a little space between them. Bake for 20 minutes, then allow to cool. *Makes 2 cups*

THE PORK, PEANUT, AND PINE FESTIVAL is held on a weekend in mid-July at Chippokes Plantation State Park, Surry, Virginia. Admission is free; there is a $1 charge for parking. All entertainment takes place (on two stages) from 10:00 A.M. till 6:00 P.M. on Saturday, and from noon till 6:00 P.M. on Sunday. Artists and artisans display their wares on both days—some on the front lawn under the flowering crape myrtle trees, others in the formal garden. The industry exhibits are in the barn area. Chippokes is a working plantation and is run as a model farm. The historic mansion is closed during the festival, but is well worth a separate visit. Pork and peanuts in countless preparations are served at individual booths, many run by local churches and civic groups. Prices range from 50¢ for peanut soup to $4 for a barbecue plate.

Chippokes State Park is located about 60 miles southeast of Richmond, off Route 10. It can also be reached from Williamsburg via the Colonial Parkway and the James River ferry. For additional information about the festival, contact Chippokes State Park, Surry, Virginia 23883.

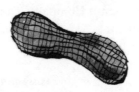

Gilroy Garlic Festival

Gilroy, California

ONE MORNING LATE IN JULY we traded the damp San Francisco fog for the hot sunshine of the Santa Clara Valley. A few miles south of Morgan Hill, the air became thick and sweet with the smell of freshly harvested garlic. We were approaching the annual Gilroy Garlic Festival, and anticipation began to grow. We had heard all sorts of tales about Gilroy and its garlic extravaganza, but would they really have garlic ice cream? "I'll bet they don't have chocolate-covered garlic," a friend exclaimed, and we were certain they wouldn't go that far, not even in California.

An oak- and eucalyptus-shaded park about the size of a small town is the setting for this very large food festival, a three-day event that is world famous for its single-minded devotion to the "scented pearl." On the festival grounds, the aroma in the air is different. There it is the smell of garlic cooking, mingled with the scent of barbecued steaks, sautéed calamari, and other familiar uses for garlic.

We eased into the fair and strolled among the booths, which were selling a host of items derived from or based on garlic. One stand featured Garlique, a fragrance made from garlic extract with rose scent added; we were reminded that garlic is known as the "stinking rose." Their flier noted, "He may forget your name, but he'll know you've been there." Another booth was hawking the Garlic Machine, similar to a garlic press but with a screw-type mechanism that pushes the garlic through the holes as you need it. Elsewhere, someone was selling a garlic squeeze, supposedly self-cleaning. Everywhere there were long braids of garlic; one local grower was selling a garlic corsage—two or three heads twined with a dried flower and a pretty ribbon.

In addition to the gadgets, we spied garlic charms (in fourteen-carat gold), garlic caricatures and cartoons, misty-looking photos of garlic in the raw, garlic appliqués on totebags, and garlic prints on potholders and dishcloths. There seemed to be no limit to the imagination when it came to garlic.

We moved along quickly to Gourmet Alley, a central area of major food booths run by the festival organizers. It is here, under a huge tent, that the large-scale cooking goes on and the best foods are offered. There are six specialties, and they rarely vary: marinated and stuffed mushrooms, pasta con pesto, pepper steak sandwich, scampi, calamari, and a vegetable stir-fry with garlic bread. Although all were good, the pepper steak and calamari were outstanding. The steaks are done Santa Maria style—marinated in rosemary, lemon juice, olive oil, and garlic, and barbecued until crisp. They are basted with the marinade, which is spread on with giant rosemary branches, then served on garlic bread with sautéed green peppers and onions. When the calamari is cooked, a show takes place as the chef flambés the strips of squid in a sauce of white wine, garlic, lemon juice, and tomatoes. Calamari has never been so tender and sweet.

Not far from Gourmet Alley, in a ring surrounding the demonstration area, are additional food booths. Here we sampled some other garlic offerings: garlots (deep-fried spring rolls filled with beef, garlic, onions, and tomatoes), garlic tamales, garlic-fried ravioli, escargot kebabs (three escargots and two mushrooms on a skewer, dripping with garlic butter and served on a baguette), pickled garlic ("garlic torsie," an East Indian food), garlic jelly (plain citrus jelly flavored with garlic, best used as a condiment), and—yes—garlic ice cream! The last surprised us. Gilroy Foods mixed up some soft vanilla ice cream with a little granulated garlic for a combination that is not too sweet and actually quite refreshing. The only garlic item we didn't like at the festival was the newly introduced garlic wine, a novelty from a local vineyard. It tasted oily, like mediocre Chablis mixed with garlic juice.

Why all the fuss about garlic in Gilroy? The Garlic Festival was begun in 1979 to boost Gilroy's image as a garlic-producing and -processing area, and it has succeeded in bringing upward of 110,000 people here each year to discover countless uses for garlic. Will Rogers described Gilroy as "the only town in America where you can marinate a steak by hanging it on the clothesline," but these Gilroy folks have turned a liability into an asset. The air does have an intense smell that strains your patience, but this festival is one of the most sophisticated we've ever attended. There's no concession to the mundane hamburgers, hot dogs, and cotton candy. Fresh garlic reigns here, in well-prepared and tasty dishes that are a cut far above the usual.

Scampi in Butter Sauce

The following is a Gourmet Alley favorite, from the *Garlic Lover's Cookbook*. It is reprinted here courtesy of the Gilroy Garlic Festival Association, Inc.

BUTTER SAUCE

2 to 1 cup (1 to 2 sticks) butter
1 tablespoon finely minced fresh garlic
8-ounce jar clam juice
¼ cup all-purpose flour
1 tablespoon minced parsley

⅓ cup white wine
Juice of ½ lemon
1 teaspoon dried basil
¼ teaspoon ground nutmeg
Salt and pepper to taste
½ cup half and half

SCAMPI

2 tablespoons butter
⅓ cup olive oil
1 tablespoon minced fresh garlic (or more to taste)
Juice of 1 lemon
1 teaspoon fresh chopped parsley or 1 teaspoon dried
½ teaspoon crushed red pepper
1 tablespoon fresh basil or 1 teaspoon dried
¼ cup white wine

Salt and pepper to taste
3 pounds of deveined and cleaned jumbo shrimp or prawns

Make the sauce first. Melt the butter with the garlic in a small saucepan over medium heat; do not let the butter brown. In a separate bowl, mix the clam juice, flour, and parsley, blending until the mixture is smooth. Pour the flour mixture into the garlic butter and stir until smooth and well blended. Stir in the wine, lemon juice, herbs, and spices, stirring constantly. Gradually add the half and half and stir until thickened. Simmer, covered, for 30 to 45 minutes, stirring occasionally.

Melt the butter for the scampi in a large saucepan over high heat and add the oil. Combine remaining ingredients except the scampi, and add to the saucepan. Stir, and add the scampi and sauté until firm and slightly pink. Do not overcook. Pour 1 cup of the scampi butter over the scampi. (Refrigerate the rest of the sauce for later use.)   *Serves 6 to 8*

Baked Sweet Elephant Garlic

Here's a simple way to prepare the gigantic elephant garlics, sweeter and milder than regular garlic.

6 to 8 heads elephant garlic   *2 to 3 tablespoons butter*

Preheat the oven to 350°F. Grease a small baking dish that will just hold the garlics.

Separate the cloves, peel them, and place them in the baking dish. Place dabs of butter on top and bake until the cloves are soft and slightly caramelized on the bottom, about 1 hour. At first, when the garlic bakes, it will give off a very strong garlic odor, but it eventually tones down as the garlic becomes very sweet. These are best served with roasted meats.

Serves 4 to 6 as accompaniment

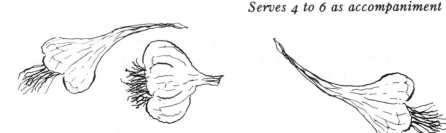

Garlots

Garlots were the invention of Sharon Kaminskas at one of the booths outside of Gourmet Alley. They were very popular with festival-goers.

2 tablespoons vegetable oil
1 medium onion, chopped
18 cloves (about 1 large head)
    garlic, peeled and chopped
1 pound chopped beef
4 tomatoes, peeled, seeded, and
    chopped

Pinch cumin
Salt and pepper to taste
8 spring roll wrappers (lumpia
    wrappers)
Vegetable oil for deep frying
½ cup grated Parmesan cheese

Heat the oil in a heavy skillet and add the onion and garlic. Cook until wilted, then add the meat, breaking up the lumps and frying until it changes color. Add the tomatoes and cook the mixture until it is dry, about 10 minutes. Add a little cumin and season with salt and pepper to taste. Let the mixture cool.

Separate the spring roll wrappers and put 1 heaping tablespoon filling on each roll along the diagonal. Fold one corner over the filling, then fold over the shorter two ends and roll the wrapper until the remaining end piece is wrapped around the filling. Moisten the end with a little water to make it stick.

Heat the deep-frying oil to 375°F and deep fry the garlots, 2 at a time, for 5 to 7 minutes. Drain on paper towels, then sprinkle with grated Parmesan cheese and serve hot. *Makes 8 garlots*

THE GILROY GARLIC FESTIVAL is held the end of July. On that weekend, "alliophiles" (garlic lovers) of the world seem to unite. There are some prefestival and off-site events (such as the Miss Garlic Festival Pageant, the Garlic Country Bicycle Tour, and the Great Garlic Recipe and Cook-off Contest), but most everything takes place at Christmas Hill Park, Gilroy. Foods are sold at the many (about one hundred) booths and at Gourmet Alley. Typical prices run about $3 to $6 per dish. Other garlickiana is also for sale: braids of varying lengths, garlic presses, garlic perfume, and so forth.

Continuous entertainment begins about 10:30 each morning and goes on till 7 at night; there are four stages, including a children's stage. In addition, there are garlic-braiding demonstrations daily as well as contests and a garlic-topping contest. Despite all the crowds, you never feel closed in; and although you might have to wait on line for a certain dish, the lines are never too long. Adequate parking is in a field adjacent to the site, and traffic in and out is handled efficiently. An admission fee ($4 for adults, $1 for children, $2 for senior citizens) is charged and is good for the whole day.

Gilroy is located about 100 miles south of San Francisco, off U.S. 101; just follow your nose! For additional information, including a schedule of events, contact the Gilroy Garlic Festival, P.O. Box 2311, Gilroy, California 95020.

Indian-Style Salmon Bake

Sequim, Washington

W E START THE FIRE with cedar to get the heat up, then put on the alder to keep the coals." That's how the Sequim Rotarians began describing their Indian-style salmon bake. They've been doing it this way since 1969, following methods developed by the Northwest Coast Indians centuries earlier. Sequim (pronounced *Skwim*) is a small town on the north shore of Washington's rugged Olympic Peninsula, a region noted for both its rich Indian culture and its abundant salmon. The temperate climate, great fishing, and lush rain forests draw a sizable summer tourist population, many of whom can be found, along with local residents, feasting at this annual event.

A day or two before the bake, one of the Rotarians comes in and rototills a small patch of the lawn by the Grange's main building, Macleay Hall. Then some members of the group lay a bed of sand a foot thick, which will hold the heat when the fire gets going well. By seven o'clock the morning of the bake the men begin to assemble, and while the fire crew gets the coals going, the rest are busy preparing the 2,400 pounds of king (Chinook) and silver (coho) salmon. First the fish are split open and the heads and tails removed. Then they are boned, butterflied, and carefully placed on long cedar stakes, tail end down. The stakes have been split in half almost from end to end, but the closed end serves as a hinge, and the slab of salmon is slipped between the two halves of the stake, then pinned to crosspieces so that the fish is spread-eagled on the stake. The fish are given a liberal dose of salt and cracked whole pepper, then the stakes are set into the sandy bed alongside the fire. By this time the heat of the fire is a steady 150 degrees. As stake after stake of salmon is added, the rows of fish begin to look like a stockade surrounding the fire. Walking around this stockade, you can see the silver skins of the salmon glisten as they are slowly baked.

"You got to have the angle just right," we were told, "so that there's no dripping off the fins. If the fins drip, the fish is cooking too fast and the oils go out. Can't cook the fish too fast." The cooking crew sees to that—walking the fire, they call it—watching each one and making whatever adjustments seem necessary: restaking, turning, shifting the angle of the stake in the sand, or moving the fish from the front row to the back row. Periodically they check the heat of the fire by holding their hands over it, and after about two hours, when the salmon are nearly baked, the fish are turned so that their skin side faces the fire and the heat gives it a last-minute crispness.

This salmon bake is one of several held in the Pacific Northwest, and one of the few that are truly "Indian-style." It is a fitting way to prepare this king of fish, producing a moist, mildly smoky fish with a very crisp skin. The bake is held in August, when the fish that is served is ocean-caught. The salmon have only just begun to muster strength for the return to their freshwater birthplaces. Thus they are juicy and plump— perfect for baking.

By noon the length of the line for tickets to the bake would rival some New York City movie houses. But then the serving begins. Dinner is plentiful: cole slaw, beans, buttered bread, and of course the salmon— about a pound apiece; and we were asked if we wanted more! Everyone sits at long tables under sunny skies enjoying themselves while L.J.'s Reminiscers play old-time songs. When the Reminiscers are ready to take a break, the Dungeness Drifters come on and serenade the happy eaters.

An announcement is made that whoever wants to can sign up for "surplus salmon," to be sold (at a ridiculously low price) after the bake. A woman comes by giving out ice cream to those who've finished their salmon. Elderly women in straw hats accompanied by elderly men in baseball caps visit friends at other tables. And by two o'clock the ticket line is still long and cars keep pouring in. The Reminiscers are back on stage singing "Stormy Weather"—funny under such a blue sky. Up on the rise of lawn, behind the tables, the last hundred salmon on stakes are being tended to, and even though we're full, it's still a mouth-watering sight.

Because of the methods involved and the unique results, it is impossible to offer any instructions on reproducing this salmon bake at home. There's really no substitute for being there.

THE SEQUIM SALMON BAKE is held at Prairie Grange, Macleay Hall, Sequim, on the first Sunday in August. Tickets are $6 and are available at the gate. The bake is from noon to 6:00 P.M. We advise getting there on the early side, as the line gets pretty long. Parking is at the Grange.

Sequim is on the Olympic Peninsula, about 17 miles east of Port Angeles on U.S. 101. There are signs in town to direct you to the Grange. For additional information, write the Sequim Chamber of Commerce, P.O. Box 907, Sequim, Washington 98382.

Other salmon bakes are held in the Pacific Northwest. There's an Indian-style bake in Depoe Bay, Oregon, and another in Klamath, California. Port Angeles has a bake, but not Indian-style. For information about these bakes, contact the local chambers of commerce or town offices.

Shaker Kitchen Festival

Hancock, Massachusetts

THE SHAKERS HAVE always paid careful attention to food and its preparation. In their earliest years they frequently gave gifts of food to victims of epidemics and disasters; all through the nineteenth century their prosperous communities hosted travelers. As the skill of the Kitchen Sisters became known, people from nearby cities came to share Saturday and Sunday dinners with them. To the Believers, these diners from outside were "the World"; and by the 1860s "the World's people" were enjoying the Shakers' hospitality in ever-growing numbers. As one Brother noted in his diary in 1883: "A load of the World from Boston today for dinner."

Fortunately, "the World" can continue to partake of those excellent meals. Every summer since 1963, Hancock Shaker Village has served World's Peoples Dinners as part of their annual Kitchen Festival. The dinners are held in the Believers' Dining Room of the 1830 Brick Dwelling, an imposing building near the center of the village that originally housed a hundred Shaker men and women. It now houses exhibits that show aspects of the Shaker way of life—food preparation, dining, health care, and meeting rooms for social and religious purposes.

In August, the Brick Dwelling becomes the center of the Kitchen Festival. Throughout the week there are demonstrations and tastings of traditional Shaker preparations: breads, pies, puddings, succotash, sweetmeats, fried cakes (such as crullers), molasses candy, and other foods. One afternoon was devoted to a study of corn.

The dinners are served each evening and also at noon on Sunday. There is a different set menu for each meal, following the style of a farm family whose pleasure is in sharing the bounty of the land.

Old accounts mention "great platters of delicious chicken with yellow gravy . . . and Shaker beans, applesauce and cake." The dinners prepared by the wise Kitchen Sisters did more than satisfy hunger and provide nutrition; their dinners were intended to "create enjoyment, joy and satisfaction to those partaking of them" as well. And they still do. Original recipes are followed, and ingredients are fresh and fine. Everyone sits at large tables and eats family style. The room is bare except for a simple chest with a vase of flowers on it. Rows of traditional Shaker pegs line the walls. The plainness of the room and its furnishings complements the simplicity and wholesomeness of the food.

As we sat down to a hearty dinner, we were handed a Table Monitor, written by a Shaker Sister, Hannah Bronson, around 1800. We were cautioned, as were the nineteenth-century visitors before us, to clean our plates:

 TABLE MONITOR

"Gather up the fragments that remain,
that nothing be lost."
                                                    —CHRIST

Here, then, is the pattern which Jesus has set,
And his good example we can not forget;
With thanks for his blessings, his word we'll obey,
But on this occasion we've something to say.

We wish to speak plainly and use no deceit;
We like to see fragments left wholesome and neat;
To customs and fashions we make no pretence,
Yet think we can tell what belongs to good sense.

What we deem good order we're willing to state,
Eat hearty and decent, and clear out our plate;
Be thankful to heaven for what we receive,
And make not a mixture or compound to leave.

We find of those bounties which heaven does give,
That some live to eat, and that some eat to live;
That some think of nothing but pleasing the taste,
And care very little how much they do waste.

Though heaven has blessed us with plenty of food:
Bread, butter and honey and all that is good;
We loathe to see mixtures where gentle folks dine,
Which scarcely look fit for the poultry or swine.

We often find left on the same China dish,
Meat, apple sauce, pickle, brown bread and minced fish;
Another's replenished with butter and cheese,
With pie, cake and toast, perhaps, added to these.

Now if any virtue in this can be shown,
By peasant, by lawyer, or king on the throne;
We freely will forfeit whatever we've said,
And call it a virtue to waste meat and bread.

Let none be offended at what we here say,
We candidly ask you, is that the best way?
If not, lay such customs and fashions aside,
And this monitor take, henceforth, for your guide.

Dinner is presented in the same way as the Shakers would have presented it to "the World" a hundred years ago. One of the waitresses sings a grace song. Then platters of steaming hot corn on the cob are set before the guests; following that come baskets of sweet breads—lemon-nut, blueberry, walnut, zucchini. The salad is served alongside. Then out come bowls full of Sister Mary's Zesty Carrots and platters of Brother Ricardo's Chicken Pudding. Most dishes are served separately, to assist the guests in not mixing things up on their plates (as per verses five and six of the *Monitor*). There is plenty of food; seconds and even thirds are cheerfully offered. Our dinner was topped off with generous slices of Mother Ann's Birthday Cake—a white layer cake with marshmallow icing—and scoops of Rose Water Frozen Cream—curiously refreshing. Other dinners give you the opportunity to sample such traditional dishes as Shaker Tomato Pudding, Meat Loaf with Herbs, Ham Baked in Cider, Ginger Beets, and Ohio Lemon Pie.

After such a rich and bountiful meal one needs a good, long walk; and Hancock Shaker Village is the perfect setting. You can stroll through the herb garden, where the herbs for all the cooking are grown. The Visitor's Center has maps of the village, and there are guides stationed throughout the buildings and grounds who can answer questions and explain aspects of Shaker life. Most of the time there are demonstrations of various crafts and chores going on—from cabinet making to herb drying.

The Kitchen Sisters often presented departing guests with a farewell gift, such as a loaf of their unforgettable bread. These breads as well as other home-baked goods can be bought in the Good Room, a shop in the basement of the Brick Dwelling. The Good Room also sells cookbooks, jellies, and herbs and spices, including rose water, which can be used for making the delicious ice cream served with many of the dinners.

The following recipes are reprinted with permission of Macmillan Company from *The Best of Shaker Cooking* by Amy Bess Miller and Persis Fuller. Copyright © 1970 by Shaker Community, Inc.

Hancock Dill Bread

This is a very soft dough; add only enough flour to make it not sticky. The dough finishes up as a light, dill-flavored loaf. Extend the baking time, if necessary, to 55 minutes if you are using metal loaf pans.

2 cups cooked and mashed potatoes
2 cups boiling water
2 packages (¼ ounce each) active dry yeast
½ cup water, warmed to 105– 115°F
¼ cup plus 1 teaspoon sugar
4 tablespoons (½ stick) butter, melted

1 tablespoon salt
1 tablespoon dried dillweed or ½ cup chopped fresh
8 cups flour
Shortening, melted
Dillweed and dill seed, crushed (optional)

Combine the potatoes and the boiling water. Mix until smooth and let cool to lukewarm.

Soften the yeast in the warm water along with 1 teaspoon of the sugar and let sit for 10 minutes.

Beat the remaining ¼ cup sugar, the butter, salt, and dillweed into the potato mixture. Gradually add about 4 cups of the flour. Beat thoroughly. Stir in the yeast mixture. Work in the remaining flour, enough to make a dough that won't stick to your hands. Turn out onto a floured board and knead until smooth and elastic. Place the dough in a greased bowl and cover. Let rise for about 2 hours, or until doubled in bulk.

Punch the dough down, cover the bowl, and let rise again for about 1½ hours, or until doubled in bulk.

Preheat oven to 375°F. Grease 3 bread pans, then divide the dough in thirds and shape it into loaves; place in pans. Brush with the melted shortening and bake for 45 minutes. Remove from the oven, brush again with shortening, and, if desired, sprinkle with crushed dillweed and dill seed, mixed half and half. Remove from pans and cool on rack.

Makes 3 loaves

Sister Mary's Zesty Carrots

6 carrots
Salt
2 tablespoons grated onion
2 tablespoons prepared horse-
　radish

½ cup mayonnaise
¼ teaspoon pepper
¼ cup water
¼ cup buttered bread crumbs

Clean the carrots and cut them into thin strips. Cook until tender in salted water, then place in a 6-by-10-inch baking dish.

Preheat the oven to 375°F.

Mix together the grated onion, horseradish, mayonnaise, 1 teaspoon of the salt, pepper, and water. Pour this over the carrots. Sprinkle with the buttered crumbs and bake uncovered about 15 minutes.

Serves 4 to 6

Rose Water Frozen Cream

1 tablespoon flour
1½ cups sugar
1 teaspoon salt
2 egg yolks, lightly beaten

2 cups milk, scalded
4 cups light cream
1 tablespoon rose water

Mix the flour, sugar, and salt. Add the egg yolks and stir until smooth. Add the milk slowly, then pour the mixture into the top of a double boiler and cook, stirring, until thick (about 15 minutes). Let cool, then add the cream and rose water. Pour the mixture into the container of an ice-cream freezer and freeze according to manufacturer's instructions.

Makes 2 quarts

THE SHAKER KITCHEN FESTIVAL is held the first week of August at Hancock Shaker Village, in Hancock, Massachusetts. There are daily exhibitions, demonstrations, and tastings—a different food or type of food being prepared each day. The dinners are held at 6:00 P.M. each night except Sunday, when there are two sittings—one at noon and one at 1:00 P.M. Each day's dinner has a set menu; there is no choice. A descriptive brochure, including a list of dinner menus, will be sent on request. Reservations are necessary and may be made by writing or calling Hancock Shaker Village, P.O. Box 898, Pittsfield, Massachusetts 01202; (413) 443–0188. As of this writing, dinner costs $9.25 per person and has to be paid in advance. There is no additional admission charge to the museum.

Of course the museum itself deserves careful attention; one could easily spend an entire day (or more) touring the buildings and gardens. A wide variety of interpretive programs are available. The museum is open daily from 9:30 to 5, June 1 to October 31; it is located on U.S. 20, 5 miles west of Pittsfield.

Maine Lobster Festival

Winter Harbor, Maine

THE LOBSTERS ARE COOKED at the water's edge, on a makeshift fireplace constructed of rocks and steel rods. Every few minutes, the man tending the fire puts on a fresh spruce log. Another uses a long pole to retrieve the net bag of cooked lobsters from one of the four 50-gallon trash cans that serve as steamers. He swings the pole and bag to one side, then drops the bag to the ground. As the steam bellows upward, a co-worker helps him open the bag and separate the tangle of bright red lobsters. They transfer the lobsters to another large pail and carry the pail to the tables, where volunteers are serving the lobster feast. This is the annual Winter Harbor Lobster Festival. It is the middle of August and the weather is perfect.

Every year the Winter Harbor Chamber of Commerce sponsors a festival celebrating Maine's foremost product—the American lobster. It is primarily a one-day event that includes a 15-kilometer foot race, a crafts fair, a softball tournament, a cannon shoot, a tug of towns, a wacky water walk, and a spectacular lobster dinner. Activities are divided between the town and Frazer Point, part of nearby Acadia National Park. The lobster boat races are held in Frenchman's Bay, the stretch of water between town and the Point.

Winter Harbor is short on parking space, so the town sets aside some fields to accommodate all the cars. They also run shuttle buses out to the Point, since the two-lane road to the Schoodic Peninsula was never meant for the traffic that this popular event generates. Catching a shuttle bus is easy, although some people walk the four miles to Frazer Point, perhaps to put an edge on their appetites.

The lobster dinner, served on the Point from 11 to 3, is a mighty good deal. Not only do you get a 1¼-pound lobster steamed to perfection and served with drawn butter, but dinner also includes an ear of the sweetest honey-and-cream corn, potato chips, a soda or coffee, and a blueberry muffin made with wild Maine blueberries. The setting couldn't be better:

a rocky beach against a backdrop of pine trees. Most people take their lobster trays and find a grassy spot in the sun or they settle on some flat rocks along the beach. The lobsters are molting at this time of year and their shells are soft, so there's no difficulty getting to the sweet meat inside. Some lobster-fanciers, though, crack the shells on the rocks, if only to feel in the spirit. There are a lot of "eat-in-the-rough" places in New England, but nothing can compare with this true rough spot.

The festival serves about thirteen hundred lobsters every year, but we found many people also come for the crabmeat rolls, crabmeat salad, and shrimp sandwiches. We also noticed that people were here from all over the country—we saw license plates from as far away as Texas, North Carolina, and Virginia. Festival-goers don't usually travel that far, but the proximity to Acadia National Park explains why this crowd was so mixed. While we enjoyed our lobster and talked with the people nearby, we also tried to understand the lobster boat races then under way. There are a total of thirteen races, each involving a different type of lobster boat—diesel or gas, four-cylinder or eight-cylinder, inboard or outboard. It would have helped if there had been an announcer for the races, but the audience (many of whom understood these races perfectly) was left to keep track of the races themselves. Nevertheless, they are exciting, as the boats charge across the bay in a manner very surprising for a squat lobster boat.

The year we attended the festival, it was possible to tour a destroyer that was anchored in the bay. The crew from the U.S.S. *Moosbrugger*, also known as "the Moose," welcomed their visitors from shore and showed them what life is like on board a modern-day battleship. Lines for the tour were quite long—clearly a popular activity.

We caught the shuttle bus back to town just in time to watch the wacky water walk at the town dock. Lobster crates had been strung tightly across a section of the boat basin, and it was up to the contestants—all kids—to "walk" across them. There were a total of twenty-three crates plus some inner tubes, held taut by a rope that stretched from the dock to the shore. One by one the boys and girls took their turns walking across—except that most of them found running the better way; that is, until they came to a slippery box and ended up in the water. Wacky it was, and lots of fun, too.

On the town dock was a trade display of the latest in lobstering equipment: propellers, marine engines, anchors, rope, and so on. Down the street was the crafts fair, with booths selling nautical and country crafts. Before long, the prizes were awarded to the winners of the lobster boat races, and the concluding parade wound its way down the main street of town.

THE WINTER HARBOR LOBSTER FESTIVAL is held mid-August and is sponsored by the Chamber of Commerce. Free parking is in lots in the town of Winter Harbor, and a shuttle bus (also free) makes regular runs from town to Frazer Point. The lobster feast is on Frazer Point from 11:00 A.M. to 3:00 P.M. and cost $7 the year we went. Other events, arts and crafts booths, and exhibits are centered around the town dock and are on all day Saturday, ending with the parade down Main Street at 5:00 P.M.

Winter Harbor is located about 25 miles southeast of Ellsworth, off Route 186. For additional information, contact the Winter Harbor Chamber of Commerce, Winter Harbor, Maine 04693; or call the town office at (207) 963-2235.

Beefiesta

Scott City, Kansas

I N KANSAS the skyscrapers in the distance are grain elevators, four or five clustered together, often near a railway siding. Nearby are a few homes and then miles of wheat fields for farther than the eye can see. "One Kansas farmer feeds seventy-five people and you," the sign at the state line says. Food for thought in these days of agribusiness. This is western Kansas—flat wheat fields and small, square-shaped counties with county seats right in the middle. Such a county is Scott, and Scott City is its seat. There, each August, the Beefiesta is held as part of the county fair.

To get to Scott City we drove over miles and miles of prairie, imagining them filled with cowboys running the big cattle drives. The closer we got to town, the more feedlots there were; crowded with cattle, their smell was overpowering. Scott City, Kansas—population 5,300; elevation 2,971. Hot and sunny all summer. The fairgrounds are located on the outskirts of town, and the exhibits are housed in old Quonset huts that look like airplane hangars. There on display are vegetables, garden crops, and flowers; home sewing and fancywork; cakes, canned fruit, and jams; hobbies; local history; and special exhibit classes for FFA (Future Farmers of America) and the Boy Scouts. Behind the exhibit halls are the livestock displays.

But the focus of the Beefiesta is the free barbecue and the free beef-tasting booths. The booths, run by local beef-related businesses, are set out in a horseshoe shape beneath a grove of trees. A huge line for the tasting snakes around the fairgrounds, while at the front of the line people pass by each booth and sample the wares. The bank serves barbecued beef cubes; next to them, the HRC Feed Lots are offering barbecued brisket. (HRC has been at the Beefiesta for six years, each year with a different recipe.) Hughes Land and Livestock is giving away "Home on the Range Burgers." A group of cattle buyers serve up plain steak (no salt or pepper)—delicious. The CowBelles, a nationwide beef promotional group, present green chili burros and hand out fliers such as "A Dozen Ways to Stretch Your Beef Dollar" or "Slim Down with Low-Calorie Beef Recipes." Beef Belt Feeders, Inc., offers beef cubes deep-fried with onions and serves them with a spicy sauce; and Scott Pro (a cattle feed supplier) presents plain barbecued top sirloin with a choice of dips—cheese, mustard, or horseradish.

Although the fair is six days long, the tasting booths are only open on Saturday; the barbecue—called the Beefiesta—is also only on that day. A real pit barbecue is dug two days before and lined with thirty inches of coals. The beef roasts are then set into stainless-steel pans and put to cook in their own juices for twenty-seven hours. When the meat is ready, it's "pulled" into shreds and piled onto a large hamburger bun. This barbecue is served plain, with no sauce. The meat is moist, and you really taste the beef itself, without unnecessary spices—just the smoky taste of a long, slow cooking. And it's not at all greasy, because the fat's all been drained off when the meat is taken up out of the cooking pans.

Dinner is served under a big tent. The barbecued beef is accompanied by canned beans (unfortunately) and pickles, raw onions, and iced tea. It's a bit hard to balance the whole meal on your lap—more chairs and tables would help—but the food is served up fast and is tasty and hot. Our dinner was interrupted by a dust storm that seemed to blow up out of nowhere, forcing everyone to run for cover; those of us in the food tent remained there while the tent swayed and flapped as the dust-laden wind blew through. "It dusted us up and it dusted us over," as Woody Guthrie sang; and for us wandering Easterners it seemed the truly quint-essential prairie experience. The sky grew darker than a thundercloud, and the few trees around us bent over almost sideways. Outside, you'd find it hard not to get the fine dusty soil in your mouth or eyes; the cars in the parking lot were covered as though with ash. And it was gone as fast as it had come.

After dinner, about eight o'clock, the rodeo begins. There's bareback riding, calf roping (hard to do), saddle broncs, steer wrestling, and barrel racing. A real Western event, and a perfect finale to the Beefiesta and the Scott County Fair.

Kansas Barbecue Brisket

4½- to 5-pound brisket
½ bottle Liquid Smoke
2 teaspoons celery seed

1 clove garlic, crushed
Salt and pepper to taste

SAUCE

1 cup ketchup
½ cup water
6 tablespoons brown sugar

½ cup vinegar
4 teaspoons chili powder

Trim the meat of excess fat. Combine the Liquid Smoke, celery seed, garlic, and salt and pepper in a bowl and rub the meat thoroughly with the mixture. Cover and place in the refrigerator overnight.

The next day, preheat the oven to 350°F. Place the meat in a pan, cover tightly, and bake for 3½ to 4 hours. Remove the meat from the pan and drain off and discard the fatty liquid. Let the meat cool, then slice.

Combine the ingredients for the sauce in a large saucepan. Gently heat, then add the meat slices. Simmer for 1 hour, basting occasionally, until the meat picks up the flavor of the sauce. Add a little water to the sauce if it cooks down too much. The sauce may seem too sweet at first, but after cooking with the meat, it turns spicy, picking up the smokiness from the meat while lending just a touch of sweetness.   *Serves 6*

Home-on-the-Range Burgers

These tasty burgers are from Hughes Land and Livestock.

1½ pounds chopped beef
1 clove garlic, minced
1 small onion, chopped
1 tablespoon chili sauce
1 tablespoon prepared mustard

1 tablespoon Worcestershire
     sauce
1 large egg, lightly beaten
Salt and pepper to taste

Combine the ingredients in a bowl, then shape the mixture into 6 patties. Broil the burgers for 5 to 7 minutes on each side, or until crisp on the outside and rare on the inside. Serve on hamburger buns, with ketchup or additional chili sauce.   *Serves 4 to 6*

Green Chili Burros

The CowBelles know how to make a spicy burro (what others sometimes call a burrito).

1 tablespoon vegetable oil	*1 large can (23 ounces)*
3 pounds boneless beef, cut into	*tomatoes, drained*
bite-sized pieces	*1 clove garlic, minced*
2 cans (4 ounces each) green	*2 large onions, diced*
chilies, chopped	*Dash cumin*
1 jalapeño pepper, minced	*Salt and pepper to taste*
(optional)	*1 dozen flour tortillas*

Heat the oil in a large skillet and brown the meat until crisp. Add the remaining ingredients except the tortillas, then cover and simmer over low heat for 2 to 3 hours, or until the mixture is soft and the meat is quite tender.

To assemble the burros, soften the tortillas by lightly sautéing them on a hot griddle or by wrapping them in foil and warming them in a 350°F oven for 10 minutes. Place about 3 tablespoons filling in the center of each tortilla, then fold the edges over and roll up so that you have a cylinder with 2 closed ends. Serve immediately. *Serves 6*

THE BEEFIESTA is part of the Scott County Free Fair and is held on a Saturday in the middle of August. The fair itself is a week-long event, but the Beefiesta is the highlight. Cooking demonstrations are in the afternoon; the tasting booths give out samples from 2:00 to 5:00 P.M. Lines are long. The barbecue supper begins at 5:00 P.M. and is free. There are also carnival rides and agricultural exhibits. Parking is in a field adjacent to the fairgrounds. There is no admission charge; the only event that is not free is the rodeo on Saturday night.

Scott City is located in western Kansas, about halfway between Denver and Topeka, at the intesection of U.S. 83 and Route 96. For additional information about the Beefiesta and County Fair, write Beefiesta, 221 West Fifth, Scott City, Kansas 67871; or phone (316) 872-3525.

Strange Seafood Exhibition

Beaufort, North Carolina

"MMM. THAT WAS GOOD! Harry, have you had the smoked clams yet?"

"Ooo. Eel! I've never had *eel.*"

"Try some of this stuff, it's good."

"Dog clams. What kind of clams are they?"

"Mussels? No we don't much eat them around here."

"Herring roe and eggs. Now I remember . . . we'd have that for breakfast where I grew up, along the Hudson."

"Those periwinkles are awful small. How many of 'em make a meal?"

When the director of the North Carolina Maritime Museum blows a conch (actually a whelk), its eerie and thrilling sound marks the start of the two-hour Strange Seafood Exhibition in Beaufort. Equally thrilling is the opportunity to sample some of the most unusual and fascinating foods ever to come from the sea. These "strange" seafoods sort themselves into three categories: first, traditional foods of coastal Carolina that are no longer eaten; second, those harvested and still consumed by many local people but seldom by others; and last, those highly prized in other countries but rarely eaten here even though they can be harvested in this area.

Each year, on the third Thursday in August, beneath the large magnolia trees alongside the old museum, the volunteers for this event set out samples of over forty different preparations—everything from seaweed relish to red porgy salad. This is intended as an educational exhibit, not a true food festival, but it is the taste buds that receive the schooling.

For many people, eel, octopus, and squid are hardly novelties, yet how many of us have ever eaten dog clams, periwinkles, or triggerfish? If you live near a good fishmonger, you might have tried rock shrimp, shark, or tilefish; but how often does your merchant have stingray, sea urchins, or red porgy? Even for those who grew up near the shore, it may be a surprise to discover that mole crabs and coquina clams are edible, even tasty.

The ridged dog clam is only an inch long, so it's not worth harvesting commercially, but you can easily pluck it up with your toes or fingers from the sandy bottom in shallow water. By contrast, the Atlantic ribbed mussel is hard to dislodge from the seawalls and jetties on which it lives. Larger than the familiar blue mussel, this one makes a good stew (and, we were told, the mussel liquid cures earaches). Coquina clams are tiny, less than an inch long. They are the small clams you find along the ocean shore as the waves break and whose shattered shells litter the high-water mark. Periwinkles are small snails that climb up the blades of marsh grass; at the festival they are served in a garlic butter, and you pluck them out of their shells with a straight pin.

Spiny sea urchins are very popular among gourmets in this country. At Beaufort, you can sample both the eggs and the testes for considerably less (financial) risk than at a fancy restaurant. The eggs are stronger than the testes, but in both you can taste the primitive smell of the sea. Dried mullet roe captured our attention. Mullet has been a major food fish for years, and since the mullet runs—or "blows"—are so large, the extra fish have traditionally been salted and dried for long-term storage. This mullet roe has been sun-dried the old-fashioned way, and it has an intense, gamy taste, slightly sticky and not meant for the fainthearted.

Triggerfish is an inhabitant of warm, tropical waters. Though it has a very tough skin, it has a mild taste like grouper or snapper and is not at all fatty; the chowder made from it is thin and delicate. Pinfish are small scavenger fish; their iridescent bodies glimmer and twinkle as they swim around the pilings in the harbor. These fish have points, or "pins," around their fins and they must be handled carefully, but they can be chopped and baked with spinach, eggs, cheese, and bread crumbs for a hot appetizer tidbit.

The tasting here is not all fish and shellfish. The sea and its environs also proffer a variety of seaweeds and grasses that can be used to make teas, soups, salads, and even a pasta. Yaupon is a member of the holly family; this shrub grows in thickets along the dunes and produces a poisonous red berry, though its leaves are edible. The tea made from yaupon was too sweet for us, and we suspect that the version made by the Indians centuries ago was probably stronger. The cream of sea lettuce soup was also not to our liking, nor was the sponge seaweed salad; but these sea greens are intriguing to sample and they represent an entirely different meaning of the word *seafood*.

Although we've enjoyed smoked eel, fried squid, octopus salad, stuffed clams, and scallop fritters before, the versions we sampled at the exhibition were good, as were the herring roe and eggs, the stingray casserole, and the whelk chowder. The marinated butterfish was cool and refreshing, the smoked shark flaky and moist. In fact just about everything here is worth sampling, though you might not rush out and plead with your fish store to order red porgy for your next dinner party.

This is a fun event, especially if you aren't familiar with the less common seafoods. Our only complaint about the exhibition is that it attempts to give too much in too little time and too little space. If there were more room around the tasting tables, people could get to what they want to try and skip the tables with foods that don't interest them. Also, staggering the admission throughout the afternoon would avoid that "bunching up" at the beginning of the line, thus allowing more people to sample more foods. But even with all the crowds, we could hear the surprised exclamations as someone tried a new taste: "Hey, this is *good!*"

The following recipes are adapted by permission of the North Carolina Maritime Museum, Beaufort, North Carolina, *Strange Seafood Recipes* cookbook, compiled from the annual Strange Seafood Exhibition. The first recipe is from Judith Spitsbergen of Beaufort.

Scallop Fritters

1 pint (1 pound) bay or sea scal-
    lops, chopped into ½-inch
    dice
1¾ cups all-purpose flour
1 tablespoon baking powder
½ teaspoon salt

2 eggs, lightly beaten
1 cup milk
2 teaspoons grated onion
1 tablespoon butter or other fat,
    melted
Shortening or oil for deep frying

Drain the scallops. Sift the dry ingredients together and set aside.

Combine the eggs, milk, onion, butter or fat, and scallops. Pour the wet mixture into the dry ingredients and stir until the batter is smooth.

Heat the shortening in a deep fryer or deep pot until hot, about 350°F. Drop the batter by heaping tablespoonfuls into the hot fat and fry for about 3 minutes, or until golden brown on all sides. Drain on absorbent paper. Serve hot.   *Serves 4*

Pickled Bluefish

Bluefish are less "strange" than most of the foods at the festival, but this pickled version will be a surprise. It tastes a bit like herring, without that herring chewiness. This is from Mary Dudley Price of Gloucester, North Carolina.

1¼ pounds bluefish fillet, skin removed
5¼ cups water
1 cup coarse salt
2 cups distilled white vinegar
½ cup sugar
½ tablespoon minced dried hot red pepper
½ tablespoon whole allspice

½ tablespoon mustard seeds
1 teaspoon crumbled bay leaves, or more to taste
2 cloves garlic, cut in half
½ tablespoon white pepper
1 lemon, sliced
1 medium onion, sliced and separated into rings

Rinse the fish and remove any small bones that may remain. Prepare a weak brine solution by mixing together 2 cups of the water and 2 tablespoons of the salt. Soak the fish fillet for 1 hour. Drain and then prepare a strong brine solution by mixing 2 more cups of the water with ¾ cup of the salt. Add the fish fillet and cover. Refrigerate, letting the fish soak in the brine for 12 hours.

Drain the fish and rinse well. Combine the remaining 1¼ cups water, 2 tablespoons salt, the vinegar, sugar, dried pepper, spices, garlic, and white pepper in a large stainless steel pot. Bring to a boil and add the fish. Cover and simmer for 10 minutes, or until the fish is easily pierced with a fork but before it gets so tender that it flakes apart. Remove the fish in pieces and place in a shallow dish. Layer on the lemon and onion rings and pour over some of the pickling solution until the fish is covered. If desired, crumble in another bay leaf. Cover and refrigerate for up to 2 months. The fish is best if served after about 1 week of pickling. It is good sliced or broken into small chunks and served with crackers, topped with an onion ring. *Serves 10 as appetizer*

Herring Roe and Eggs

This recipe is from Mrs. L. W. Moore, of Beaufort, North Carolina.

3 tablespoons vegetable oil
1 pound fresh herring roe (or
substitute mullet, flounder,
or another mild roe)

4 large eggs
Salt and pepper to taste

Coat the bottom of a 10-inch skillet with the oil and place over moderately high heat. Add the roe, breaking it up with a fork. Cook for 2 minutes, then separate the mass of roe to make 4 wells open to the surface of the skillet. Crack an egg into each and allow to set until the egg white solidifies slightly. Then stir the eggs into the roe and mix, continuing to cook the roe and eggs until the mixture is dry. If desired, serve with hot grits. *Serves 4*

THE STRANGE SEAFOOD EXHIBITION is held the third Thursday of August in Beaufort, at the North Carolina Maritime Museum. The exhibition is from 2:00 to 4:00 P.M. Tickets should be obtained in advance, as this is a sell-out event, and there are only a thousand spaces available. Tickets cost $3 and can be had by visiting or writing the museum (see below) after May 1. The exhibition is an educational program of the museum.

The museum itself is well worth visiting, either before or after the food. Admission is free. Our only complaint about the festival is that there isn't enough room for all the people and tables. Lines become unwieldy at times, and not everyone has the opportunity to taste everything. There's also no place to sit down. Despite the fact that everyone inevitably begins to eat at once, we advise arriving early, studying the "menu," and deciding what you want to try first.

Beaufort is located on the coast, about 170 miles southeast of Raleigh, on U.S. 70. Parking for the exhibition is on the street. Additional information is available from the North Carolina Maritime Museum, 120 Turner Street, Beaufort, North Carolina 28516; (919) 728–7317.

Watermelon Festival

Hope, Arkansas

*T*HEY GROW BIG WATERMELONS in Hope. Really big. Melons from Hope regularly tip the scale at 100 pounds, and many of them reach over 150 pounds. Record watermelons have been coming out of Hope since 1925, when the Laseter brothers produced one weighing 136 pounds. That melon was sent to President Calvin Coolidge, but the Laseter brothers continued growing the big ones, edging their way up to 152 pounds in 1929. There were other record-setting growers, including O. D. Middlebrooks, whose 1935 melon weighed in at 195 pounds and was sent to movie star Dick Powell. The records are still being set. In 1979, Lloyd and Ivan Bright raised a melon that weighted 200 pounds, establishing a top place for Hope in the *Guinness Book of World Records*.

"We're pretty proud of our watermelons. We don't just produce the best. We also produce more giant watermelons than any other place. If you want to see a hundred-pound watermelon, come to Hope in August and we'll show you hundreds of them." That's how the flier for Hope, Arkansas, invites people to the annual Watermelon Festival. Hope offers "a slice of the good life," as all the T-shirts and banners say, and that slice is a generous cut from a frosty cold melon.

The Watermelon Festival was first held in 1926, and since then has grown in size but still retains the character of a small-town fair. Hope itself is small, with a population of just a little over ten thousand people. It is located in southwest Arkansas, about a thirty-minute drive from the Texas border. This is a very active festival, with such an assortment of contests and activities that there surely is something for everyone. A loudspeaker announces the upcoming events in Fair Park, where almost all the contests are held: the tennis tournament, four-mile run, basketball shooting, swim meet, horseshoe pitching, hula hoop contest, sack races, egg toss, arm wrestling, and cow chip toss. Elsewhere (but not far away) are the dog show, tug-o'-war, chess tournament, break dance contest, softball tournament, tricycle races, and Ping-Pong tournament. Every evening of this four-day event produces a variety of entertainment, including a country-western dance, a country music show, disco dancing, and square dancing with the Hope Melonaires. The gospel singing is on the afternoon of the last day of the festival.

Since most of the activities take place in Hope's shady Fair Park, we couldn't really object to the hundred-degree temperatures. In fact, the heat made eating watermelon the natural thing to do. There's plenty of watermelon to eat, and it's all free. The melons are kept cold in a refrigerated tractor trailer until the moment they are cut into large slices and handed out to the waiting crowd. Over a thousand melons are donated by ten local growers.

At the table where the melon slices were being given out, we picked up a slice that was a deep rosy red and another that was lemon yellow. The red melon was sweet, but the yellow even sweeter. Yellow watermelons are grown regularly down here, but they don't seem to make it to our market very often.

We're from the dig-in school of melon eating, and we were surprised to find that most of these folks use spoons or forks. "Melon just isn't any good without salt," someone declaimed as he poured it on. Another commented, "I never could eat watermelon with a spoon. I need a fork." We tried a fork, we tried a spoon, but we found them both a pest. It's much more fun to just bend over and get right into it mouth-first. We dug our way to the rinds, then tossed them into the back of the pickup truck parked nearby for that very purpose.

We'd just about swallowed our last mouthful of watermelon when the seed-spitting and watermelon-eating contests were to begin. The spitting contest was largely a matter of wind and pucker power, with the contestants sending their seeds across the stage to distances of up to ten or twelve feet. The eating contest seemed to generate more excitement, perhaps because of the barker-type emcee, who encouraged or chided the contestants in their eating styles. Announcing, "We goin' to have a watermelon-eatin' time," he advised the contestants not to "worry about the seeds; they come out tomorrow." As the kids, ranging in age from five to about fifteen, took their places in a line on stage and set about the task before them, the crowd cheered and the emcee yelled, "Quit that chewin', gal! EAT that watermelon. Eat those melons!" Juice ran down their arms as they plowed through the melons. No "rakin' it out" was allowed, meaning they couldn't squeeze the water from the melon as they ate it or suck up only the pulp. When it was over—five frenetic minutes later—the winner was asked what he thought of watermelon. A boy of about ten, he answered, "Not much."

"Not much?" the emcee exclaimed. "Look what you done put in there!" patting the boy's stomach. Everyone laughed; then the boy was asked his name, and where he was from, and who his father was—important questions in small cities where most everyone knows everyone else.

The whole city of Hope gets into this festival. Windows of shops and businesses in town are not only painted with watermelon cartoons but are decorated as well. One of the cleverest was the beauty parlor's, where a watermelon, with a face painted on it, sat under a hair dryer. Stores sell Hope T-shirts. Posters in windows announce the festival. The motels and restaurants in town give away coupons that serve as chances for winning a hundred-pound melon. The Dairy Queen makes a watermelon shake (melon juice, milk, and ice cream—quite tasty). Even the arts and crafts are watermelon-related. At the festival people wear watermelon hats, watermelon jewelry, watermelon T-shirts. Not far from the entrance to the festival was a woman sitting under a watermelon parasol and wearing watermelon socks.

We were curious to discover why Hope produced such good watermelons and why so many of them were of record-setting weights. We asked a local farmer, who was proudly displaying Black Diamonds and Jubilees in the back of his pickup. "Lots of moisture . . . and fertilizer. This· was a good year," he said and gestured toward his truck, which held several dozen mouth-watering specimens. The people of Hope are proud of their watermelons, and they go all out to show it. It is indeed a "slice of the good life."

THE WATERMELON FESTIVAL is held in Hope, Arkansas, in the middle of August. It's a four-day event, with most activities on Saturday. There are dances or musical entertainment on Thursday through Saturday nights. The four-mile run starts things off on Saturday morning. All other contests, games, arts and crafts booths, food booths, the band concert, and the watermelon are at Fair Park. Only the dancing and cake walks are held in the downtown plaza.

Admission to the festival is free; the watermelon is also free. Hamburgers and barbecue sandwiches cost about $1. It is hot, but the coliseum building (in the park) is air-conditioned; for 25¢ you can buy a bingo game and sit down inside. The park is shady, and there are plenty of benches and bleachers to sit on. Parking is on side streets or in nearby fields and lots. If you get there real early (9:00 A.M.), you might find a spot in the park itself.

Hope is in southwestern Arkansas, just 120 miles southwest of Little Rock, off I-30. For additional information, including a schedule of events, contact the Hope-Hempstead County Chamber of Commerce, P.O. Box 250, Hope, Arkansas 71801; (501) 777-3640.

State of Maine
Blueberry Festival

Union, Maine

THE SIGN READ, "Fog-Nourished Blueberries." But by midmorning the fog had lifted and we could see miles of blueberry barrens. Upon closer examination, we could see the blueberries, too. Little wild ones, growing close to the ground. Across the road, people were using blueberry rakes (similar to cranberry scoops) to harvest the blueberries. It seemed that everywhere we drove in Maine that summer, we saw blueberries. Small wonder, then, that there are at least two blueberry festivals each August. We chose the one at the Union Fair, since it seemed to offer us the greatest opportunity to eat those precious berries.

The Union Fair is one of the longest-running agricultural fairs in Maine—well over a hundred years old—and it features all you'd expect of a country fair: from horse and oxen pulling to a pig scramble, from 4-H and Grange exhibits to harness racing. There are cows and sheep of nearly every breed; flowers, fruits, and vegetables; organic-farming displays; needlework; paintings; preserves and baked goods; a baby-beef auction; and a farm parade. The Union Fair is one week long, and Friday is Blueberry Festival Day. Blueberries are featured all week—in exhibits, pottery (for sale), and all manner of goodies to eat—but Friday is the big day.

The festivities begin with a blueberry pancake breakfast in Sherman Park, an area of the fairgrounds. Big, thick pancakes are flipped over on the griddle and then onto your plate. The butter melts all over them and mixes with the syrup. Even in August, Maine mornings are cool, and there's nothing like this hot breakfast to take the chill off. Picnic tables are full of happy breakfasters too busy eating to notice the cold. "Princesses"—contestants in the blueberry queen pageant—cheerfully serve seconds to those who want them. It's real easy to put away a few platefuls.

The Union fairgrounds is also the home of the Matthews Museum of

Maine Heritage. There we saw elaborate exhibits of eighteenth- and nineteenth-century life, including farm equipment, carriages, and home furnishings. A series of special displays showed an old-time post office, a cooper's shop, a farmhouse kitchen and pantry, a schoolroom, and a library. The library had an extensive collection of books, letters, and clippings about the town of Union. Among all the artifacts in this well-stocked museum was a big Moxie display, celebrating the hundreth anniversary of the Maine soft drink.

We strolled around the fairgrounds and watched some of the competitions. In particular we were captivated by the oxen pulls, an event we had never seen before. Here was a test of strength—both of the oxen team and of the handler. We watched the 3,600-pound pull; that is, a team of oxen weighing 3,600 pounds was to pull a sled with weights totaling 6,000 pounds. No simple matter, these handlers coaxed and chided their teams to pull almost double their weight down and back across the arena.

Just as popular as the pulls were the home- and handcraft competitions and displays. We marveled at the needlework and quilting, done by local women, hanging in the center of the exhibition hall. Across one aisle was an extraordinary display of Maine's wild edible foods, done by the Warren Evening Extension. At one end of the hall was a special exhibit from the Wild Blueberry Association of North America, which included, among other memorabilia, Margaret Chase Smith's recipe for blueberry cake. The first blueberry festival was announced in the *Enterprise* with a headline that ran, BEHOLD THE BEAUTIFUL WILD MAINE BLUEBERRY, RESPLENDENT AND DELICIOUS. Another early headline was printed in blue ink.

But enough reading about blueberries for us. It was time to visit the Blueberry Hut. Here, in a small booth alongside the exhibition hall, were the bakers, all wearing blueberry corsages and blueberry barrettes. They were handing out free blueberry pies to the fair-goers. Your admisison ticket to the fair entitles you to a free pie, but if one isn't enough, you can buy more for only a dime apiece, though there's a limit of six per person. Some 3,600 pies are given away (or sold) during the day. We saw several people take their pies, still hot from the oven, into the exhibition hall. We followed and found that a booth inside was selling homemade blueberry ice cream. Heavenly, especially atop the pie.

Across from the ice cream stand, the Methodist Church was selling a variety of baked goods, including a very good blueberry cake. On other days, the Blueberry Hut devotes its energies to selling blueberry cookies, doughnuts, muffins, and pies. There is also a sit-down restaurant on the fairgrounds; it's Burns Old Homestead, where home-style cooking (and table service) is featured. They, too, were selling things blueberry, mostly pies and muffins (in addition to hot meals).

All the blueberries at the festival—and in all of Maine, as well—are wild, low-bush berries. The blueberries have not been planted; they're indigenous to a soil that was conditioned by the glaciers and a climate that offers cold winters and cool summers. Wild blueberries have an intense flavor that develops with minimal assistance from humans. The fields are periodically burned and rotated, but nature does the rest.

The Indians gathered blueberries and dried them in the sun. The colonists called them bilberries or whortleberries and used them in cobblers, grunts, buckles, and slumps. Farmers in Maine refer to them as low-bush blues and harvest them carefully by hand. Wild blueberries are small and dark. Putting low-bush blues into your muffins or pancakes gives them a flavor boost unequaled by commercial high-bush berries.

The job of the blueberry festival queen is to promote blueberries in Maine and around the nation. From the size of the crowd at this festival, it looks like not much promotion is necessary. Almost everyone seems to know about wild blueberries, and many come to Maine at harvest time, especially for the Blueberry Festival.

Blueberry "Pie"

The pie that is served at the festival is really a cobbler, and here is a recipe for it, adapted to family-size proportions.

1 quart fresh wild blueberries
¾ cup sugar
Ground cinnamon
2 tablespoons lemon juice

3 tablespoons cornstarch
1 cup Bisquick
½ cup milk

In a bowl, combine the blueberries with the sugar, 1 teaspoon of the cinnamon, the lemon juice, and the cornstarch. Mix well, but carefully so as not to break the berries. Place the filling in individual 1-cup baking dishes, then set aside briefly.

Preheat the oven to 350°F.

In a small bowl, blend the Bisquick with the milk until the mixture is moist and spreadable. Spoon some of the topping onto each dish of blueberry filling, then sprinkle the tops with additional cinnamon. Bake for 30 minutes, or until the tops are lightly browned and the fillings begin to ooze up around the sides. Serve hot with ice cream, either vanilla or blueberry. *Makes four 1-cup servings*

Blueberry Muffins

These aren't as sweet as most blueberry muffins, and they'll seem a little denser, too, but the taste is unbeatable. This recipe is by Arley Carman Clark, a local blueberry fancier.

2 cups all-purpose flour
½ teaspoon salt
3 teaspoons baking powder
¼ cup sugar
1 large egg, lightly beaten

1 cup milk
¼ cup vegetable oil
2 teaspoons lemon juice
¾ cup fresh wild blueberries

Preheat the oven to 425°F. Lightly grease a 12-cup muffin tin.

Sift the dry ingredients together. In a separate bowl, combine the egg with the milk, oil, and lemon juice. Add the dry ingredients quickly. The mixture should be lumpy; don't overbeat. Fold in the berries and then fill the muffin cups about two-thirds full. Bake for 25 to 30 minutes, or until lightly browned on top. Let sit for 10 minutes, then remove the muffins from the tin and serve immediately with butter or let cool on a rack. *Makes 1 dozen*

Uncooked Blueberry Pie

In season, most Maine cooks make their wild blueberry pies this way, with a baked crust and an unbaked filling. The berries retain their fresh taste, yet the small amount of cornstarch helps the filling keep its shape.

1 quart wild blueberries
½ cup sugar
¼ cup water

1 tablespoon cornstarch
One 9-inch pie shell, baked
¾ cup heavy cream

Set 2 cups of the berries in a bowl and add the sugar and water. Let sit for 1 hour to allow the juices to be released from the berries and combine with the sugar.

Place the sugared berries in a saucepan and add the cornstarch. Stir to dissolve over low heat, then increase the heat to medium and stir until the mixture is thickened, about 5 minutes. Allow the mixture to cool slightly, then pour into a large mixing bowl. Add the remaining blueberries and toss well. Pour the mixture into the pie shell and let cool to set completely. When ready to serve, whip the cream and cover the top of the pie with it. Serve.   *Serves 6*

THE STATE OF MAINE BLUEBERRY FESTIVAL is held in conjunction with the Union Fair. It is always on the Friday of the fair, and the fair is usually the third week of August. Admission (which includes parking) is $3.50. The blueberry pancake breakfast (all you can eat) is $2.50 and begins at 8:00 A.M.; pancakes are served until 11:00 A.M. The free pies are given out from noon till 8:00 P.M. (extra pies are 10¢). Blueberry ice cream is about 65¢ a scoop; blueberry cake and muffins run 50¢. In the restaurant, a sandwich is about $1.25; full meals cost about $5.

The fair is a week long. Games and rides (provided by Billy Burr's Fun-O-Rama) and harness racing are on every day. Other days have special events, and various exhibits are judged. The exhibit halls and the museum are open daily. There's a $1 admission to the museum.

Union is in the middle of Knox County, about thirty miles east of Augusta, off Route 17. For further information, contact the Union Fair, Knox Agricultural Society, Union, Maine 04862.

The other blueberry festival of note is in Machias in mid-August. Machias is in northern Maine, on the coast, about 80 miles east of Bangor. Contact the Blueberry Festival Committee, Machias Congregational Church, Center Street, Machias, Maine 04654.

International Zucchini Festival

Harrisville, New Hampshire

THE INTERNATIONAL ZUCCHINI FESTIVAL is probably the funniest food festival around. But then, zucchini can become a pretty funny vegetable. If you've grown your own, you know what we mean—expecially at the end of the summer. By August, you've given zucchini away to all your friends, relatives, and neighbors. You've made zucchini pickles, zucchini hash, and zucchini ice cream.

And that's just when the International Zucchini Festival comes along—perfect timing. You and your zucchini can do things together. You can enter it into competitions such as the Farthest Traveled Zucchini or the Longest or Heaviest Zucchini. You can make something of your zucchini and enter it as the Best Zucchini Needlework or the Best Off-Color Zucchini. If you have more than one, there's the Best Matched Zucchini. And if you have only inspiration left, there's the Best Zucchini Essay.

If you have been able to grow more than just zucchini this summer, you could enter the Best Vegetable "Old Masters" Reproduction or the Most Peaceful Use of a Vegetable. Should your talents lie in the performing arts, open to you would be the Best Vegetable Song (but you must sing it to an appreciative audience). We found clever entrants in all thirty-two classes—from the Rube Goldberg Memorial Award for Best Vegetable Chopper right on down to the Best Vegetable Prepared for Space Travel. Our favorite Designer Vegetable was a large zucchini carved "Calvin Klein," and our favorite Patriotic Zuke was one wrapped in a 1040 form.

Should your zucchini not feel up to entering an agricultural exhibit, perhaps you should consider the Motorized Vegetable competitions or the Flight of the Airborne Vegetables. Of course the Greased Zucchini Toss is a crowd pleaser, but your vegetable might not like it.

And if you have no zucchini but still want to have fun, try the Vegetable

Look Alike Contest (most people dress up as a zucchini, though there was an eggplant one year) or the Zucchini Peel Off, for which the festival committee supplies the zucchini. For the athletic, there's a Vegetable Olympics, including a Pentathlon—five events performed with five different vegetables.

The Zucchini Power Lifting competition called upon the strong to lift crates filled with zucchini. For the Vegetable Diving Contest, entrants stood on the end of a diving board; they executed the dive by tossing the vegetable into the center of the pool. The dive was judged on accuracy, entry into the water, and form. There is also a Regatta, with prizes for both the zucchini boat that sinks the fastest and the one that stays afloat the longest. Zucchini carving is a popular activity, and there's a display of zucchini cars.

At noon everyone gathers around Zuke Central for the Flight of the Airborne Vegetables. We watched a carrot rocket shoot into space, a zucchini rocket launched from a pumpkin pad, and a bunch of okra (another funny vegetable) sail off attached to balloons, with a sign that read, UP with OKRA.

After the excitement of the blastoff, we assembled the makings for lunch from the various food booths that were scattered about. The icy-cold Gazuccpacho was tangy, with bits of tomatoes, onions, peppers, and—you guessed it—zucchini. For those willing to wait on a twenty-minute line, there were unexpectedly tasty grilled lamburgers and lamb sausage heros served with sautéed zucchini and onions. Also gingered spareribs and lamb kebabs with rice and zucchini. For the vegetable devotees, another booth was serving a vegetarian sandwich—including zucchini—in a pita bread. Dessert was a slice of zucchini bread spread with cream cheese. Food is purchased with Zukes and Gadzukes, the currency of the festival. And there are many signs warning, NO CUKES!

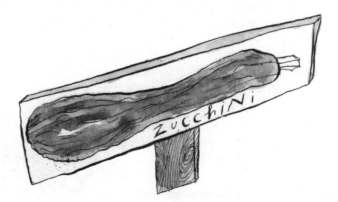

THE USES OF ZUCCHINI

I write an ode to a vegetable greeny
The lowly, tasteless, common zucchini.
The survival of this hardy garden species
Requires no lime or pesticides or cow feces.
The prolific vines of this family of squash
Will produce in the desert, bog, or marsh.
Much like kudzu in a Georgia patch,
The fecundity of this plant is hard to match.

And as soon as these vines begin to produce
We eat zucchini casseroles, bread, and mousse.
Zucchini on granola, ice cream, and pies
A zucchini facial to relax the eyes.
Zucchini daiquiris give a change of pace
To zucchini pickles and soup base.
We try zucchini jellies, jam, and juice
And zucchini stuffing for our Christmas goose.

We're served zucchini doughnuts, fried zucchini.
We eat it raw and marinated in linguini.
On restaurant menus are zucchanoes.
But here's an idea we'd be wise to use
We could get zucchinis growing on the global scene
With an Agricultural/Industrial Zucchini Machine.
To show we care for kids and dads and moms
We could stockpile zucchini instead of bombs.

         —E. A. CALDWELL
           winner of the 1983
           zucchini poetry contest

Zucchini Gazpacho

Though we normally expect cucumbers in a gazpacho, this version substitutes raw zucchini for a change of pace.

*1 small zucchini, cut into 1/4-
    inch cubes (about 1 1/2 cups)*
1 small onion, minced
1 green pepper, minced
1 clove garlic, minced
*2 medium tomatoes, peeled,
    seeded, and diced*

*1 1/2 cups chicken broth,
    skimmed*
2 cups tomato juice
2 tablespoons lemon juice
1/2 teaspoon Tabasco sauce
1 teaspoon salt
2 tablespoons olive oil

Place the zucchini, onion, pepper, garlic, and tomatoes in a blender and add the chicken broth. Spin for 1 minute, so that the ingredients are minutely chopped but not pureed. Then pour the mixture into a large bowl and add the remaining ingredients. Stir and chill for a couple of hours. Serve ice cold. *Serves 4 to 6*

Sweet Zucchini Bread

The zucchini breads at the festival are individual loaves baked by many cooks. What follows is a general recipe for zucchini bread that approximates those you'd be served at Harrisville.

*1/2 cup (1 stick) butter or
    margarine*
1 cup dark brown sugar
2 large eggs, lightly beaten
1 cup shredded zucchini
2 cups all-purpose flour

1 teaspoon baking powder
Pinch salt
1/2 cup buttermilk
1/2 teaspoon vanilla extract
2 teaspoons ground cinnamon

Preheat the oven to 350°F. Generously grease a 9-by-5-by-3-inch loaf pan.

In a large mixing bowl, cream the butter or margarine with the sugar. Add the eggs and stir, then add the zucchini and blend well.

In a separate bowl, sift together the flour, baking powder, and salt.

Fold the dry ingredients into the zucchini mixture, alternating with the buttermilk, until the mixture is blended. Add the vanilla and cinnamon, then pour into the prepared pan.

Bake the loaf for 50 minutes, or until a cake tester comes out clean. Let cool briefly, then invert the pan and remove the loaf. Let the loaf cool completely on a rack. *Makes 1 large loaf*

THE ZANINESS of the International Zucchini Festival takes place in Harrisville, New Hampshire, on the last Saturday in August. There is a $3 admission ($1 for children), which goes to benefit the Harrisville School. Zukes (25¢) and Gadzukes ($1) are on sale and are used to purchase food, crafts, balloons, face painting, and so on. The festival begins at 9:45 and goes on till 4:00 P.M. Free parking is in the fields to the north and south of town; it's a short (five-minute or less) walk to Zuke Central.

Food prices are modest; a lamburger served with zucchini and onions is $1.50; the vegetarian sandwich (including zucchini) is $2. Zucchini bread is 50¢ a slice, $2 a loaf. There are events every minute, sometimes two or three at once.

Harrisville is in the southern part of New Hampshire, about 85 miles northwest of Boston, 5 miles north of Route 101 in Dublin. For information about the festival, contact the International Zucchini Festival, P.O. Box 128, Harrisville, New Hampshire 03450; (603) 827-3033.

Fall

Hatch Chile Festival

Hatch, New Mexico

O N LABOR DAY WEEKEND the Hatch Municipal Airport is closed to air traffic. This is to accommodate the Hatch Chile Festival, which fills the hangar with chile exhibits and spills out onto the tarmac with booths and rides. Hatch is seventy-nine miles from El Paso and has a population of nearly nine hundred. There's a hospital, a movie theater, three parks, and lots and lots of chiles.

Strange things, these chiles. People in the Southwest make a big fuss about them, especially about how different each one tastes and which chile is correct for what use. Some of their names change, depending upon whether you're looking at a fresh chile or one that has been allowed to dry and shrivel up. Even the spelling is controversial. The plural of *chile* out West is *chiles*, whereas misguided Easterners tend to spell it *chilies* because they think the singular should be *chili*. But no matter how they're spelled, these peppers are all from the same basic plant, genus *Capsicum*, though they come in different shapes and sizes as well as degrees of hotness. Native Americans and early settlers knew chiles to be a food preservative and an herbal medicine. Chiles are also high in vitamins A and C, although the C is completely lost after the peppers are dried. Red chiles are merely green chiles that have been left on the plant longer; they turn red as they ripen.

Chiles are New Mexico's biggest cash crop. About eight hundred families grow chiles in and around Hatch, as soon becomes obvious when you approach the airport and pass row upon row of shining green plants growing in the rich soil of the Rio Grande Valley. There are over 350 days of sunshine each year—plenty to provide the even, dry heat necessary for growing these anchos, serranos, jalapeños, Bahamians, and Big Jims. Most of the green chiles are processed (that is, canned or frozen), whereas the red chiles are most often ground into powder or red pepper.

Chile-growing is in strong evidence at the festival, where *ristras* (ropes made of ripening red chiles) decorate the booths and growers hawk their produce from the backs of pickup trucks. Buy a *ristra*, as we did, and carry home with you the sweet, spicy smell of peppers. We let our fresh pepper chain dry on the shelf in the back of our car for two weeks, and every time we returned to the car, it was like jumping into a bowl of chile. For others not traveling as far, there are a few growers who will roast the peppers for you on the spot, so that you can rush home to make the sweetest bowl of chile you've ever tasted.

The Hatch Chile Festival is far from glamorous. Most activities take place in the aging airport hangar, which provides good shade and allows cooling breezes to blow through. People come dressed in Western hats, boots, and jeans, and speak a mixture of Spanish and English while they stroll around the booths that sell chile jewelry or tacos and burritos. When the winners of the various contests are announced, all attention is turned to the stage to watch the Little Miss Chile Festival Queen be crowned or the prize given for the best *ristra*. The cooking contest is always competitive, expecially since the recipes have to be totally original. Eloise Mendez, a past winner eager to gather another prize, entered her lovely (and delicious) red chile bread, chile noodles, tamales and enchiladas, and empanadas. For her Cheese with Green Chile she made her own cheese, called *acedero*. Also an attention-getter is the chile judging, in which the growers compete for the highest-quality produce. The favorite here is the Big Jim, a large, long, and straight chile that is a cross between a jalapeño and a poblano; it is best stuffed with cheese and batter-fried as a chile relleno.

There's also an auction, a midway with rides, a dance on Saturday night, and an art show featuring paintings of chiles. But the highlight of this annual event is clearly the chile meal, served both days although on Sunday a pit-barbecued beef brisket takes the place of the green chile enchiladas. This meal is chile heaven. The green chile con carne has been cooking for five days and is kept at a simmer on the giant commercial stoves at the far end of the hangar. Served with tortillas and beans, the chile stew is studded with tiny mincings of beef; flavorful but not devilishly spiced, it's just hot enough to make your nose run a little. The tortillas are folded in quarters, providing the perfect scoop for that last bit of chile at the bottom of the bowl. Beans are large red kidneys in a thin sauce, almost a broth. As if that were not enough of this chile madness, the dinner platter also includes some green chile enchiladas topped with Cheddar cheese (a bit too soft and mushy for our taste) and a red chile tamale that is fiery hot and just right.

Chicken Enchiladas
with Green Chile Sauce

These enchiladas straddle the line on hotness, but you can increase the fire by adding more jalapeños to the sauce.

1 medium chicken (about 3 pounds), cut up
Salt and pepper to taste
1 dried red chile
2 tablespoons lard
2 medium onions, cut up
3 cans (4 ounces each) green chiles
1 clove garlic, minced
1 tablespoon cornstarch

1 cup grated longhorn or Cheddar cheese
12 corn tortillas
1 jalapeño pepper, seeded and minced
2 cups (½ pound) grated Monterey Jack cheese

Rinse the chicken and remove the skin. Place in a large kettle of water and bring to a boil. Add the salt and pepper and drop in the red chile. Bring to a simmer, cover, and let cook for 25 minutes, or until the meat is tender. Let cool, then remove the chicken from the bones. Reserve the stock.

Heat the lard in a large skillet and add the onions and green chiles. Mash the chiles until they form a puree, then add the garlic and sauté until all ingredients are blended, about 5 minutes. Add the cornstarch and stir well, then slowly add 1 cup of the reserved stock. Stir until smooth and let simmer for 10 minutes.

Shred or dice the chicken meat and measure out about 3 cups. Mix the chicken with the longhorn or Cheddar cheese and about one third of the sauce. You should have a thick, semimoist mixture.

Wrap the tortillas in foil and place in a warm (200°F) oven to soften for about 10 minutes. Spoon a little sauce into the bottom of a baking dish large enough to hold the 12 enchiladas. Take a tortilla and place a cylinder of filling down the center. Roll the tortilla and place, seam side down, into the baking dish. Continue to form the enchiladas, placing them side by side in the dish. Add the minced jalapeño to the remaining sauce and pour it over the enchiladas; top with the grated Jack cheese. Cover the dish with foil and bake for 30 minutes in a 350°F oven, or until the sauce is bubbly. Serve with cornbread.   *Serves 4 to 6*

Red Chile Tamales

Making tamales is a lengthy affair, and it helps if you have a friend to assist with the assembling. These tamales are made with chile powder instead of fresh chiles because for most people the powder is more readily available. Be certain, however, that you use pure chile powder, not the blended powder that is commonly sold in supermarkets.

1½ pounds boneless chuck steak
1 package (8 ounces) corn husks
  (see note)
5 tablespoons lard
4 tablespoons flour

Salt and pepper
½ cup pure chile powder
½ cup water
1 cup boiling water

MASA

1 cup lard
2½ cups masa harina
1 tablespoon chile powder

2 teaspoons salt
1¾ cups reserved beef broth

Place the chuck steak in a large pot and cover with water. Bring to a boil over high heat, then reduce the heat, cover the pot, and simmer for 3 hours. When the meat is tender, drain and let cool. Reserve the broth and shred the meat.

Meanwhile, soak the husks in hot water for 2 hours, or until soft.

Melt 3 tablespoons of the lard in a saucepan and add 2 tablespoons of the flour. Blend well until smooth and season with 1 teaspoon of the salt. In a small bowl, mix the chile powder with the water to make a paste. Stir the paste into the melted lard, then gradually stir in the boiling water. Stir the sauce until it is smooth.

Melt the remaining 2 tablespoons lard in a saucepan over medium heat and blend in the remaining 2 tablespoons flour. Add the chile sauce and simmer over low heat for 5 minutes. Be careful, because chile burns easily; keep stirring. Add the shredded meat and simmer the sauce, uncovered, for 30 minutes, stirring frequently. Season with salt and pepper to taste and then let cool.

To make the masa, beat the lard with an electric mixer until it is light and smooth. Add the masa harina, chile powder, and salt, then stir in the beef broth. Mix well. To test if the masa is light enough for the tamales, scoop up a ball of it with a teaspoon and then float it in a small glass of warm water. If the masa floats, it is ready to use; if it sinks, then beat in more lard and test again.

Drain a few of the corn husks and pat them dry. Spread a husk out onto a counter so that the narrow end points away from you. Spread about 3 tablespoons masa on the husk so that you have covered almost up to the narrow tip and 4 inches down the length of the husk. Spread the masa sideways across to the left edge of the husk and across to the right side, leaving about ½ inch on the right side. Then spread about 2 tablespoons filling down the center of the masa and fold the left side of the tamale over, then the right side, using the bare edge as a seal. It should stick well; if not, moisten it lightly. Fold over the wide and narrow edges and fasten with a strip of corn husk or with string.

Arrange the tamales on the rack of a steamer, with the narrow edges of the tamales pointing up if possible. Bring the water in the steamer to a boil and put in the tamales, being sure that the water does not touch the tamales themselves. Cover the steamer and steam for 1 hour, or until the masa firms up and separates from the husk (you'll have to open a tamale to see if they are ready.) *Makes 4 dozen tamales*

NOTE: If corn husks are not available, you can wrap the tamales in foil, but pierce a few holes in it to allow the steam to escape.

Green Chile con Carne

This recipe is adapted from one by Jesse Morales, included in the cookbook compiled by the Hatch Valley Chamber of Commerce.

2½ tablespoons lard
1 pound lean boneless chuck steak, cut into bite-sized chunks
2 tablespoons all-purpose flour
2 medium tomatoes, peeled, seeded, and chopped

4 cans (4 ounces each) whole green chiles, drained and chopped
1 clove garlic
Salt to taste
2 cups water

In a large skillet or cast-iron pot, heat the lard over medium-high heat and add about half the meat chunks. Brown well, turning frequently for about 15 minutes, then remove and drain. Continue browning the remaining pieces of steak.

When all the meat is browned, return the chunks to the pot and add the flour. Stir to coat the meat, then add the tomatoes, chiles, garlic clove, and salt. Add the water, stir, and bring the mixture to a boil. Reduce the heat to a simmer, cover the pot, and cook for 2 hours, or until the meat is quite tender and a lovely green sauce forms.

Serves 2 to 3

THE HATCH CHILE FESTIVAL is held annually on Labor Day weekend. Everything happens at the Hatch Municipal Airport. The events are pretty well distributed over both Saturday and Sunday. A different meal is served each day: the chile meal on Saturday and the barbecue on Sunday. The concert and dance are on Saturday night, but there is also a dance on Sunday night. There is no admission to the festival, although a parking charge ($2) is levied. The meals are $5 per person; tickets are sold at the entrance. Other foods, soft drinks, and chiles are for sale from individual wagons and stands. (Our *ristra*, 3 feet long and enough red chiles to last a long time, cost $6.)

Hatch (New Mexico) is about 70 miles north of El Paso (Texas), off I-25; the airport is just outside of town (there are signs to point the way). For additional information, write the Hatch Valley Chamber of Commerce, P.O. Box 38, Hatch, New Mexico 87937.

National Hard Crab Derby

Crisfield, Maryland

HEY'RE OFF AND RUNNING, so to speak, at the National Hard Crab Derby. In only eighteen seconds, Crazy Annie crosses the finish line, beating out stiff competition from Thunder Road and Sing Sing. After a series of heats, the finalists go against one another for the prized trophy, while Claws, Lil' Nipper, One-Armed Bandit, Rock Bottom, Rolling Ralph, Shackles, Compromise, Willie, and other dalliers are claimed by their sponsors or relegated to the steam pot.

This is Saturday of Labor Day weekend in Crisfield, a small town at the southern tip of Maryland that sticks out into the Chesapeake Bay. The crab races are going strong today, as the Annual Hard Crab Derby honors the mighty blue crab of the Chesapeake. The Governor's Cup Race is the highlight of this festival, with crabs from over thirty-five states competing for first place. Well, the crabs aren't really from states like Kansas or South Dakota; the governors of most states enter Maryland crabs to race in their name. The entrants are given names such as Seward's Folly, Arkansas Traveler, Connecticut Yankee, and Spirit of Massachusetts. As with the regular derby, the crabs are placed in individual gates. The starting gun is fired and the row of gates tipped downward, sending the racers off across a sloping platform. The first crab over the bottom edge is the winner, with all the glory that winning brings.

Not all the crabs are racing, however. There are plenty to eat, too. The tender, young soft-shelled crabs are hot and crisp from the fryer, served two to a bun. Crab cakes are spicy and speckled with herbs, also on a bun. But the special treat is the steamed crabs.

Maryland steamed crabs come coated with peppery Chesapeake Bay seasoning. Buy them by the dozen, and the server will pluck them from the large pot and pile them into a cut-down cardboard box that acts as a tray. You'll be handed some sheets of newspaper and offered a knife or mallet. If you haven't brought your own knife, buy one now, because it will help you to pry all the sweet meat from the shell. Grab a beer and take your mess of crabs over to a picnic table that overlooks the bay. Spread the papers on the table and select a crab. Pull off the claws and set them aside, within reach for later. Peel back the apron, that grayish section on the underside that connects with the shell at one end. Break off the apron, then rip off the top shell. Pick off the "dead man's fingers" or "devil fingers"—fingerlike extensions that are the lungs. Break off the mouth of the crab and remove the yellowish fat if its taste is too strong for you. Snap the remaining portion in half, then use your knife or fingers to dig into the individual sections where the legs and claws were attached, to extract the sweetest meat this side of a lobster. If you've cracked some large crabs, then you'll want to go after their claw meat as well. Crack the claw with the mallet, or your teeth, and pull the meat out, using the pincher of the claw as a handle. The claw meat isn't as refined as the backfin, but well worth the effort nonetheless.

Eating steamed crabs can be pretty messy, but as you crack and pick, the spicy coating gets onto your fingers and combines with the crab meat for an unbeatable taste. Choose the heavier crabs; those will have more meat. And while you're having fun eating, you can refine your crab-picking technique.

If you'd like some tips on picking crabs, watch the pros do it at the crab-picking contest, usually just preceding the races on Saturday. These contestants are almost all from the processing plants in the area, and they know how to get the most from a crab in the least time. As a crowd cheers, they deftly strip off the legs, shell the crab, then thrust their knives into the body, flicking out the tender lumps onto a pile on their laps. For fifteen minutes they pick their way through a mountain of crabs, displaying their individual styles and techniques. "Look at her," someone remarked, "she's quivering her knife." At the signal, they pack the crab meat into containers to be weighed, then the winner is announced: three and one half pounds of clean, cartilage-free crabmeat, which is later sold to spectators for only six dollars a pound. (Just to put things into perspective, it took us an hour to pick out half a pound.)

What with the crab races, the crab-picking contest, and the crabs to eat, this is a very "crabby" festival. There's also a Miss Crustacean Beauty Pageant, a Crabbers Ball, and a crab-cooking contest to prolong the enjoyment. But we think that at this festival the eating is the most fun, second only to bringing home some lump crab meat or whole crabs in your cooler.

Deviled Crab

This recipe, adapted from one by Miss Nicki Dixon of Crisfield, is re-printed from *Crabbiest Recipes from the Annual Crab Cooking Contest.* It was grand-prize winner in the 1967 contest.

5 tablespoons butter or margarine	*Dash cayenne pepper*
½ cup finely chopped onion	*½ teaspoon salt*
¼ cup finely chopped green pepper	*2 teaspoons Worcestershire sauce*
3 tablespoons flour	*1 tablespoon prepared mustard*
1½ cups half and half	*1 tablespoon finely chopped chives*
2 large eggs, separated and yolks lightly beaten	*1 pound lump crab meat*
	1 cup soft bread crumbs

Preheat the oven to 375°F. Generously grease a 1-quart baking dish.

Melt 3 tablespoons of the butter or margarine in a heavy saucepan and then add the onion and green pepper. Sauté until tender, then add the flour. Mix until smooth. Stir in the half and half gradually over medium heat; keep stirring until the sauce thickens. Remove a small portion of hot sauce from the pan and mix into the egg yolks, then add the yolk mixture to the saucepan.

Heat the sauce for 2 minutes more, then remove from the heat and add the cayenne, salt, Worcestershire sauce, mustard, and chives. Mix well. Stir in the crab meat and spoon the mixture into the casserole.

Melt the remaining 2 tablespoons butter or margarine, then combine with the bread crumbs and sprinkle the mixture on the crab meat. Bake for 20 to 25 minutes, or until the crumbs are golden brown.

Serves 4

Seasoned Crab Cakes

These spicy crab cakes took first place for Betsy Hedemen in the 1983 Crab-Cooking Contest.

3 tablespoons mayonnaise	*1½ teaspoons Old Bay Seasoning*
2 large eggs	*1 tablespoon butter, melted*
3 tablespoons half and half	*1½ slices white bread, crusts*
1 tablespoon lemon juice	*removed*
1 teaspoon Worcestershire sauce	*1 pound backfin crab meat*
1 teaspoon salt	*Vegetable shortening for frying*

In a small bowl, mix together the mayonnaise, eggs, half and half, lemon juice, Worcestershire sauce, salt, Old Bay seasoning, and butter.

In another bowl, break the bread into very small pieces (fingernail size). Pick over the crab meat carefully so as not to break up the lumps, then add to the bread crumbs. Pour the liquid mixture over the crab meat, then shape into 8 cakes or patties. Place the cakes on a platter and chill for about 5 hours.

Melt enough shortening so as to be ½ inch deep in a heavy 10-inch skillet. Heat until very hot, about 350°F, and add the crab cakes. Fry on one side for about 2 to 3 minutes, or until nicely browned, then turn and fry on the other side for an equal amount of time. Drain on paper towels, then serve hot.   *Serves 4*

THE NATIONAL HARD CRAB DERBY is held on Labor Day weekend in Crisfield, Maryland. Most events are on Saturday (including the parade, the crab-picking contest, and the crab races). There are some contests and band concerts on Sunday, ending with a fireworks display. The parade is in town, but most events (and all food booths) are at the Legion grounds. Admission to the grounds is $2 and includes parking.

A dozen steamed crabs costs about $5; the crab cakes and soft-shelled crabs are less. If you want to enter a crab in the derby, entry fee is $3 (they supply the crab).

Crisfield is on a finger of land that juts out into the Chesapeake Bay, on the Delmarva Peninsula. It's about 30 miles south of Salisbury on Route 413. For information, write National Hard Crab Derby & Fair, P.O. Box 215, Crisfield, Maryland 21817.

Castroville Artichoke Festival

Castroville, California

RTICHOKE SOUP, frittata, antipasto, and pastries. Pastries? We wondered. So we decided to head, without further delay, to Castroville, California, for the twenty-fourth annual Artichoke Festival.

"You can't miss it," we were told. "Just turn off Route One at the giant artichoke." We made our right turn and drove into the small town of Castroville, where everything seemed to be "artichoke"; but this was to be expected in the Artichoke Center of the World. Castroville is the heart of California's central coast, and artichokes are the heart of Castroville.

This clumsy-looking vegetable, first encountered by many in French restaurants, is botanically related to the thistle, but is not itself a thistle, although it is often referred to as such. The artichoke was first cultivated in Italy around the middle of the fifteenth century, gradually spread to other European countries, and was brought to the United States by French settlers (in Louisiana) and Spanish settlers (in California). Artichokes were first grown commercially in Castroville in 1921, and since then have grown into a $30 million crop. Castroville is not only the center for growing artichokes in this country, it is also the home of several packing plants and a marinating operation.

While many think of California as a land of perpetual sunshine, this section of the coast—along Monterey Bay—is subject to ocean breezes and cooling fogs, just what the artichoke thrives on. Although they are available all year long, the peak season for artichokes is April and May, so the festival is held in September, which is a less busy time for the growers. You could have fooled us, though, because the just-picked summer 'chokes were fabulous, and we heard talk of the truly delicious "winter-kissed" artichokes that come during the frosty winter months.

In 1959, when the festival was started, it was little more than a barbecue and a parade. But the growers got behind it (forming the California Advisory Board) and began to use the festival as a way of promoting artichokes, then quite foreign to most Americans. Much of the food prepared at the festival is Italian or Portuguese in origin, brought here with the people when they came to California in the early 1900s. The food booths, run by local civic groups, featured an astonishing variety of preparations, some more successful than others. We relished the peppery artichoke soup and were puzzled by its contents until we learned that it was made with marinated artichokes, which sounds awful but results in a surprisingly good soup. Certainly outstanding was the artichoke frittata, a cakelike omelet two inches thick and filled with chopped onions and artichoke hearts. Equally good was a savory artichoke appetizer—marinated bottoms filled with tiny California bay shrimp and topped with a tart mayonnaise dressing. Although they were a novelty, we found the greenish artichoke cake and pie quite plain-tasting and not very artichokey, as well as visually unappetizing.

By far the greatest eating fun at the festival was the French-fried artichoke hearts, particularly those prepared at the Lions Club booth. The older woman behind the counter—a grandmother sort—carefully picked through the frozen artichoke hearts and placed them in layers on paper towels, separating and drying them as they thawed. Then she shifted back to the stove, where she gave her batter a stir, dipped in some thawed hearts, and plunged them into the hot fat. As she tended the deep-frying hearts, her hips gave a subtle sway to the music coming from the nearby stage. We tried the other fried artichoke hearts at the festival, but at this booth they were made by the woman who introduced them to America, right here in Castroville. They were the best, of course, and best eaten hot with a dash of salt.

Eating is not all the fun at the festival, however. There's a flea market each year in which all sorts of artichokiana are sold, including artichoke salt and pepper shakers, dishes, and the ever-present T-shirt. Continuous music fills the streets with rhythm while the audience sits around on bales of hay. The festival features a beauty pageant, a foot race with some stiff competition, and a parade. Windows of the shops along the main street are decorated with artichoke pictures, and a banner stretches across the street heralding the festival. The fourth and sixth grades of the local school have an artichoke-decorating contest; making queens out of the artichokes was the most popular, but some were more unusual, especially the artichoke Christmas tree. At the twenty-fifth festival, in 1985, there was a recipe contest, too.

Perhaps one of the greatest bonuses of this festival is the opportunity to buy artichokes of different sizes, packed in sacks to take home. Since artichokes are high in minerals and vitamins, including calcium, and also have more protein than most other vegetables, you are toting home a bag of nutrition as well as the raw ingredient for many satisfying dishes. The theme of the festival is "Have a Heart," and in Castroville during this three-day event you'll get not only to the bottom but also to the heart of artichokes.

French-fried Artichokes

2 packages frozen artichoke
    hearts
⅔ cup all-purpose flour
2 teaspoons baking powder

1 large egg, lightly beaten
1 cup milk
Pinch salt
Vegetable oil for deep frying

Thaw and drain the artichoke hearts on paper towels, with cut sides down. They must be completely dry; this will take at least 1 hour.

Mix together the flour, baking powder, egg, milk, and salt for the batter. Meanwhile, heat the oil in a deep fryer or large pot until it is 360°F. Plunge the artichoke hearts into the batter, then drop them into the hot oil. Deep fry for 7 to 10 minutes on each side, or until they are evenly browned. Drain on paper towels and sprinkle with additional salt.

Serves 4

Cream of Artichoke Soup

This recipe is adapted from one by the Artichoke Advisory Board and served at the festival. It is made with marinated artichokes, which give the soup a piquantness.

2 jars (6 ounces each) marinated
    artichoke hearts
½ cup chopped onion
½ cup chopped celery

1 cup chicken stock
2 cups half and half
2 teaspoons cornstarch

Drain the marinade from the artichokes, saving half the marinade. Cut the larger artichokes from one jar in half and set aside. Place the marinade in a saucepan over medium heat. Sauté the onion and celery in the marinade until they are limp. Then add the chicken stock and simmer the mixture, covered, over medium heat for 10 minutes.

Combine in the container of a blender the whole artichokes with ½ cup of the soup liquid. Whirl until it is the consistency of a puree, then pour into the soup pot. Mix the half and half with the cornstarch, then add the mixture to the soup. Add the reserved artichokes and stir. Cover and simmer for about 5 minutes, or until thoroughly warmed. Garnish with croutons, if desired. *Serves 4 as an appetizer*

Artichoke Frittata

This is very much like the artichoke frittata served at the festival, easiest made with frozen artichoke hearts, although you could boil up tiny fresh ones and remove the tough outer leaves.

1 package (9 ounces) frozen
  artichoke hearts, thawed
4 large eggs

¼ cup chopped onion
1 cup milk
Salt and pepper to taste

Remove the artichokes from the package and break apart. Let drain on paper towels until all the moisture is off the leaves. The artichokes must be completely dry.

Preheat the oven to 350°F.

Cut the artichokes up into pieces about ½ inch in size. Mix with the eggs, onion, and milk in a bowl.

Grease a 1-quart baking dish and pour in the artichoke mixture. Bake for 30 to 45 minutes. Insert a thin knife into the center of the frittata; if done, it should come out clean. Transfer the baking dish to the broiler for about 3 minutes to brown the top. *Serves 4*

THE CASTROVILLE ARTICHOKE FESTIVAL is held the second weekend in September. There are continuous events and music on both days, from 9 to 4. The foot race is on Saturday, the parade on Sunday. All the artichoke delicacies are available from individual booths on both days from 9 till 4. Frittatas, soup, and pastries run about $1 per item; some things, naturally, are more expensive. There is no admission charge; parking is on side streets (the main streets are closed off for the festival).

Castroville is on U.S. 1, about 110 miles south of San Francisco and 16 miles north of Monterey. For more information, you can write or call the Castroville Artichoke Festival, P.O. Box 1041, Castroville, California 95012; (408) 633–CHOK (2465).

McClure Bean Soup Festival

McClure, Pennsylvania

T HE ENVELOPE containing the information about the Ninety-first Annual McClure Bean Soup Festival is embossed in the upper left-hand corner with the United States flag as it was during the Civil War—that is, with thirty-six stars: 8-6-8-6-8; and in the right-hand corner is a picture of a kettle of steaming hot soup hanging over an open fire. Under the flag is a cannon and "Largest Celebration of Its Kind in the World!" Under the kettle it says, "Attendance Increases Annually!" Centered: "2 Big Days— 5 Big Nites."

Civil War veterans had been meeting in McClure regularly since 1883, and had been holding soup festivals, no doubt a re-creation of the bean soup dinners they had eaten in the field; but it was not until 1891 that the public was invited to partake of a real Civil War bean soup dinner. Records show that Comrade Ner B. Middleswarth was chairman in charge and he managed to get the War Department to supply hardtack to be served with the soup. Today, fortunately, crackers are served.

By the early 1900s, the ranks had thinned considerably, and so the sons of the "boys who wore the Blue" took over. Now their great-grand-sons are in charge, and the festival is lots bigger and more elaborate (attendance does increase each year), with political speeches, games and rides for children, and people selling everything from belts to mobile homes. But the highlight is still the bean soup, made from the original recipe: hamburger, beans, and lard.

The soup kitchen is a large section of a vast white wooden shed. There, eight men—several in Civil War hats and uniforms—stir sixteen 35-gallon cast-iron kettles of soup boiling over wood fires. At serving time, a pulley is brought over, the entire kettle is lifted off the fire, and the kettle is carefully placed behind a serving counter. The fire is stoked up and another kettle brought in. All told, upward of fifteen thousand people are served each year.

The soup is a dinner in itself. The year we went to McClure, it cost 95¢ for a serving, plus an additional dime for crackers. The soup is literally boiling as it's served. It is thin, but with a distinctive smoky flavor and a very beany taste. No wonder, since it is chock-full of navy beans. All it needs at table, besides half an hour to cool down, is salt, pepper, and the crackers.

The line for soup tickets snakes around the booths selling souvenirs and cotton candy. This line is long but moves quickly; the portions are ladled out soup-kitchen style and are ready for you as you approach the serving table. There's lots of talk about when the soup cost only fifteen cents and the crackers were free, but it's still a good deal. People eat their suppers at long tables under the shed, while gospel music from the stage drifts in from behind the kitchen. There's other food too, including barbecued pork platters and pork barbecue sandwiches. But these are just supporting attractions; the soup is the star.

McClure is a modest town north of Gettysburg, in the valley that is formed between the Shade Mountains and the Jack Mountains of the Alleghenies. Their Bean Soup Festival has been going strong for nearly a century—it's one of the oldest festivals we know of. What began as a reunion in 1883 continues today as families and friends throughout the valley get together during festival days.

Civil War Bean Soup

This is how the North fed its hungry, in a recipe plentiful enough to serve a small army.

½ pound navy beans
2 tablespoons lard
½ pound chopped beef
2 quarts water

Soak the beans in water to cover overnight, or until they have swelled. Drain and set aside.

Melt the lard in a heavy cast-iron casserole set over medium-high heat. Add the meat and break up the clumps. Continue to cook over medium heat until the meat no longer has any pink color. Add the beans, stir once, and add the 2 quarts water. Bring to a boil, then cover and reduce the heat to a simmer. Let cook slowly for 45 minutes, or until the beans are quite soft.

Scoop up some beans with a slotted spoon and smash them against the side of the pot. Repeat this two or three times, until the soup has become cloudy and slightly thickened. Bring the mixture back to a boil and boil vigorously for 15 minutes. Serve very hot, with saltines.

Serves 8

THE McCLURE BEAN SOUP FESTIVAL is held annually in McClure, Pennsylvania, in mid-September. All events take place in Cold Springs Grove, a large park in town. Parking is in lots scattered around the area, but attendants are there to direct traffic and to help you. There is a parking charge of $2, otherwise there are no entrance fees.

The bean soup is served Wednesday and Thursday night (after 4:30 P.M.) and on Friday and Saturday from 11:30 A.M. on. There is entertainment each evening as well as on Saturday afternoon. All booths are open throughout the festival; the midway rides operate every evening and all day Saturday. The bean soup dinner costs about $1 and is served in a pavilion where there are plenty of picnic benches and tables. Other food is available from concessionaires; some have table service.

McClure is in central Pennsylvania, about 70 miles northwest of Harrisburg, on U.S. 522. For further information, write the McClure Bean Soup Committee, McClure, Pennsylvania 17841; or call (717) 658-8425.

Sorghum Sopping Days

Waldo, Alabama

A SUNNY DAY, a covered bridge over a rippling brook, a nineteenth-century mill converted into a barn, and the air sweet with the smell of autumn. In Hocutt Park, just beyond the brook where the mill faces the road, people are standing in line to buy sorghum molasses and to have a sorghum-and-biscuits breakfast. It's time again for Sorghum Sopping Days in Waldo, Alabama, an annual September event since 1973.

This is sorghum made the old-time way, and country biscuits with sausage and sorghum is the old-fashioned way of enjoying sorghum. Even for people in this rural part of east-central Alabama, sorghum is a touch of nostalgia because good sorghum is getting hard to find. Fewer people grow the canes now, and almost no one takes the time to squeeze out the sweet juice and boil it down, then strain it through cheesecloth into jars. At Waldo, though, they even use a horse to turn the gears that power the sorghum press. This press is about a hundred years old, made by the Chattanooga Plow Com'y, and as the gears turn, they squeeze the canes until a thin yellow-green liquid trickles out. This cane juice is boiled down in a copper evaporator until it is thick and syrupy. It takes about forty minutes to cook down a batch, and as it cooks, the men tending the cooker skim the impurities off the top. They strain and bottle the syrup right on the spot, and after you've had the sorghum breakfast, you're very inclined to take a few jars of syrup home with you.

The sorghum breakfast is served all day long. You buy your "ticket" for the meal at the door of the mill-cum-barn: "Here's your ticket. It doesn't turn into a fork until you begin eating." As you enter the mill to pick up your food, you're handed a plate with Frank Bannister's whole-hog sausage patties and two mammoth baking-powder biscuits. Next stop is in front of two crocks—one of hot melted butter (real butter), the other warm sorghum syrup. Most people just pour the butter and syrup right onto their biscuits. We were more timid and put the sorghum off to the side; but we quickly discovered the wonder of butter and sorghum. In fact, we made "sandwiches" of the biscuit with the sausage and sopped the whole thing in the butter and syrup all together. Wonderful. Sorghum sopping, you bet!

Sorghum canes are speckled, red at the base. Kids used to suck on the ends of the canes as a snack, especially when just about every farm in the South grew its own sorghum. Sweet sorghum—grain sorghums are different, grown mostly as feed or for flour—was at one time considered a more dependable crop than corn because it is more resistant to heat and drought. The syrup was a common sweetener during the nineteenth century, but it was eventually replaced by refined sugar, although many rural southern cooks continue to prefer sorghum for baking. It is thinner and lighter than molasses (which is made from sugar cane), and it has much more flavor and character than sugar. One woman we spoke to swore by it for her gingerbread.

While the sorghum is being cooked down and as people file out of the mill with their breakfast plates, the stage is readied for the day's entertainment. Waldo's "sound system" consists of a 1950s portable record player and a loudspeaker set up in front of a makeshift stage that has been constructed in front of the brook. The announcer starts the record, then calls out the name of the tune. The entertainment—local cloggers—begin to dance. Each dancer gets her or his chance at "center stage," though their abilities vary considerably. The audience applauds the different groups, while kids run into the brook, splashing each other and cooling off. We look up and see half a dozen horse-drawn carts coming down the road to the festival, and as they cross the bridge, we wonder if, perhaps, time has suddenly stood still.

❧

You'll probably come away from Sorghum Sopping Days with at least one jar of syrup. You can use sorghum in any recipe that calls for molasses, for a stronger, more pungent taste. And, of course, you can make biscuits for your own sorghum sopping. Here are a couple of other uses for sorghum, equally good as breakfast sweets.

Sorghum Butter

½ cup (1 stick) sweet butter, at
room temperature

¼ cup sorghum syrup

Beat the butter with an electric mixer until smooth. Slowly add the sorghum to the bowl, beating all the while. The mixture may curdle the butter if you add it too fast, but if that happens, melt the mixture, then let it cool until solid again. Spread the sorghum butter on toast, muffins, or pancakes.

Makes ¾ to 1 cup

Sorghum Toast

Slices of white bread (preferably stale)

Sorghum syrup (see note)
Butter

Pour the sorghum into a shallow bowl, then dip each slice of bread in it, coating both sides. Don't let the bread absorb too much sorghum; you want a thin coating only.

Heat the butter in a skillet, about ½ tablespoon per slice, and quickly fry the bread over medium heat until warmed. Spread the slices with butter or something cool and mild in contrast, such as yogurt, whipped cream, or sour cream.

NOTE: If you can't pick up your syrup at the Sopping Days, you'll find sorghum sold at many country farm stands in the South and Midwest. It is also found at tourist shops that feature country wares.

SORGHUM SOPPING DAYS in Waldo are usually the third weekend of September. The meal is served on both days and costs $2.50. Other than that, there are no charges, although it is customary to put a dollar or two into the volunteer firemen's bucket as you leave. (The festival is a fundraiser for the department.)

Sorghum is made and sold on both days, and the crafts festival and entertainment are also on both days. Everything is right there at the old mill; no reservations are necessary, and tickets for the meal are sold as you enter the building. It's a great way to spend the morning or afternoon.

Waldo (it's not on the map) is 6 miles south of Talladega at milepost number 58, off Route 77. (Altogether, it's about 50 miles southeast of Birmingham.) For additional information, write Town of Waldo, Route 3, Talladega, Alabama 35160.

Persimmon Festival

Mitchell, Indiana

PERSIMMON ICE CREAM. Persimmon pucker balls. Persimmon pancakes with persimmon sauce. Persimmon bars, fingers, fudge, cookies, and candy apples. Don't look for these on your supermarket shelf. There won't be recipes for them in your cookbooks either. About the only chance you'll get to sample such treats is at the Persimmon Festival in Mitchell, Indiana, where Hoosier cooks compete to invent new uses for this strange and wonderful fruit.

You may have thought you've eaten persimmons. You may even like the large orange oriental persimmons you find in the market. But chances are, unless you are from the southeastern United States or southern Midwest, you haven't seen a native American persimmon, let alone savored its unique, fragrant flavor.

The American persimmon tree has a short, slender trunk with spreading branches that flower in May and June to form juicy oval fruits that grow in tight clusters of five or six. In fall, their dusty blush turns from pale orange to yellowish brown. This fruit is a world apart from the more common Asian persimmon, a cultivated tree from Japan now grown in California.

The botanical name for the native persimmon is *Diospyros virginiana*, meaning "the fruit of Jove." Its habitat is mostly southern, from New York to Florida and westward into southern Ohio, Indiana, Missouri, and southeastern Iowa and Kansas (there's even supposed to be one somewhere in New York's Central Park). The Catawba Indians of South Carolina gave it its common name. They used to strip the bark and boil it to make a mouth rinse. The Choctaw Indians along the Natchez Trace dried the fruits for winter use. Settlers in Pennsylvania made persimmon wine, while others brewed beer from the fruit. No one uses the bark anymore, but today some smart people in towns like Mitchell still harvest the fruit and use it in puddings, pies, cookies, and cakes.

During festival days, the few streets that run through downtown Mitchell are closed to traffic, and the local charities and clubs set up booths to sell hamburgers, hot dogs, soup, chili, and—of course—persimmon pudding and pie. There are as many different persimmon puddings as there are booths. And the pie, lest you be fooled, is really just a pudding baked in a piecrust. Both are dark, dense, and delicious. One booth also sells persimmon ice cream, a great idea that could be made even better with a little more persimmon. Nevertheless, it is possible to buy containers of persimmon pulp to take home so you can try your own hand at the ice cream, or pudding, or fudge.

The Persimmon Festival has many of the customary food festival events: a five-mile run, a fifty-mile bicycle tour, a dance, an arts and crafts exhibit, a flea market, carnival rides, the crowning of a festival queen, a chicken barbecue, and a grand parade. One of the major attractions is a candlelit tour of the nearby Spring Mill Village, a re-creation of a pioneer village. But the emphasis here is on the persimmon itself, and the cooking contest and persimmon food samples are the highlights of this week-long event.

The cooking contest has two divisions: one for persimmon pudding (the ultimate use of persimmon pulp) and the "other" category for everything else. Pudding can vary from light to dense, from creamy to rough, and from dark brown to beige, depending on who is making it and the particular persimmons they are using. The key to a winning recipe is to make the pudding with a minimum of flavorings, so that the true taste of persimmon can come through. Persimmon pudding here in Mitchell is a specific thing: it is always a soft baked square made with spices, sugar, milk (or buttermilk), eggs, and baking powder. When it comes from the oven, it's puffed up, but soon it sinks in the center to resemble a squashed pillow. The taste is mildly sweet and the texture soft; whipped cream seems the perfect accompaniment.

And how does this mystery fruit taste? At the festival we sampled raw pulp, persimmon pudding, ice cream, pie, fudge, and cookies. We took pulp home and made more pudding, pies, fudge, ice cream, and upside-down cake. The pulp tastes very fragrant, a puree similar to applesauce with a mildly bitter aftertaste. Cooked up in a pudding, the pulp loses that aftertaste and gains a flavor reminiscent of figs or dates, which is why it has sometimes been called a date plum.

Perhaps it was because the fruit from the persimmon tree was unreliable—some trees bore well while others nearby didn't—or maybe too many people tried the fruit before it was ready (it used to be a southern trick to play on strangers). Whatever the reason, this native fruit lost favor with the American people. A few years ago Raymond Sokolov bemoaned the gradual disappearance of this fruit, noting that they are "of a sophistication worth commercial exploitation." More recently, a few articles have appeared in national food magazines describing the persimmon and its many uses. Yet today it seems to be only a local favorite, in pockets of the Midwest such as Mitchell.

The persimmon's secret is easy to uncover: If the fruits are ripe enough, they'll lose their tannic astringency and turn sweet. This means either waiting until after the first frost, when they fall to the ground, or picking the fruit earlier and allowing it to ripen to a gushy softness. There's a Tennessee saying, "Gather the persimmons after the frost as the mistletoe begins to whiten." Thus, each September, when the air is cool and the leaves have begun to change color, folks in Mitchell gather up the persimmons and turn them into a rich, flavorful harvest.

Persimmon Pudding

This is Bessie Cooper's pudding, winner of the 1981 festival cooking contest.

2 cups persimmon pulp (see note)
2 cups sugar
2 large eggs, lightly beaten
1 teaspoon baking soda
1½ cups buttermilk
1½ cups all-purpose flour
1 teaspoon baking powder
⅛ teaspoon salt
½ teaspoon ground cinnamon
1 teaspoon vanilla extract
4 tablespoons (½ stick) butter
¼ cup heavy cream, whipped

Combine the persimmon pulp, sugar, and eggs in a large bowl and stir well. Add the baking soda to the buttermilk and stir until the foaming ceases, about 1 minute. Add the buttermilk mixture to the persimmon mixture and stir. Sift the flour, baking powder, and salt into the persimmon mixture and mix well. Add the cinnamon and vanilla.

Preheat the oven to 350°F. Lightly grease a 10-inch square cake pan.

Melt the butter and add to the mixture; beat well. Pour the batter into the cake pan and bake for 45 minutes, or until firm to the touch. Serve at room temperature with whipped cream. *Serves 8 to 10*

NOTE: In and around Mitchell you can buy persimmon pulp—fresh in season and frozen later in the year. Persimmon pulp is also available in cans from Dymple's Delight, Route 4, Box 53, Mitchell, Indiana 47446. The pulp from Dymple's Delight is sweetened, so for 2 cups regular pulp you should substitute 1 can (20 ounces) sweetened pulp and then not add the 2 cups sugar.

The following two recipes are from *Old-Fashioned Persimmon Recipes*, The Old-Fashioned Recipes Series & *Backroads Travel* Magazine and Guide, Bear Wallow Publications, Nashville, Indiana.

Brown County Persimmon Fudge

This is a creamy fruit-flavored fudge, less like a hard fudge and more like a jelly or soft taffy. Once it is made, you need to keep it chilled, or it will run all over your counter, but the fresh-fruit flavor makes this fudge worth the effort.

1 cup persimmon pulp (see note above)
6 cups sugar
2½ cups milk

½ cup light corn syrup
½ cup (1 stick) butter
1 cup chopped nuts

Combine the pulp, sugar, milk, and corn syrup in a large, heavy-bottomed saucepan. Cook, uncovered, for 1½ to 2 hours, or until the mixture reaches the soft ball stage (or 230°F on a candy thermometer). Stir often; do not let the mixture stick to the bottom of the pan.

Remove from the heat and allow the fudge to cool in the pan to lukewarm. Stir often, then add the butter, beating well. When the mixture begins to thicken (about 3 minutes), stir in the chopped nuts. Spread the mixture in a buttered 8½-by-13-inch pan and let cool completely before serving. Cut individual pieces as you want them.

Serves 10 to 12

Persimmon Upside-Down Cake

This is a light cake with a chewy caramel topping and a layer of persimmon in the middle.

4 tablespoons (½ stick) butter
2 cups sugar
1½ cups persimmon pulp (see
*   note to previous recipe)*

3 eggs, separated
1 cup cake flour
1 teaspoon baking powder
½ teaspoon salt

Melt the butter in a 10-inch skillet. Add 1 cup of the sugar, stir, and cook until lightly caramelized. Remove from the heat, let cool slightly, and pour the pulp over the mixture.

Preheat the oven to 350°F.

Beat the egg yolks until thick and gradually add the remaining sugar. Sift the flour, baking powder, and salt together, then fold into the egg yolk mixture. Beat the egg whites until they form stiff peaks, then fold the whites into the batter. Pour the batter over the pulp in the pan and bake for 45 to 50 minutes, or until the cake is firm to the touch. Invert the cake onto a platter and serve warm.   *Serves 6*

THE PERSIMMON FESTIVAL is held in Mitchell when persimmons are ripe, the last full week of September. Festivities are on Main Street from Monday through Saturday, with most events on Saturday (including the parade and square dance). During the week, most stands are open from noon to 6:00 P.M., the carnival is on from 6:00 to 11:00 P.M. Persimmon goodies are available every day. All foods are sold from individual stands, operated by civic groups in Mitchell. Persimmon pudding runs about $1.25 a serving. Persimmon pulp is available (mostly frozen) to take home. There are no admission charges; parking is on side streets.

Mitchell, Indiana, is about 35 miles south of Bloomington, on Route 60. For additional information about the festival, contact the City of Mitchell, P.O. Box 2, Mitchell, Indiana 47446; (812) 849-2151.

Marion County Ham Days

Lebanon, Kentucky

THERE ARE NO ROAD SIGNS in Marion County beckoning the visitor to Ham Days. There are no posters, no advertisements, no markers showing where to turn. We follow the map closely, for we realize that the very best festivals are those without signs—they're already so well known by people in the area that there's no need for directions.

The road cuts across the knobland of central Kentucky, to the county named for General Francis Marion, the Swamp Fox of the Revolutionary War. On a late September morning, the fields glisten from an early frost, and in the tobacco barns the drying leaves hang like bats in a cave. The air is heady as the road nears the bourbon distilleries. Warehouses filled with barrels of aging bourbon resemble prisons—tall, straight-sided, metal-clad buildings with bars on the windows and chain link fences around the perimeters.

Sour mash bourbon and tobacco are Kentucky traditions. So is real country ham. Marion County celebrates their ham tradition with a glorious two-day festival featuring a "pigasus" parade; pig-calling, pipe-smoking, and tobacco-spitting contests; an auction of the champion ham; a 10-kilometer "pokey pig" run; country music; crafts exhibits; and a country ham breakfast that rivals the best. The streets of downtown Lebanon are cordoned off, and tables are set up in front of City Hall for the breakfast. And the crowds eat. Five hundred volunteers serve fried apples, scrambled eggs, country ham with red-eye gravy, sliced tomatoes, and biscuits to hungry townspeople and visitors.

If your only experience with ham has been a tasteless, brine-cured, boiled ham, you're in for a real surprise. These somewhat saltier hams are dry-cured with a salt rub for six weeks, then rinsed and rubbed with sugar and smoked for a few hours on a damp day over hickory chips. They then are aged for from six months to two years. The dry cure and light smoking treat the hams gently, allowing the untamed character of the pork to come through. With aging, the hams mellow remarkably; and hams aged between one and two years are usually considered best.

The hams at the breakfast are supplied by Tony Lyvers, a farmer in nearby Loretto, who also has a booth at the festival, a small wooden stand with thin beams overhead from which hang tawny-skinned hams of varying sizes. As you select your ham, Mr. Lyvers will pull it down and insert an ice pick into its depths, bringing it back out again to reveal the ham's nose, its honest, old-fashioned aroma.

Ham is not the only country skill on display at the festival. Most recently, Roby Cogswell, a folklorist at Indiana University, assembled a group of people from the neighboring counties to demonstrate regional crafts. George Miles used a froe (a type of hatchet) and mallet to make tobacco sticks; Clotine Rogers dipped strips of brown paper into water, then twisted them to rush chair bottoms; Martha Cramer demonstrated basketmaking; Tom Walston played the harmonica, and Eric Swan showed water yoke making; Dorothy Rice spun yarn while Bernard Ryan twisted tobacco; Gloria Bright made butter; and Fred Douglas sang gospels. These are old-time crafts and occupations of this region, all but lost in the rush to industrialization.

Ham Days is a very local affair. The windows of the Victorian storefronts along Main Street display exhibits assembled by schoolchildren in the county. All along the parade route the posters for the festival, also made by children, are imaginative reflections on the role of pigs in rural life. Perhaps the most charming aspect of the entire festival is the children's parade. One year some clever children dressed up as the toenails of a foot—the five little piggies who went to market. Husband- and wife-calling contests engage the adults, as do the flea market and antique car show. In between events onstage, there is the chance to stroll past the food booths and sample the homemade bean soup and cornbread, the freshly pressed apple cider, country ham sandwiches, ham biscuits, hot dogs, and soft drinks.

If all this activity isn't enough, or if you need a little diversion between helpings of ham biscuits, there's the chance to tour the Maker's Mark distillery, a few miles away. This is the only distillery in the United States granted National Historic Landmark status, and even if you aren't a bourbon fan the tour is well worth the trip. (There are no samples or sales at the distillery; it's against the law.) A little farther afield, in Bardstown, is Federal Hill, Stephen Foster's "Old Kentucky Home," also open for tours. But these other sights of Kentucky will be there another day, another time. For two special days, once a year, Ham Days is the reason to be in Lebanon.

Fried Kentucky Country Ham
with Red-Eye Gravy

Here's how the country breakfast ham is fixed at the festival.

1 large ham steak (about 1½   *½ cup water (see note)*
   pounds)

Place the ham steak in a heavy skillet, with just enough water to cover the bottom of the pan. Over medium heat, allow the water to evaporate and cook the steak until it is brown, about 3 minutes on each side. Place the ham on a platter and add the ½ cup water to the pan. Bring to a boil and scrape up any particles that might have adhered to the bottom of the skillet. As it boils, stir and blend them into the liquid to form a golden-brown natural gravy. Replace the ham in the gravy for a minute before serving. (Do not overcook.) Serve with fried apples.

NOTE: If you want a more robust gravy, add half water and half coffee to the skillet.   *Serves 2*

Country Fried Apples

1 apple, peeled, cored, and sliced
1 tablespoon butter
1 tablespoon brown sugar

Melt the butter in a heavy skillet and add the apple slices, stirring to coat them with the butter. When the apple starts to brown, cover and simmer until soft. The apples will start to give off a little liquid, and the slices will brown slightly. Remove from the heat and sprinkle on the brown sugar. Stir, and serve immediately.   *Serves 2*

MARION COUNTY HAM DAYS in Lebanon are two days of fun and food, the last weekend of September. There are plenty of events on both days, including the country ham breakfast (served on Saturday from 6:00 to 11:00 A.M. and on Sunday from 8:00 A.M. to 2:00 P.M.). Contests are on both days; the parades are on Saturday, but the gospel music is Sunday. Also on Saturday are the folklore/craft demonstrations. All events are held on Main Street, and everything (except the breakfast) is free. Tickets for the breakfast cost $4.50 and are purchased on the spot. Parking is on side streets. Additional parking is at the Marion County High School; shuttle bus service runs from 10:00 A.M. till 7:00 P.M.

On Saturday, the Maker's Mark distillery sponsors free bus tours starting at 10:00 A.M. We found the tour worth our while.

Lebanon, Kentucky, is about 60 miles southwest of Lexington, off U.S. 68. For additional information about Ham Days, contact the Lebanon/ Marion County Chamber of Commerce, Lebanon, Kentucky 40033; (512) 692–2661.

Apple Harvest Festival

Southington, Connecticut

THEY CALL IT New England's Little Apple. Southington, Connecticut, is in the heart of one of the best apple-growing areas in the state, and it puts on just about the best apple festival we know of. As New Yorkers, we naturally assumed that there'd be a fantastic festival upstate, somewhere around Cortland or Rome, where apples are king. But, as hard as we searched, we were never able to find a celebration that really gave the apple its due in the state known for the fruit; we had to go next door to Connecticut. Here, in a town with four large orchards, one of which dates all the way back to 1809 and another to 1880, people come each year to toast the wonderful, versatile apple.

The apple agenda is jam-packed with fun. Activities are scheduled for two consecutive weekends and include a talent showcase, pancake breakfast, bed race, antique show, beautiful-baby contest, five-mile road race, battle of the bands, plus comedy show, concerts, and dances. One of the most exciting events is the parade, held on Sunday of the first weekend. We've never seen so many people gather for a festival parade, but as soon as it got under way, we knew why. The Southington High School Band, dressed in crisp blue and white uniforms, marched sprightly by us playing a rousing tune. Soon followed the J.F.K. Junior High School Band, another large and brassy group, dressed in green and white. That afternoon we were to see a succession of school bands from all the towns in the area. They were great, and they kept everyone's spirits high as the politicians, beauty queens (in their traditional Corvettes), Scouts and Indian Guides, antique cars, farm machinery, and fire engines moved by. The crowds cheered and clapped as their school band, children, or favorite float came along.

The parade passes around two sides of a triangular park in the center of town, the village green. In this triangle, as well as an area across the main street, are the twenty food booths that make up the "Festival of Foods." These booths, run by the local churches and civic groups, offer the expected hot dogs, hamburgers, and pizza; but there are also a few surprises, such as bratwurst and bauernwurst sausages from the Concordia Society, pasta e fagioli from Hose Company No. 3, and delicious Conestoga steak sandwiches and spiced apple cider from the Historical Society. Apple fanciers can dote on the chunky apple fritters offered every year by the Zion Lutheran Church, or the apple sundaes made with hot apple topping and vanilla ice cream. There were also caramel apples and candied apples. Both the American Legion and the First Congregational Church were selling slices of homemade apple pie. We headed for the church for a piece of pie served with a wedge of Cheddar cheese. Of course we couldn't pass up the apple crisp with brown sugar topping. Then we heard that the Kiwanis Club was serving some wonderful fried apple rings, so there was no time to waste. As we waited on line for our dozen, we watched the cooks core and slice the apples, then dip them in batter and deep fry them until their coatings puffed up and turned golden brown. With a little sprinkling of cinnamon sugar, they were soft and sweet, crisp and tart all at once.

We'd been to another apple festival a couple of years ago in Kentucky, where they also grow a lot of apples. There the big event was a three-thousand-pound apple pie that they lifted out of the oven with a forklift. Though we had fun at that festival too, the pie wasn't all that good, and the pie was just about the only thing made from apples that we saw. At the Southington Apple Harvest Festival, the apples were all around us— in snacks and desserts, as cider, even just plain straight apples. And that's a wonderful reason for coming to Southington, the Little Apple in Connecticut.

Hot Apple Sundae

3 medium apples, peeled,
  cored, and cut into ½-inch
  dice
½ cup sugar
1 cup water
1 teaspoon cornstarch

¼ teaspoon ground cinnamon
Pinch nutmeg
1 pint good vanilla ice cream
Whipped cream (optional)
Maraschino cherries (optional)

In a saucepan, combine the apples with the sugar and water. Cook over
low heat until the apples are tender but still chunky. Stir in the cornstarch
and spices, simmer for another minute, then remove from the heat and
let cool slightly.

Scoop the ice cream into individual dishes and pour over the apple
topping. If desired, top with whipped cream and a cherry.   *Serves 4*

Fried Apple Rings

If you've got an apple corer, making these rings will be very easy. If
not, use a sharp knife to cut around the core from both sides and then
pop or scrape out the core.

4 large apples, such as Cortlands
1 cup all-purpose flour
1 large egg, lightly beaten
1 cup milk
2 teaspoons baking powder

1 teaspoon sugar
Pinch salt
Vegetable oil for deep frying
Cinnamon sugar

Core the apples and have them ready.

In a bowl, mix the flour with the egg, milk, baking powder, sugar,
and salt. Stir until the batter is smooth.

Heat the oil for frying until very hot, about 375°F.

Slice the apples crosswise (without peeling them) into ¼-inch-thick pieces and dip each slice in the batter. Drop the slices into the hot oil and deep fry each for about 5 minutes. Do not add more than a few rings at a time to the oil or the temperature will drop too much. The rings will turn lightly brown and puff up a little. Remove and briefly drain on paper towels. Quickly sprinkle with cinnamon sugar and serve while still hot.

Serves 4

THE APPLE HARVEST FESTIVAL is held in Southington, Connecticut, on the last weekend of September and the first weekend of October. There are no admission charges. Free parking and free shuttle buses are provided, and there are signs to direct you to the lots. There are events on both weekends, and the food booths are open throughout the festival. The parade is at 1:30 P.M. on the Sunday of the first weekend.

Apple goodies (and other foods) are sold at individual booths. Apple rings were $2.50 a dozen; the hot apple sundae was $1.50; pie runs about $1 a slice; and cider is about 25¢.

Southington is located about 20 miles southwest of Hartford on Route 10. For additional information, including a schedule of events, contact the Greater Southington Chamber of Commerce, 7 North Main Street, Southington, Connecticut 06489; (203) 628–8036.

Cranberry Festival

South Carver, Massachusetts

THE CRANBERRY—called crane-berry by the Indians because it was a favorite food of those large birds—is one of the few native North American fruits. The Indians had many uses for the wild cranberry. In addition to eating the fruit, they used its juice for a red dye when weaving, and a cranberry poultice was fairly common for treating arrow wounds. They shared this crisp, red fruit with the early English settlers, and cranberries have been a part of Thanksgiving Day feasts ever since 1621.

As cranberries became more popular, the wild fruit fell into short supply. In 1816, the first cultivated berries were grown on Cape Cod. This early venture was very successful, and throughout the last century, people drained swamplands and turned them into cranberry plantations.

The cranberry is a low-growing vine that thrives in peat and sand. At harvest time (late September) the bogs are often flooded. The ripe berries are then knocked off the vines (by the harvesters) so that they float to the surface, creating vast crimson patches all over the flooded area. Dry harvesting, done with the old-fashioned scoop (or rake) is another method but less favored.

The Massachusetts Cranberry Festival, begun in 1948, is held in South Carver each September. This is the heart of cranberry country, with over three thousand acres of cranberry bogs. The site is the Edaville Railroad Park, a family amusement center with a cranberry bog in the middle. Several other bogs are elsewhere on the grounds. There is a narrow-gauge railroad that encircles the cranberry bogs, and a highlight of the festival is a forty-five-minute ride on the old-fashioned train. The railroad was originally constructed to serve the bogs: hauling sand out to them in the winter and bringing the harvest back in the fall.

Other events at the festival include the woodsmen's competition, a sheep-to-shawl spinning and weaving contest, a puppet theater, and a spinning bee. Under the Cranberry Tent you can watch cranberry-screening demonstrations, cranberry-cooking demonstrations (with samples for the tasting), and refresh yourself with glasses of free cranberry juice. There is also a display of antique harvesting equipment. The "Make It Better with Cranberries" contest is held to encourage the imaginative use of cranberries in everyday cooking. Winning entries are exhibited.

Over in the Center Green area is a tent featuring the National Cranberry Quilt display. The theme of a recent quilt patch contest was "Cranberry Scoops, Baskets, or Boxes," and it focused on the decorative and functional use of cranberrry containers. The winning patches—from all over the country—are then pieced together and quilted for the national quilt. Past themes include "Harvesting," "The Berry Itself," and "The Cranberry in All Seasons."

Along the walkways that encircle the central cranberry bog, one can find other, delicious diversions: a chicken barbecue served with cranberry sauce (what else?), a local bake sale featuring cranberry cakes—some of them past winners in the cooking contest, and all of them irresistible—and a stand selling cranberry sherbet. There is also an arts and crafts sale. The 4-H has its fair at the same time, so there are various animal exhibits, shows, and contests. All afternoon you can hear the Edaville Roundhouse Ramblers Dixieland Band strike up their cheerful tunes.

After the festival you may want to visit the Cranberry World museum in nearby Plymouth. Founded in 1977, Cranberry World is an exhibit that traces the cranberry from the seventeenth century to the present. There are movies, dioramas, and even a scale-model cranberry farm. Most interesting was the Indian exhibit, showing how crane-berries were used for food, medicine, and dyes. Downstairs are more modern applications, including cooking demonstrations and gallons of free juice.

Just driving along any road in Plymouth County you are apt to pass by a bog flooded for harvest. The cranberries lie like rubies, clustered together in the afternoon sun. People in chest-high waders are raking them up, boxing them, and sending them off to be screened, bagged, and sent to stores. Most people only know a bagged berry, unless they have been lucky enough to come to cranberry country during harvest time.

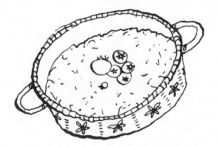

Dandy Cranberry Bars

This is a dense cookie with a thin cheese filling and a nutty cranberry layer. It won Best-of-Show for Lillian Harju in 1979.

CRANBERRY FILLING *(see note)*

1 quart fresh cranberries
1 cup water
1½ cups sugar

3 tablespoons tapioca
½ cup chopped nuts

CHEESE FILLING

1 package (8 ounces) cream cheese
2 tablespoons butter or margarine

½ teaspoon vanilla extract
1 tablespoon cornstarch
1 large egg
2 tablespoons milk or cream

DOUGH

1½ cups light brown sugar
1 cup (2 sticks) butter or margarine
2 eggs

2½ cups all-purpose flour
1 teaspoon baking soda
1 teaspoon salt
3 cups old-fashioned rolled oats

Combine all the ingredients for the cranberry filling except the nuts in a saucepan and cook gently for 10 minutes, stirring often. Set aside to cool, covering the pan lightly. When cool, add the nuts.

Mix the ingredients for the cheese filling until well blended; set aside. Preheat the oven to 350°F.

Make the dough. In a large bowl, using an electric mixer, blend the sugar, butter or margarine, and eggs. Add the remaining ingredients and mix well. Place half the cookie dough in a greased 15-by-10½-inch pan and pat down firmly. Spread the cheese filling evenly over the cookie dough; spread the cranberry filling over the cheese filling. Flatten the pieces of the remaining cookie dough in your hands and place over the fillings, patching together until the fillings are covered and all the dough is used. Bake for 20 minutes. Let cool, then cut into individual bars.

Makes 35 bars

NOTE: These cookies are best kept cold and served cool. To save time, you could substitute 2 cups (or one 8-ounce can) of whole cranberry sauce for the cranberry filling. Add ½ cup nuts just before spreading on top of the cheese filling.

Cranberry Kitchen Cookies

This recipe was a winner for Amy McDermott in 1978.

½ cup (1 stick) butter or margarine
1 cup sugar
¾ cup brown sugar
¼ cup milk
2 tablespoons orange juice
1 large egg, lightly beaten

3 cups all-purpose flour
1 teaspoon baking powder
¼ teaspoon baking soda
½ teaspoon salt
1 cup chopped nuts
2½ cups chopped fresh cranberries

Preheat the oven to 375°F. Lightly grease a cookie sheet. Cream the butter or margarine and the sugars together. Beat in the milk, orange juice, and egg. Sift together the dry ingredients, then combine with the creamed mixture and blend well. Stir in the chopped nuts and cranberries. Drop by teaspoonfuls onto the cookie sheet and bake for 10 to 15 minutes.   *Makes 12 dozen cookies*

Cranberry Sherbet

Because this is a milk sherbet, the sharpness of the cranberry juice is toned down, for a smooth and mild frozen dessert.

2 cups cranberry juice cocktail
3 cups whole milk

Approximately ½ cup sugar
⅛ teaspoon salt

Pour the cranberry juice and milk into the container of an ice-cream freezer. Add the sugar, increasing the quantity to ¾ cup if desired, then add the salt. Stir until dissolved, then freeze in an ice-cream freezer according to manufacturer's directions. Pack into freezer containers and store in the freezer until ready to eat.   *Makes 1½ quarts*

Cranberry Sour-Cream Coffee Cake

This was a winning entry from Helena Blum in 1979.

*½ cup (1 stick) butter or
  margarine*
1 cup sugar
2 large eggs
1 teaspoon baking soda
1 teaspoon baking powder
2 cups all-purpose flour
½ teaspoon salt
1 cup sour cream

GLAZE

⅔ cup confectioners' sugar
2 tablespoons warm water
½ teaspoon almond extract

1 teaspoon almond extract
*1 can (8 ounces) whole
  cranberry sauce*
½ cup chopped nuts

Preheat the oven to 350°F. Grease a 10-inch tube pan. Cream together the butter or margarine and sugar. Add the eggs one at a time and mix well. Sift together the dry ingredients. Add the creamed mixture alternately with the sour cream, then stir in the almond extract. Spoon half the batter into the prepared pan and spread with half the cranberry sauce. Sprinkle with half the chopped nuts. Repeat these two steps with the batter, cranberry sauce, and nuts. Bake for 40 to 55 minutes, or until a cake tester comes out clean. Let cool. While cake cools, prepare the glaze. Beat the sugar with the water until smooth, then flavor with extract. Spread glaze on cake and let set before serving.

Serves 6 to 8

THE CRANBERRY FESTIVAL (and 4-H Fair) is held the last weekend in September and the first weekend in October at the Edaville Railroad Park in South Carver, Massachusetts. Admission to the grounds (which includes a ride on the old Edaville Railroad) is $5 for adults, $3 for children. There are many events on both days of both weekends. If you only want to come for one day, you should get a program and pick the day that interests you the most. (The Plymouth County 4-H Fair is only on the second weekend.)

Cranberry cooking and screening demonstrations (and samplings) are held every day; and the harvest machinery and national cranberry quilt are on continuous display. Festival hours are from 10 to 5:30, during which time you can take your 5½-mile rail ride through the cranberry bogs. Food is available from individual vendors, ranging from a cranberry sherbet ($1.25) to an entire cranberry cake ($6.50). There is plenty of entertainment, including puppet shows for children.

The Edaville Railroad Park is on Route 58, in South Carver, Massachusetts; the festival is well sign-posted. South Carver is about 15 miles southwest of Plymouth. (Plymouth is where Cranberry World is located; it's well worth a visit.) For additional information about the festival and a schedule of events, contact the Massachusetts Cranberry Festival, P.O. Box 7, South Carver, Massachusetts 02366.

There is also a cranberry festival in Warrens, Wisconsin, during the last weekend in September. For additional information, contact the Warrens Cranberry Festival, P.O. Box 146, Warrens, Wisconsin 54666.

Okra Strut

Irmo, South Carolina

O KRA IN IRMO. According to local radio personality Gene McKay, okra and Irmo go well together. "Okra is just funny," he says, "and it's incredibly symbolic of Irmo." We weren't sure of what that symbolism was, but we agreed that it's pretty hard to be serious about okra. So we went to join the Irmese in their annual Okra Strut.

Irmo, South Carolina, is like an adolescent with growing pains. Originally it was a water stop for trains on their way to Columbia, but in 1890 it was declared a town and named after two railroad officials: C. J. *Ir*edell and H. C. *Mo*seley. Since then, Irmo has experienced several large housing developments, but as far as we could ascertain, there still is no real center to the town. Almost everything, except the housing developments, is stretched out alongside the railroad tracks. Even the new mall isn't far from the tracks.

St. Andrew's Road runs parallel to the tracks, and it is a wide street perfectly suited as a parade route. This festival parade is huge, with more politicians than any other we've seen. Even candidates for coroner were campaigning. Interspersed among the okra-theme floats were school bands, beauty queens in convertibles, and marchers from a whole range of local civic groups and clubs, including a float by the Columbia Mothers of Twins.

At the conclusion of the parade, the spectators all follow the marchers to the grounds of the Irmo High School. There in the parking lot are booths selling foods as well as arts and crafts. We saw ceramic animals and vegetables (including okra), patchwork pillows, 'tater boxes, wooden toys, and lots of "country" crafts. We found the food booths more rewarding (as we frequently do) and followed the exotic scent in the air to the booth run by the Hindu Temple and Cultural Center of South Carolina. A woman in a sari was serving an Indian version of the southern American favorite, fried okra. In this spicy dish, whole okras had been coated with a fritterlike batter and deep fried. Okra is a traditional Indian food, and we were pleasantly surprised to see it represented here.

At another booth we discovered that Irmo Food Distributors, a local business, had only that day begun to sell their new pickled okra. Packed in vinegar, hot peppers, garlic, spices, and salt, these Okra Strut Brand pickles were attractively arranged in one-pint glass jars to take home. The pickled okra is crisp and tart.

The large crowds surrounding the Lake Murray Women's Club booth then drew us to the only southern-fried okra stand at the festival. These ladies—who had originated the festival as a fundraiser in 1974, then turned it over to the town—were selling absolutely delicious French-fried okra. Though it was a twenty-minute wait for our dish of okra, when it came, the okra was hot from the fryer and lightly sprinkled with salt. It was perfect: crunchy on the outside and soft on the inside, with none of the gumminess that usually characterizes okra. We realized then that though many vegetables are French-fried, okra is superbly suited to this treatment.

The star attraction of the strut is the Shoot-out at the OKra Corral. This is the annual okra-eating contest. The nine contestants (seven men and two women) included the mayor of Irmo, a policeman, members of local civic groups, and a beauty queen. They sat onstage at a long, bare table and watched as the officials placed before each of them a large bowl of limp, boiled okra.

The contestants would be allowed no salt, no beverage. Warnings were given to the audience to move back, lest they be in the way if a contestant threw up (incidentally, disqualifying himself). A slew of okra jokes followed—"Ate so much boiled okra when I was a boy that I couldn't keep my socks up." As the audience laughed, the nine onstage steeled themselves for the task ahead. The okra looked dead. There is nothing more vile to eat than okra that has been boiled until it's so soft that its mucilaginous qualities are the only forces holding it together.

The starting gun was fired, and the nine tore into their okra. Well, not exactly tore. One man daintily picked up a piece (hard to separate the individual okra) and ate it slowly, dabbing his lips with a napkin after each bite. Guess he didn't plan on winning. "Mayor Heizer has his two-finger technique from last year," the announcer pointed out. We heard the contestants mutter, "This stuff is nasty," and "I'll never eat okra again."

Before long, one of the women took the lead with her "close-to-the-plate" shovel-in style. We heard a man call out, "You gonna let that girl beat you?" But beat them she did, eating an amazing 2.17 pounds of okra in five minutes. Why did she do it? "It looked like fun," she said.

As we left the festival grounds, we spied a man we'd seen in the parade.

He was dressed as an okra: green from head to toe (including his hair and beard), with an okra necklace, an okra belt, and a bouquet of okra in his hand. You might say he was doing the Okra Strut.

Fried Okra

For this recipe, choose okra that are large—on the average of 3 inches long.

½ cup all-purpose flour	Vegetable oil for deep frying
½ cup white cornmeal	4 cups sliced okra,
1 large egg, lightly beaten	cut ½ inch thick
1 cup milk	Coarse salt
Salt and pepper to taste	

In a large bowl, combine the flour and cornmeal. In a smaller bowl, mix the egg with the milk, then stir into the cornmeal mixture. Season to taste with salt and pepper.

Heat the oil to 375°F. Place about 1 cup of the okra in the batter and stir to coat the pieces, then place the okra in the hot oil. Deep fry the okra, being sure to separate the pieces in the oil and to turn them so that they brown on both sides. Remove as the pieces brown, in about 5 minutes. Repeat with the remaining okra, never frying more than about 1 cup's worth at one time, or you'll risk lowering the temperature too much. Drain the okra on paper towels and sprinkle with coarse salt. Serve while very hot. *Serves 4*

Okra Skillet Dish

This was Mrs. H. W. Reid's winning recipe in the 1984 okra-cooking contest. Use very small okra for this dish—no larger than 2 inches long.

3 tablespoons butter	1 medium tomato, peeled,
1 pound okra	seeded, and diced
1 onion, sliced	Salt and pepper to taste
½ cup chopped green pepper	½ cup grated Parmesan cheese

Heat the butter in a large skillet over high heat and add all the vegetables except the tomato. Sauté until tender, about 5 minutes. As the okra softens (don't cook it too long or it will become gummy), add the tomato pieces. Heat through and then season to taste. Sprinkle Parmesan cheese on top and serve at once. *Serves 4*

THE OKRA STRUT is held the first Saturday in October. The parade begins at 9:30 in the morning, and the festival booths open right afterward. Entertainment goes on throughout the day; the Shoot-out is usually at noon.

There are no admission fees; parking is in pay lots or free on side streets. If you want to street-park, you have to get there early, since many streets are blocked off during the parade. A helping of fried okra costs $1; barbecue sandwiches (for one does not live by okra alone) are $2.

Irmo is about 12 miles north of Columbia, South Carolina, on Route 60. For additional information, write Town of Irmo, P.O. Box 406, 1239 Columbia Avenue, Irmo, South Carolina 29063; (803) 781–7050.

Arkansas Rice Festival

Weiner, Arkansas

RICE WAS FIRST grown in China in 3000 B.C. Over four thousand years later it was grown in Charleston, South Carolina; and in 1906, it came to Weiner, Arkansas, where it has been a major crop ever since. The United States is one of the largest rice-exporting countries in the world, and Arkansas is the largest rice-producing state in the country.

Here in Weiner, though, it's not all planting, harvesting, and milling. There's time for some fun, too, and that's what the Arkansas Rice Festival is all about. Held each year since 1975, the festival draws thousands of visitors to this small town in northeastern Arkansas. On the way to Weiner you can't help but notice the stubble that remains in the fields, making them look as though they'd been given a giant crew cut. The rice plant itself is quite pretty; its grain-laden strands bend gracefully atop slender green stalks.

The highlight of the festival is the "rice tasting," an event that has people lined up over an hour ahead. The tasting is a free sampling of about five hundred rice dishes. They're not all served at once; most people sample about fifteen to twenty of the dishes. The dishes, all made by local people, mostly wives of rice growers, are constantly rotated. Many of them tend to be gelatin salads (which we found unappealing, but were popular with other eaters) or casseroles. A few dishes, though, really stand out. We were lucky enough to be served an étouffé, a boudin, and dirty rice—recipes from neighboring Louisiana. There was also a good steak-rice-pepper dish, a meat loaf with rice, Spanish rice, and duck with rice.

The University of Arkansas was demonstrating an experimental canned rice product. The rice goes into the can dry, water is added during processing, and it ends up as a puree. It comes out of the can like a loaf; you slice it, dust it with cornmeal, and fry it up. Is there no limit?

Fortunately, we were able to top off our covered-dish luncheon with some pretty tasty desserts: vanilla pudding with rice, chocolate-covered rice balls, and wonderful peanut-butter/Rice Krispies balls rolled in chocolate.

After the tasting extravaganza, we relaxed and listened to the Rainbow Senior Citizens Band, who had set up an electric organ, washboard, tambourine, drums, trumpet, and other instruments near the antique farm equipment. Across the street were the new machinery displays. A $100,000 combine had become a jungle gym for some local boys; while back where we were sitting, the antique threshing machine showed us how things used to be done.

At the other end of town was the commercial building, where people were busy entering drawings, buying rice, and learning about new machinery and products. Although rice is a common dish throughout most of the world—indeed, many people subsist entirely on it—there are a few uses for the grain that surprised us. The hulls make a very fine abrasive used in polishing operations; they're also used in hand soap. Rice oil is a high-quality cooking oil. Rice flour can be used in place of wheat for baking; and brewers rice, the smallest size fragments, is used in making pet foods and beer.

Very popular at the festival are the tractor pulls—from 1,750-pound mini-rods all the way up to 20,000-pound farm tractors—and these contests generate a lot of excitement. Competition, albeit of a different sort, is equally stiff in the beauty pageant; Miss Arkansas Rice goes on to promote rice throughout the nation, so more than just beauty is involved. For the athletic there's a 10-kilometer (sanctioned) run; for the greedy, a rice-eating contest; and for the creative, a rice agriculture photo contest. For kids there are puppet and magic shows; and for everyone there's music, dancing, and lots of fun. The motto of the festival is "Have a Rice Day." We did and hope you do, too.

These dishes are typical of those you'd find served at the rice tasting. This first recipe is from the Rice Council of America.

Arkansas Cumin Rice

2 tablespoons bacon drippings or vegetable oil
⅓ cup chopped onion
¼ cup chopped green pepper
1 cup uncooked rice

2 cups beef broth, boiling
1 tablespoon Worcestershire sauce
¾ teaspoon each salt and cuminseed

Preheat the oven to 350°F.

Heat the bacon drippings in a skillet and sauté the onion, pepper, and rice until the rice is golden brown. Stir often to prevent overbrowning. Turn the mixture into a shallow, greased 2-quart casserole. Add the remaining ingredients and stir well. Cover tightly with a lid and bake for 30 minutes, or until the rice is tender and the liquid is absorbed. Fluff lightly with a fork and serve. *Serves 6*

Sausage and Rice Casserole

2 tablespoons vegetable oil
1 medium onion, chopped
1 bell pepper, chopped

1 pound sweet sausage links
½ cup uncooked rice
1½ cups chicken broth

In a heatproof casserole, heat the oil and sauté the onion and pepper until wilted. Add the sausage links and brown on all sides.

Preheat the oven to 350°F.

When the sausages are nicely browned, add the rice and stir until the kernels are glistening. Add the broth, then cover and bake for 35 minutes, or until the rice is tender and plump. *Serves 2*

Duck with Rice

Wild ducks feed among the stubble of the cut rice fields, and it seems only natural to combine duck with rice. This recipe is best made with wild duck, but is almost as good with domestic.

1 duckling (about 5¾ pounds)
2 stalks celery
1 onion, cut in half
Salt and pepper
1 cup uncooked rice
2½ cups water
3 tablespoons vegetable oil
2 cups chopped mushrooms

1 medium onion, chopped
1 red bell pepper, chopped
¼ cup all-purpose flour
¼ cup chopped fresh parsley
¼ cup bread crumbs
¼ cup slivered almonds
*   (optional)*

Place the duck in a large pot along with the celery, onion halves, and a pinch each of salt and pepper, and add water to cover. Bring to a boil, cover, and simmer until the meat falls off the bones, about 1½ hours. Let cool and remove the duck; strain and reserve about 2 cups stock. Remove the meat from the bones and skim the fat from the broth.

Cook the rice in the 2½ cups water until firm but done. Set aside. Preheat the oven to 350°F.

Heat 1 tablespoon of the oil in a skillet and add the mushrooms. Sauté until lightly browned, then set aside. Add the 2 remaining tablespoons oil to the skillet and sauté the chopped onion and pepper until wilted. Add the flour and stir to coat the onion and pepper pieces. Gradually add the reserved stock and stir until blended. Cover and simmer until the sauce is thickened, about 3 minutes. Season to taste with salt and pepper.

In a bowl, combine the mushrooms, rice, duck pieces, and parsley. Add the sauce and blend well, then pack into a greased 2-quart casserole. Sprinkle the top with bread crumbs and the almonds, if desired. Place the casserole in the oven to bake for about 35 minutes, or until heated through. Serve immediately.   *Serves 4*

THE ARKANSAS RICE FESTIVAL takes place on the second weekend in October (National Rice Month) in Weiner, Arkansas. Events are held in the center of town on both days. There are tractor pulls, demonstrations of antique threshing machinery, and continuous entertainment (on three stages) from noon till 6:00 P.M. On Saturday night there is usually a concert and a square dance; the parade is on Sunday morning. In the commercial building, various companies hold drawings for prizes and/ or merchandise. Agricultural products and machinery are also on display both days.

The focal point of the festival is the rice tasting, which takes place from 11 to 4 on Saturday at the Catholic Hall. This is a free, covered-dish supper (served cafeteria style), where the visitor can sample at any one moment about seventy-five (of five hundred or so) different rice dishes. The line gets pretty long; people begin lining up as early as 10:00 A.M. No tickets or reservations are available, and there are no charges for any of the events. Parking is on side streets, wherever you can find a spot.

Weiner, Arkansas, is located in the northeast corner of the state, about 20 miles south of Jonesboro, off U.S. 49. For additional information, contact Weiner City Hall, Weiner, Arkansas 72479; (501) 684–2284.

Chincoteague Oyster Festival

Chincoteague, Virginia

But four young Oysters hurried up,
    All eager for the treat:
Their coats were brushed, their faces washed,
    Their shoes were clean and neat—
And this was odd, because, you know,
    They hadn't any feet.

—LEWIS CARROLL
"The Walrus and the Carpenter"
from *Through the Looking-Glass*

WE, TOO, were eager for the treat—the treat of oysters. Chincoteague's annual oyster festival (held every year since 1973 on Columbus Day weekend) features the bivalve in a mouth-watering array of preparations: oyster fritters, oysters raw, oysters steamed, oysters fried, and oyster stew. On the side you can enjoy hush puppies, potato salad, and cole slaw. And in case that's not enough, there are also steamed crabs, hamburgers, and hot dogs. It's all-you-can-eat here at the Maddox Family Campground on Chincoteague's breezy shore.

Oysters have long been a popular food. Greeks farmed oysters as long ago as the fourth century B.C. The Romans ate them in prodigious quantities; they even transported them overland from France. In the United States, oysters were favored by Indians of both coasts. Oysters were so plentiful in the eighteenth century that they were a staple food of the lower classes. By the nineteenth century, oysters were being transported inland to satisfy the appetites of those who had settled the Midwest. (A cookbook of that time calls for two hundred to be put in a stew.) Oyster vendors were common on street corners, and oyster cellars were as much a part of city life then as coffee shops are today.

Oyster festivals have been almost as popular as the oysters themselves. In Colchester (Great Britain) what is surely the oldest oyster festival in the world has been celebrated the last Friday of each October since before 1318. That year was the first recorded festival, but they had been held for long before then. The Colchester oyster festival, actually, is so ancient that no one knows when it began. There are a number of more modern oyster festivals—in Louisiana, Maryland, Virginia, New York, Connecticut, Maine, and Washington State. But the one at Chincoteague is oysters unlimited! Big, juicy Chincoteague salt oysters.

The festival-goers follow bravely in the footsteps of such renowned oyster-eaters as Henry IV, who once ate three hundred before dinner; Casanova, who ate fifty a day; and Diamond Jim Brady, who thought nothing of putting away three or four dozen before dinner. (In Mobile, Alabama, the famous Winzell's restaurant has an ongoing contest: If you can beat the oyster-eater who currently holds the record—nineteen dozen in twenty-five minutes, as of May 1984—you get your oysters for free.) Although there's no eating contest at the festival, you do have only four hours in which to consume as many as you are able. Eight baseball-capped young men were doing exactly that. They had constructed a pyramid of oyster shells (decorated with beer bottles) in the center of their picnic table; and their display would have warmed the hearts of their forebears—it was easily three feet high and six feet long, and that was only at three o'clock. Who knows to what heights it had risen by the end of the afternoon.

Most true oyster fanciers immediately head for the raw oysters, which are cold and briny. Other choices, though, are not to be missed. The oyster fritters are light and crisp, packed with soft oyster bellies. The steamed oysters are piled so high in their bowls that you have to eat a few just to get them to your table. (We found a pocket knife invaluable for prying open some of the more reluctant shells.) The oyster stew is a creamy, oyster-packed broth. Should your appetite begin to wane, you can perk it right up with the crunchy and dark fried oysters, great plain, with salt, or dipped in tartar sauce.

Other good oyster festivals include the East Coast Oyster Shucking and Eating Championships in Leonardtown, Maryland, and its West Coast counterpart held in Shelton, Washington. There is also an Oys-terrific Oyster Festival held annually in Oyster Bay (Long Island), New York. But we think Chincoteague the pearl of oyster festivals. Partly that has to do with our undying love for the Chincoteague salt oyster. We find it superior to almost any other variety. And what can surpass the opportunity to eat as many of them as you'd like? Truly, if you want a wonderful time, head over to Chincoteague and let oysters be your world for an afternoon.

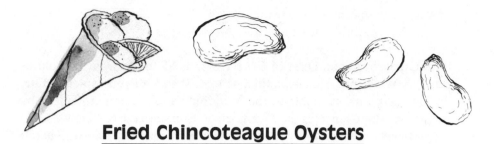

Fried Chincoteague Oysters

If possible, use large Chincoteague salt oysters, because they hold up to deep frying so well.

2 pints shucked oysters
¾ cup all-purpose flour
1 large egg, lightly beaten

⅓ cup milk
Salt
Vegetable oil for deep frying

Separate and drain the oysters on paper towels.

In a bowl, mix the flour with the egg, milk, and salt until smooth. Pour the oil into a 10-inch skillet until it is 1 to 2 inches deep. Heat until very hot, about 375°F, then drop in a couple of the oysters. Fry on one side for 2 to 3 minutes, or until browned, then turn and fry on the other side. Drain on paper towels while you continue to fry the remaining oysters. Don't add too many oysters to the skillet at once, or the oil temperature will decrease too much. Serve hot, sprinkled with salt or dipped in tartar sauce. *Serves 4*

Creamy Oyster Stew

1 pint shucked oysters
2 cups half and half
4 tablespoons (½ stick) butter

Salt and pepper to taste
Cayenne pepper

Place the oysters along with their liquor in a large saucepan. Put the pan over low heat and cook until the edges of the oysters just begin to curl, about 3 minutes. Add the half and half, butter, salt, and pepper. Heat slowly until hot; do not boil. Just before serving, sprinkle with cayenne. *Serves 4*

THE CHINCOTEAGUE OYSTER FESTIVAL is held on Saturday of Columbus Day Weekend, from noon till 4:00 P.M. It's an all-you-can-eat affair. Tickets ($15) are available at the Maddox Family Campground or by mail from the Chincoteague Chamber of Commerce (see below). Only 1,650 tickets are available, so it's advisable to get them ahead. There's plenty of parking at the campground, and there are lots of tables and benches.

Chincoteague is on the Eastern Shore of Virginia, about 185 miles southeast of Washington, D.C., at the end of Route 175. For information and tickets, write the Chincoteague Chamber of Commerce, Box 258, Chincoteague, Virginia 23336.

Gumbo Festival

Bridge City, Louisiana

UMBO. The very word sounds mysterious. Gumbo filé. Filé gumbo. Either way, it's a highly seasoned stew developed and cultivated to its fullest among the Creoles and Cajuns of southern Louisiana. It is thought that the word *gombo*, of Bantu origin, was brought to the bayou country by African slaves, who used it as a name for okra or soups made with okra. Before long, *gombo* got changed to *gumbo* and came to mean a seafood or meat stew at first thickened with okra and now commonly with filé powder—ground sassafras leaves. It's a drab, olive powder with a faint, fruity scent and almost no taste by itself. But put into a seafood stew, the powder awakens to impart a distinctive earthy flavor.

Gumbo is what brought us again to Louisiana, this time to Bridge City, the other end of the Huey P. Long Bridge from New Orleans. Gumbo is taken seriously here all year long. On the second weekend of October over seventy-five thousand people come to Bridge City for its Gumbo Festival, a three-day event where King Creole Gumbo and Miss Creole Gumbo hold court. In 1973, then governor Edwin W. Edwards proclaimed Bridge City the "Gumbo Capital of the World," and since that time the people of Bridge City have taken it upon themselves to serve up gallons of gumbo to visitors looking for a good time and some great food. Although there are the usual hamburger and chili dog stands, gumbo is the thing to eat here, possibly supplemented with some red beans and rice or jambalaya.

Gumbo can (and has) been made of almost any edible substance, but at the festival two major types are offered: a seafood gumbo, made with shrimp, crab, and oysters; and a chicken and andouille gumbo, flavored with the smoky taste of andouille sausage. (There's an entire festival devoted to andouille; see page 227.) The gumbo here is prepared in huge vats in a shed on the fairgrounds and served in the large community building. Each serving is assembled individually as the women behind the counter first place a scoop of fluffy white rice in a bowl, then ladle out the gumbo of your choice while you watch. The gumbo is served in a china bowl and, incongruously, you're given a plastic spoon to eat it with. There's additional hot sauce on the tables for those who feel the brew isn't hot enough, and we spied a few people who brought their own bottles of filé, too. "Gumbo without filé just isn't gumbo," the woman across the table from us remarked. That's probably true, since the thickening properties of filé only do their job when added just before eating.

The festival gumbo is made the traditional way, from a roux, or browned flour-and-fat paste. This roux forms the base for the mixture, to which is added water, onions, celery, green peppers, and herbs, plus the seafood or chicken and sausages, and lastly the filé. Gumbo itself is a muddy green stew, not very appealing to look at, but who cares about looks when something tastes so good? The chicken and andouille gumbo had great flavor, although the liquid itself seemed a little thin. The seafood gumbo, however, couldn't have been better—spicy but not overly fired up, a nice balance of flavors and seasonings enhanced by the filé. The portions are large and the service fast. Even the cleanup is efficient; we don't think we've ever seen a festival so spotless.

Outside the dining area, the crowds collect around the gambling booths and the beer wagons while others line up for their turn on the Ferris wheel, the merry-go-round, and other more unsettling rides. At the soda booth, along with the usual Cokes and 7-Ups, is another regional favorite—pop rouge, a carbonated strawberry drink. Too sweet for us, but after all, this is the South.

The year we came to Bridge City there was another novelty: gumbo popcorn. They wouldn't give away their secret, but our guess is that they tossed the popcorn with crab boil, filé, and onion or garlic salt. Delicious, although rather salty, allowing us to indulge in an old festival tradition—lining up for another beer.

Along with the T-shirts, aprons, and cookbooks on a gumbo theme, this event has for sale something that we had been noticing at the more trendy festivals—designer posters. These graphically very attractive posters are sold as future collector's items, and they cost anywhere from $25 to $150. Although lovely, often striking, the posters lend a touch of professionalism to the festivals that doesn't seem to belong. What does belong at a food festival (and is here in force) is the excitement of the crowds for their favorite food—gumbo.

YUM.

Seafood Sausage Gumbo

This gumbo is adapted from one by John Noel, King Creole Gumbo VII, and is provided courtesy of the Gumbo Festival.

1 gallon water, boiling
*1 cup cold roux (available in a
    jar or you can make it your-
    self by browning 1 cup flour
    in 1 cup butter until it is the
    consistency of thin paste and
    the color of chocolate)*
2 cups chopped onions
1 cup chopped celery
1 cup chopped fresh parsley
1 cup chopped green bell peppers
*1½ pounds sliced smoked
    sausage*
4 pounds peeled shrimp
2 pounds crab meat
*2 pints shucked oysters, with
    liquid*
1 tablespoon salt
1 tablespoon Tabasco sauce
1 teaspoon black pepper
½ teaspoon cayenne pepper
1 teaspoon filé powder

Dissolve the roux in the boiling water and blend until smooth. (If you have just made the roux and it is hot, substitute cold water for the boiling water and then bring to a boil.) Add the onions, celery, parsley, and peppers and boil for 30 minutes. Add the sausage, shrimp, crab meat, oysters, and oyster liquid to the pot. Add enough water to cover the ingredients, then add the salt, Tabasco, and peppers. Simmer for an additional 1 hour on a low boil, then remove from the heat and let the mixture sit for approximately 5 minutes. Skim off any excess fat and add the filé. Serve with boiled long-grain rice.   *Serves about 12*

Chicken and Sausage Gumbo

2 quarts water
½ cup roux (see previous recipe)
1 tablespoon vegetable oil
1 chicken (about 3 pounds),
   cut up
1 cup chopped green peppers
2 cups chopped onions
3 cloves garlic, minced
1 cup chopped celery

½ pound chicken gizzards
½ pound andouille sausage
½ pound smoked sausage
1 tablespoon Tabasco sauce
½ teaspoon cayenne pepper
½ teaspoon black pepper
¼ cup chopped parsley
1 scallion (both green and white
   parts), chopped

Bring the water to a boil in a heavy pot and add the roux. Dissolve the roux and boil it down for about 30 minutes.

While the roux reduces, heat the oil in a heavy skillet and brown the chicken; set aside. Add the peppers, onions, garlic, celery, and chicken to the roux pot along with the gizzards, andouille, smoked sausage, Tabasco, peppers, parsley, and scallion. Simmer for 2 hours, then serve with boiled long-grain rice. *Serves 4 to 6*

THE GUMBO FESTIVAL is always held in Bridge City ("Gumbo Capital of the World") on the second weekend in October. Entertainment begins on Friday at 6:00 P.M. (we don't know at what hour of the night it lets up); but the festival really gets going on Saturday with the gumbo-cooking contest at noon. There is entertainment on both Saturday and Sunday from noon until. . . . The gumbo-eating contest is on Sunday at 5:00 P.M.

Gumbo is served to festival-goers all day (and night) Saturday and Sunday. You buy a ticket, good for a bowl, at a booth outside the community center. Eating is a stand-up affair at long tables. A bowl of gumbo costs about $4; other foods and beverages are available from individual vendors (gumbo popcorn was $1). The festival takes place at the community park; parking is in an adjacent field. There are no admission fees.

Bridge City is just across the Huey P. Long Bridge from New Orleans; follow the signs. For additional information about the festival, write the Gumbo Festival, P.O. Box 9069, Bridge City, Louisiana 70094.

West Virginia
Black Walnut Festival

Spencer, West Virginia

NUTTY, BUT NICE. That's the West Virginia Black Walnut Festival, held each October high in the Appalachian Mountains. This is a part of West Virginia that missed the coal boom and the heavy industrialization. At festival time the trees are changing color, and they give the fifty thousand annual visitors a show that doubles the pleasure of attending this hill-country fair.

Though Spencer is a small town, this is a big festival. During its four-day run, there are gospel sings, a Queen's ball, a carnival and midway, fishing contests and canoe races, a chicken-flying contest, a 10-kilometer "nut run," photography exhibits, arm wrestling, a quilt exhibit, clogging, muzzle-loading contest, a parade, and a banjo-picking contest. And if this weren't enough, there's also a flea market with collectibles and crafts, plus an agricultural exhibition with ribbons for the finest vegetables, preserves, and baked goods.

Though all these activities might be in full swing, the visitor never loses the sight or taste of black walnuts. They are in the cooking contest, in the bake sales, and at the food booths. The cooking contest each year hinges on a different theme: one year it was fudge (a natural for black walnuts!), another year it was pie, then cake, and so forth. The bake sales offer homemade black walnut cakes, cupcakes, brownies, and pies. The Linden Order of the Eastern Star, conveniently located in the entranceway to the exhibits, was selling a moist apple-walnut cake and some very dark walnut fudge. The food booths are located with the crafts booths, which fill three of the four streets that square off the courthouse. These booths sell barbecue sandwiches, hot dogs, and hamburgers, but also offer their own varieties of black walnut fudge and black walnut brownies. The fudge from the Spencer Assembly of God Women's Ministries was a bit short on the nuts but had a mellow, milk chocolate taste. Brownies from the Liverpool United Methodist Youth Group were cakelike with a dense interior. Their black walnut cake was a light yellow cake with black walnut flecks and a black walnut icing. But regardless of whose brownies or cookies you eat, they're all made with West Virginia black walnuts.

Black walnuts are not just for eating, of course. Though the nuts add a distinctive flavor to cakes and brownies, the elegant taupe wood of the black walnut tree produces durable and beautiful furniture. The wood brings a high price, when you can get it at all, so this is a rare opportunity to see, and buy, items made from black walnut wood.

Most black walnut trees are wild, and the quality of both the wood and the nuts is subject to the whims of nature. The festival includes a judging of black walnuts, probably one of the most interesting aspects of this festival. We peeked inside the room where the judging was under way and watched as volunteers used an odd-looking horizontal vise to crack open the nuts. Then they picked out the nutmeats and arranged them on a paper plate. The plate was handed to one of the judges, who weighed the nuts. Another judge examined the color of the nutmeats. For each entrant, five walnut kernels were judged. The judges look for nutmeats that are heavy, without a high water content, and that have a pale, almost ivory flesh with a pale tan skin. It's a statewide competition and part of research into the development of commercially viable black walnut trees. The terminal bud from the winning tree is grafted onto a tree stock in the hope that someday there will be West Virginia black walnut orchards.

A black walnut is a tough nut to crack. You have to crack your way not only through a hard, rough shell, but past a puckered round husk surrounding the shell. Most people wait for the late fall, after the nuts have fallen off the trees and the hulls have begun to soften. In the beginning of fall, when the walnut trees have dropped their leaves, the walnuts remain on for a while, hanging like big green Christmas ornaments from the bare branches. By October, they've begun to drop to the ground, just in time for the Black Walnut Festival.

You can substitute black walnuts in any of your favorite brownie or cookie recipes and get a very different flavor. Black walnut meats are sold at the festival; you can also order them by mail from the Missouri Dandy Pantry, 212 Hammons Drive East, Dept. V-11, Stockton, Missouri 65785.

The following two recipes are past winners from the festival cooking contest. They are adapted courtesy of the West Virginia Black Walnut Festival, from their book *Walnut Winners Cookbook*.

Glazed Black Walnut Ring

½ cup (1 stick) butter, softened

2 cups brown sugar

3 large eggs, separated and yolks
    lightly beaten

2 cups all-purpose flour

3 teaspoons baking powder

½ teaspoon salt

⅔ cup milk

1 teaspoon vanilla extract

1 cup finely chopped black
    walnuts

NUTTY GLAZE

4 tablespoons (½ stick) butter,
    melted

10 tablespoons brown sugar

¼ cup evaporated milk

1 cup chopped black walnuts

Preheat the oven to 350°F. Grease a 10-inch tube pan.

In a large mixing bowl, cream the butter and add the sugar, beating until smooth. Add the egg yolks and mix well. In another bowl, stir the dry ingredients together and add to the creamed mixture alternately with the milk. Add the vanilla and walnuts and mix well.

Beat the egg whites until stiff, then fold into the batter. Pour the batter into the prepared pan and bake for 45 minutes. Let cool briefly, but keep the oven at 350°.

While the cake cools, prepare the glaze. Mix the butter, sugar, and milk until smooth. Add the nuts.

Remove the cake from the pan and transfer to a large cookie sheet lined with foil. Spread the glaze evenly over the cake and return it to the oven to bake for an additional 10 minutes. The glaze will harden and the nuts will adhere to the cake.   *Serves 8*

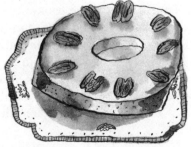

Black Walnut Harvest Pie

CRUST

⅓ cup shortening

¼ teaspoon salt

1 cup all-purpose flour

3 tablespoons water

½ teaspoon vinegar

FILLING

½ cup heavy cream

½ cup dark corn syrup

3 large eggs

¼ teaspoon salt

1 cup sugar

1 teaspoon vanilla extract

2 tablespoons butter, melted

1½ cups chopped black walnuts

Preheat the oven to 400°F.

Mix the shortening, salt, and half the flour for the crust until the mixture resembles small crumbs. Add the water, vinegar, and the remaining flour and mix until the dough cleans the sides of the bowl. Chill the dough for 30 minutes, then roll it out and line a 9-inch pie pan.

Blend the cream with the corn syrup, eggs, salt, sugar, vanilla, and butter. Add the walnuts, stir, then pour the mixture into the pie shell. Bake for 10 minutes, then reduce the heat to 350° and bake for 25 minutes more. The pie will rise up in the center, then gently sink a little.

Serves 6

THE WEST VIRGINIA BLACK WALNUT FESTIVAL is held in Spencer, West Virginia, on the second weekend in October. The festival officially opens on Thursday and runs through Sunday. Most events are on Friday and Saturday, though the exhibits are open from Thursday noon on. The Black Walnut Festival Sweepstakes (judging of the best black walnuts) is on Thursday, and the cook-off is on Friday. Kids' Day is also Friday, with a special parade; the grand parade is at noon on Saturday. Carnival rides are open from Tuesday night on.

Parking is on side streets and also in local lots; a free shuttle bus runs from the lots to the center of town. All events take place in the center of town (streets are closed), and all exhibits are at the armory, a few blocks away. There are no admission charges to the festival. Food is sold at booths: a barbecue sandwich costs about $1 (depends where you buy it); black walnut fudge and brownies are about 50¢. Bags of nuts were $6 a pound, shelled.

Spencer is located about 60 miles northeast of Charleston, at the intersection of U.S. 33 and U.S. 119. For additional information, including a schedule of events, write West Virginia Black Walnut Festival, P.O. Box 77, Spencer, West Virginia 25276; (304) 927-3708.

Burgoo Festival

Utica, Illinois

ACCORDING TO *Carey's Dictionary of Double Derivations*, burgoo is literally a soup composed of many vegetables and meats delectably fused together in an enormous caldron, over which, at the exact moment, a rabbit's foot at the end of a yarn string is properly waved by a preacher whose salary has been paid to date. These are good omens, which fortify the burgoo. We doubt that anyone waved a rabbit's food over the four 55-gallon pots of burgoo that were cooking in Utica, Illinois, at the burgoo festival. But omens or not, they served up some mighty good stew.

Burgoo is a soup or stew (depends on your frame of reference) made famous by Mr. J. T. Looney of Lexington, Kentucky, around 1900. It's usually made in vast quantities, and historically was served at political rallies, horse sales, barn raisings, and other outdoor events. In Kentucky, it's also served on Derby Day. The origin of the name, unlikely as it may seem, is generally believed to be from an oatmeal porridge eaten by British seamen in the mid-eighteenth century. Most probably it was a mispronunciation of the Turkish grain bulgur; and it drifted into America as meaning any sort of mess cooked up in large quantities. In the West (at that time Kentucky and Illinois were the West), bulgur was not readily available, but squirrel was very available. Thus, burgoo became a game and vegetable stew.

In the 1940s, in Winchester, Illinois, the American Legion sponsored an annual Burgoo Soup Picnic. Each August they served up hundreds of gallons to thousands of people. But that's how it is with burgoo. One recipe we found calls for six hundred pounds of meat, two hundred pounds of fat hens, two thousand pounds of potatoes, and more. Should squirrel be included? Another recipe, from the *United States Regional Cook Book*, says, "Use squirrels in season—one dozen squirrels to each 100 gallons." Mr. Looney used no squirrel, just beef and fowl. We must admit to being squeamish on the subject, and were reassured by the festival coordinators that in Utica they don't use squirrel, either.

When we reached Utica, cars were parked on every street and across some driveways, too. We finally located a parking place and walked back to the center of town, where the action was. It was lunchtime, so we headed immediately for the burgoo.

The LaSalle County Historical Society sponsors this festival and is also the organization that serves the burgoo. Before long we saw the smoke rising from their cookfires and smelled a hearty stew cooking. There, next to the community building on a side street of town, were four 55-gallon kettles, each resting in a makeshift metal "stove." Beneath each pot was a hot wood fire, and from the back of each "stove" was a long, L-shaped chimney that directed the smoke away from the cooks. In front of the pots were volunteers stirring the contents of each pot with a canoe paddle.

We bought tickets for the meal and, upon turning them in, were handed big bowls of steaming-hot burgoo, cole slaw, rolls and butter, and a piece of pie or cake of our choosing. A section of the street was blocked off and tables and chairs were set up for the burgoo dinners. "I'm gonna like it," we heard someone say even before taking the first spoonful.

"Tastes like beef. What's in it?"

"Secret recipe," one of the cooks said with a smile. Some elementary detective work on our part revealed that Utica's burgoo is beef with carrots, potatoes, hominy, celery, tomato, cabbage, beans, onions, peppers, and thyme. The trick is that the burgoo is cooked for so long that it becomes one uniform soupy brew. The cooking begins at 10:00 P.M. the previous night, and the burgoo is cooked at a steady simmer until it's all gone—up to fifteen hours later. The stew has a tendency to stick to the bottom of the pot, so stirring is constant throughout the night, as well as the whole next day. All the food preparation is done by volunteers, from peeling the thousands of potatoes to baking the hundreds of delicious pies and cakes that are served with the meal. We chose a soft apple pie, but the sweet potato pie, the cherry pie, and the chocolate cake were tempting, too.

After our burgoo lunch, we walked around town. We had expected to see the prairie craft demonstrations that had been advertised, but all we found were some people making apple butter and a blacksmith forging iron rings and hooks. Most of the booths were selling handcrafts and antiques, but there was nothing really new or exceptional. The festival seems tilted a bit too far in favor of crafts, while we would have preferred more attention to burgoo and its historical significance.

The Historical Society has a museum in town, and they have an excellent collection of household furnishings, farm implements, and Indian artifacts from pioneer days. The building itself dates to 1848, and was originally a general store serving the needs of early travelers along the Illinois-Michigan Canal. The canal was a major thoroughfare of the mid-nineteenth century—their interstate highway. Should you be traveling a modern interstate highway through the Midwest in October, the Burgoo Festival would be worth a stop.

Burgoo

There's no one single recipe for burgoo, but this is how it's made in Utica.

2 tablespoons vegetable oil
2 pounds lean boneless beef
    (rump or bottom round),
    cubed
6 cups water
1 medium onion, chopped
2 carrots, chopped
1 stalk celery, chopped
1 green pepper, chopped
1 cup chopped green cabbage
½ cup lima beans
1 large potato, peeled and
    chopped

1 cup white hominy
1 tablespoon salt
½ teaspoon black pepper
1 teaspoon dried thyme

Heat the oil in a heavy stewpot or Dutch oven and add some of the meat. Brown a few cubes at a time, then remove and add more. Don't brown too many pieces at once or the moisture will steam them rather than seal the edges. Continue until all the pieces are browned, about 20 minutes. Then place all the meat in the pot and add the water. Cover and bring to a boil, then reduce the heat to a simmer and cook the meat until quite tender, about 1½ hours. As the meat cooks, skim any scum from the top of the broth.

When the meat is fully cooked, add the onion, carrots, celery, pepper, cabbage, limas, potato, and hominy. Season with the salt, pepper, and thyme. Bring the liquid back to a boil, then reduce the heat, cover, and let cook at a gentle boil for 3 to 4 hours. The mixture will seem overdone: That is correct. Burgoo is basically an overcooked stew. If the mixture seems to be getting too dry, add additional beef broth. Stir a few times during the cooking and also scoop up some of the ingredients with a spoon and mash them against the side of the pot. All the ingredients will become soft and will break apart. Stir well and serve in deep soup bowls.

Serves 4 to 6

THE BURGOO FESTIVAL is held in Utica, Illinois, the second Sunday in October (rain or shine) from 11:00 A.M. to 5:00 P.M. All booths and demonstrations are in town; the center streets are closed to cars. Parking is on side streets. There are no admission charges, except to the Historical Society Museum ($1). The burgoo meal costs $4 and is plentiful.

Utica is about 75 miles southwest of Chicago, between LaSalle and Ottawa, south of I-80 on Route 178. For additional information, contact the LaSalle County Historical Society, P.O. Box 278, Utica, Illinois 61373; (815) 667–4861.

National Shrimp Festival

Gulf Shores, Alabama

SHRIMP IS America's favorite shellfish. In New York City alone, nearly two million pounds are consumed each week. Most of it comes from the Gulf of Mexico; and Gulf Shores, Alabama, is right in the heart of the shrimp-fishing industry. That's where the National Shrimp Festival is held each year, and although it is only one of several shrimp festivals held along the Gulf Coast, it guarantees good times and good food.

The festival has been an annual event in this coastal resort town since 1970. There used to be a Blessing of the Fleet—a splendid parade, down the canal, of decorated shrimp boats—and we were told that it may again be featured. Meanwhile there are plenty of other shrimp events going on to keep festival-goers busy. Arts and crafts booths are set up on the boardwalk, along with food vendors, and visitors stroll among the pottery, leather, stuffed animals, and other handmade items. One artist had some Japanese-style shrimp prints (a monoprint made by inking shrimp and printing them on paper), which were really extraordinary. The 10-kilometer Shrimp Run gets off to an early start, and later in the day there are square dances, gospel music, a regatta, beauty pageants, and a cooking contest.

We were also able to take some time to find out about shrimping itself. We talked with the owner of the *Desperado*, a shrimp boat tied up at the dock at Bon Secour, the largest fish house in the area. It isn't a particularly easy job, and the fishing isn't always good. Most smaller boats—those about fifty or sixty feet long—go out into the Gulf for four days at a time; larger boats have more extensive facilities and are out for as much as two weeks at once. But in and around the Gulf Shores area, the boats that are the most noticeable are the older, small crafts, trolling the waters with outriggers that stick out like big arms into the water. These are poles from which trail the heavy shrimp nets—odd, cone-shaped contraptions with large doors that swing open when the net sinks to the water's bottom. A tickler chain in front of the net coaxes the shrimp up and into the net; and a drag line holds the net close to the bottom. When the net is hauled up on board, the crew sort through the catch, using a paddle to push the trash fish through the deck's scuttle holes back into the water. Once on board, the shrimp are quickly beheaded and packed in ice. (The *Desperado*, for example, carries forty-five thousand pounds of ice on board.)

If you've thought that shrimp with their heads on were fresher than the headless ones, that's partly true, in that they have probably been unloaded sooner; but since all shrimp die within fifteen minutes of being caught, the difference is not that great. If you've wondered, as we did, about the different colors of shrimp you've seen in the market, it's amusing to learn that shrimp are like chameleons—they change color to match the pigmentation of the bottom where they are at the time. When caught, that coloration is fixed, so the same species of shrimp may vary in hue from green to brown, white to gray.

There are different varieties of shrimp, however. In the Gulf, fishermen catch white, brown, and red shrimp as well as a few others, such as pink or rock hoppers. The location of the shrimp depends partly on the salinity of the water—brown shrimp, for example, can't tolerate water with too little salt in it and are found farther out; whereas the whites are taken mostly in the shallower water near shore. They catch browns more in the summer and at night; in the fall, the whites predominate. Also in fall, all types of shrimp are larger as well. Browns are the shrimp most served by restaurants. Royal, or ruby reds, are highly praised for their special sweetness and crisp texture. Should you find a shrimp with its head on, you could venture a guess as to type by examining its whiskers. Whites have long, black whiskers, whereas browns' are shorter and brown in color.

When the shrimp boats dock and unload their catch, the shrimp are taken by conveyor belt through a sorter, which sorts the shrimp by size. They are then packed in ice again and taken to a processing plant nearby to be graded and frozen. All this is demonstrated at the Bon Secour plant in Gulf Shores, a fish plant so spotless that a New York City health inspector could eat off the floor. After seeing all this shrimp pass us by on the conveyor belt, we asked the captain of the *Desperado* if he ate a lot of shrimp. "Very seldom," he laughed. "I'm sick of it."

Well, not having spent the last dozen years on a shrimp boat, we were just gearing up to gorge ourselves. It was time to return to the festival and head for the boardwalk, where a respectable number of food booths were offering shrimp in various forms: steamed, fried, shrimp fried rice, and shrimp eggrolls. We found the fried shrimp bogged down by a breading that would have sunk the *Queen Mary*. The fried rice and eggrolls were passable, but the steamed shrimp was what we headed for. Crisp, succulent shrimp, simply plunged into a spicy shrimp boil, drained, and served with a seafood sauce. We sampled a few efforts and found that we preferred to retreat off the boardwalk into the lower-level bar of the nearby Barefoot Restaurant. There, alongside the boardwalk and amid ear-splitting music, we sat on high stools at a long wooden bar and peeled several dozen shrimp apiece, forgoing the seafood sauce because these shrimp were just so sweet and fine that sauce of any kind would be a sacrilege. We asked the bartender what kind of shrimp he was serving up that day. He replied, "Dunno. I just head 'em, peel 'em, fry 'em, and gumbo 'em." We decided that it didn't make any difference either and ordered another plate and another beer.

Steamed Shrimp

When shrimp are fresh, the simplest preparation is the best. For these, make fresh cocktail sauce, too.

COCKTAIL SAUCE

¼ cup ketchup
*2 tablespoons prepared horse-
    radish*

1 tablespoon vinegar
½ teaspoon cayenne pepper

SHRIMP

*1 pound medium shrimp in the
    shell*
1 tablespoon lemon juice
1 bay leaf

2 teaspoons cayenne pepper
Dash black pepper
Pinch salt

Blend the ingredients for the cocktail sauce and let its flavor develop at room temperature for about 15 minutes.

Rinse the shrimp, but leave on the shells. If desired, remove the feet before steaming, although most people in Alabama prefer to take them off after steaming.

Fill a large pot with water and bring to a boil; stir in remaining ingredients and add the shrimp. Cover and boil over medium-high heat for about 5 minutes, or until the shrimp change color (they should turn bright pink). Remove from the heat and serve immediately.   *Serves 2*

THE NATIONAL SHRIMP FESTIVAL is held the third weekend in October in Gulf Shores, Alabama. Although most activities take place on Friday, Saturday, and Sunday, there are some preweekend events, such as the National Shrimp Festival Ball and the Multi-Hull Regatta. The seafood boardwalk opens Friday at 9:00 A.M. and is open all weekend from 9:00 till 11:00 P.M. Entertainment is provided all three days, too.

Food, mostly shrimp, is sold at individual booths on the boardwalk. A plate of shrimp costs about $3, depending on whom you buy it from. If you go to one of the many restaurants on the boardwalk, you can sit down; otherwise it's strictly a stand-up affair. There are no admission charges; parking is on side streets in town.

The year we were there, Fort Morgan (built in 1833 and used during the Civil War) hosted a historical exhibit in conjunction with the festival. Even if there is no festival "connection," a trip out the 14 miles from town is worthwhile.

Gulf Shores is located, as its name implies, on the Gulf of Mexico, midway between Mobile (Alabama) and Pensacola (Florida), at the end of Route 59. For information about the festival, including a schedule of events, contact the Gulf Shores Chamber of Commerce, Gulf Shores, Alabama 36542.

Boggy Bayou Mullet Festival

Niceville, Florida

MULLET? Where I come from even the cats won't eat it." This is what one man from Florida told us. Of course, in some parts of the state the shoreline is muddy, and so the mullet, which are bottom feeders, taste a lot like what they eat. Mullet are considered trash fish in many places, but along the Boggy Bayou on the Florida panhandle, mullet are a staple food—so much so that they are eaten for breakfast, lunch, and dinner.

During the third weekend in October, the friendly people of Niceville hold a festival to show the rest of the world just how tasty mullet can be. A mixture of crafts booths and food stalls fill the fairgrounds, so you can wander down the aisles and sample the fried mullet from one booth, move along to buy a T-shirt or handcrafted leather belt from a traveling craftsperson, then step up to another booth where they might be serving smoked mullet. You could, of course, eat hamburgers and Polish sausages at the festival, but it seems that most people crowd the fish booths.

The Florida mullet is the migratory *Mugil cephalus*, commonly called the black, silver, or striped mullet because of the long black lines that run the length of its body. It has a tapered nose that broadens out to a flat, wide head. When it feeds along a shallow bottom, its tail points skyward. The mullet is a fish that can make a rapid switch from salt water to fresh water by making a chemical change in its body that science has yet to understand. It leaves the Gulf of Mexico and swims up the shallow bayous each year to spawn. If caught with its delicate roe, the mullet commands a very high price. Unfortunately there is no roe at the festival, and not many people seem to prize it particularly—perhaps because it has been part of the northern trade for so many years. When Floridians here do eat the roe, they usually deep fry it.

Sport fishermen catch their mullet with cast nets. They stand in waist-high water or lean from a pier and wait for a school to swim by. Then they fling their nets out in a graceful sweep. Commercial fishermen generally use seine boats and go out into Choctawhatchee Bay for their catch. The Boggy Bayou has been an important center for mullet production for over a century, although the fishing was at its height during the Depression, when large quantities of mullet were sold fresh, packed for shipment, or salted down for later use. People down here are trying to revive the industry and hope they can again interest consumers in their versatile fish. The festival is one of their methods.

The Boggy Bayou Boys—a local sportsmen's club—fixes the mullet in two very appealing ways. They've been doing it since the festival began in 1977, and they assured us that they will be there in years to come. The fried is the most popular, and it's easy to know why. They head the fish, split them open, and remove the bones. Then they butterfly the fillets, dust them faintly with a mixture of flour and cornmeal, and fry them in vegetable oil. The fish emerges virtually greaseless and very crisp, especially around the edges. It's served either with just hush puppies, or on a platter with cheese grits, beans, and hush puppies.

The smoked mullet has also been headed, cleaned, and boned. It's then sprinkled with lemon juice, Worcestershire sauce, and melted butter. The fish is given a "heat smoke"—more a combination of smoking and cooking—for an hour to an hour and a half. When the fish starts to change color, the cooks baste it with more of the lemon juice mixture. The mullet finishes up as a very moist, lightly smoked fish—not at all salty because it hasn't been cured first. We found that the white meat on the fish picks up the smoky flavor divinely, while the dark meat seems to retain more of its fresh fish taste.

Most of the mullet at the festival is fried, but one enterprising stand, with a wonderfully aromatic barbecue pit, prepared barbecued mullet sandwiches: pieces of smoked mullet were placed briefly on the pit, then served up on a bun with a spicy tomato-based barbecue sauce.

Although thousands of people attend this festival each year, a comfortable, small-town feeling pervades. The grounds are shaded by giant live oaks, and there are large round tables placed conveniently near the food booths so that you can rest your plate and drink while you are eating. One part of the lawn is a center for recycling the beer and soda cans that usually litter most festivals. On stage, there is a bang-up performance by the Golden Eagles, the high school band—so large it must include the entire school population. The other entertainment includes country music, clogging, jazz, and rock. This is a festival without any rides, but with the usual beauty pageant, foot race, and evening dance.

The festival organizers tend to refer to this as a party, and explain that they try to follow the example of the mullet, "the plentiful fish of the area which has, over the years, given so much for so little."

❦

Deep-Fried Mullet

From the Boggy Bayou Festival, here is T. H. Lovell's recipe for fried mullet.

2 pounds mullet fillets	*Cornmeal for dusting*
Salt and pepper to taste	*Vegetable oil for deep frying*

Rinse the fillets, then dry them thoroughly. Season with salt and pepper, then dust generously with cornmeal.

Heat the oil in a large pot or deep fryer until it is 350°F. Put half the fillets in the pot, being sure not to crowd them. Fry with the skin side up first, until nicely browned, about 5 minutes, then turn and fry skin side down until browned, about 5 minutes more. Drain on paper towels while you fry the remaining fillets. Serve with cheese grits.   *Serves 4*

Cheese Grits

1 quart water	*1 cup grated Cheddar cheese*
1 cup uncooked grits, preferably	
coarse, southern style	

Bring the water to a boil in a large pot. Add the grits and cook, uncovered, over low heat until done, about 30 minutes. Just before serving, stir in the cheese.   *Serves 4*

Smoked Mullet

This "heat-smoked" mullet can be done on a covered barbecue.

2 whole mullet (about 1½	*½ lemon*
pounds each)	*2 tablespoons Worcestershire*
2 tablespoons butter	*sauce*

Light briquets in a covered grill and allow them to get very hot. This may take at least 1 hour. As they burn, add a few more briquets to keep the fire at peak level. When ready, add about ½ cup hickory chips to the coals and allow them to smoke and fill the grill with their aroma for about 30 minutes.

Remove the heads from the fish but leave on the tails. Clean the fish, then cut along the inside of the backbone almost to the tail. Spread open. The fish should lie flat in one piece.

Oil the grill, then lay the fish on it, skin side down. Add about ¼ cup more hickory chips, then place the grill about 4 to 6 inches above the coals. Shut off almost all the air from the coals, allowing the fire to smoke heavily. As the fish smokes, it will also cook. You want to keep it from cooking too fast, so that it has time to absorb the smoke. When the fish begins to change color, baste with lemon juice, butter, and Worcestershire sauce and continue to smoke the fish for 1 hour. Serve immediately, or allow to cool and serve cold as an appetizer. *Serves 4*

THE BOGGY BAYOU MULLET FESTIVAL is held the third weekend in October in Niceville, Florida, at the old Saw-Mill site—a large city park just to the north of town. There is some entertainment on Friday night, complete with dignitaries and opening ceremonies. Most activities are on Saturday starting at 8:00 A.M. (though when we got there at 9, not a whole lot was going on yet). The Golden Eagles (Niceville's high school band) kick things off mid-morning on Saturday with an hour-long concert. After that, most people seem ready to eat. A fried mullet plate runs about $3. Cokes, barbecues, hamburgers, and sno-cones are also for sale at various booths. The music goes on all day and a good ways into the night as well.

There is no admission charge; parking is well organized in a large field adjacent to the festival site. There are some large shade trees, with benches under them for cooling one's heels after lunch. There are bleachers in front of the stage. Although the Mullet Festival draws upward of 150,000 people (over the three days), we never felt crowded or jostled.

Niceville, Florida, is on the panhandle, about 60 miles east of Pensacola; take Route 85 south off I-10. For further information, write or call Boggy Bayou Mullet Festival, Inc., P.O. Box 231, Niceville, Florida 32578; (904) 678-3099.

Circleville Pumpkin Show

Circleville, Ohio

*I*T WAS POURING RAIN as we gloomily approached Circleville, Ohio. When we got to the Pumpkin Show, it was still pouring; the weather didn't improve, but our spirits sure did. "Nothing stops the Pumpkin Show," we were told by a blond teenager selling T-shirts. And, indeed, nothing seemed to.

The streets of Circleville were full of people in bright slickers and ponchos—we have never seen such festivity in such awful weather. Booths selling homemade pumpkin delicacies were doing a brisk business as their customers ducked under awnings and overhangs to keep dry. Many of the rides were closed down—at least till the rain let up—but, undaunted, people were buying pumpkins to take home for jack-o'-lanterns and pies, or visiting the agricultural exhibits, or marveling at the fifteen-foot pumpkin "tree" in the center of town. And, of course, they were also sampling a myriad of pumpkin goodies: pumpkin bread, pumpkin ice cream, pumpkin butter, pumpkin cookies, and pumpkin pies.

This is *the* pumpkin festival in the United States, billed by its sponsors as the "Greatest Free Show on Earth." It is the sixth-largest festival in the country, a popular event that has been going strong since 1903. What began as a small exhibit of pumpkins and corn fodder has grown into a four-day extravaganza with seven parades (fifty bands and forty floats), many contests (pie-eating, egg-tossing, and hog-calling, among others), extensive agricultural exhibits, and a wide variety of entertainment— including clowns, band concerts, a magician, a ventriloquist. One year the Zaleski Lariateers were featured. And not to be missed is the world's largest pumpkin pie—three hundred fifty pounds and five feet in diameter.

The Pumpkin Show is largely an agricultural show, and much attention is paid to the farming and home economics exhibits. Inside the display buildings are rows of preserves and vegetables in Mason jars, like the shelves in a farmer's cellar in fall. The children's competitions take place here, too; they include contests for the best poster (on a pumpkin theme) and for pumpkin decorations—carved and painted "heads" with elaborate hairdos, funny expressions, odd hats.

Outside, at the center of the festival, is the large pumpkin "tree" (actually a pyramid), surrounded by an exhibit of squashes, gourds, and pumpkins. It's a colorful display, with squashes and pumpkins in all hues of orange, yellow, beige, powdery blue, and ashy gray in oblong, squat, bulbous, and knobby shapes. When the pumpkins get very big, they take on real personalities.

How does a pumpkin get that big? We asked the farmer with the winning (385 pounds) heavyweight that year. "To grow large pumpkins," we were told, "you have to give them plenty of water and lots of TLC. Some people inject fertilizer straight into the vines, but you can risk losing them that way." Constant, tender attention seems to be the key.

This is truly a festival devoted to the pumpkin in all its possibilities. Everyone knows that the Pilgrims ate pumpkin pie at their second Thanksgiving dinner; yet even before that, settlers were making pumpkin stew and pumpkin soup, as well as drinking pumpkin beer. Today most people only know pumpkin pie, and often only what comes from a can— but at the festival visitors can sample new uses for pumpkin: pumpkin crepes with a praline sauce topped with whipped cream; pumpkin-flavored doughnuts, waffles, and pancakes; pumpkin fudge and taffy; pumpkin burgers, hot dogs, and pumpkin Joes (like sloppy Joes); French-fried pumpkin chips (delicious with a little salt!); even pumpkin pop. Admittedly, the pumpkin burgers wouldn't justify a trip to Circleville, but the pop is surprisingly refreshing, and the pumpkin fudge is creamy and light with a touch of cinnamon.

After a pumpkin-based lunch, we watched Bob Spohn carve pumpkins. Then we walked around town to find that the shop windows had been painted and decorated with a pumpkin theme. Corn shucks were tied up on lampposts (as they had no doubt been the first year of the festival). From one window, the winking Circleville pumpkin, the mascot of the festival, smiled out at us. The jack-o'-lanterns in front of most houses completed the town's pumpkiny atmosphere. We went back to the center of town to marvel once again at the many varieties of pumpkins and squash on display and realized that for every variety there was a recipe, or perhaps several. Before leaving, we stopped off at the Lions' booth to buy one of their delicious pies to fortify us during the trip back home.

Pumpkin Pie

This was the championship pumpkin pie from the 1964 and 1977 Pumpkin Show cooking contests, adapted from the *Pumpkin Recipe Book*, compiled by the Crusader Sunday School Class of Calvary United Methodist Church, Circleville.

1¾ cups pumpkin puree
½ teaspoon salt
1½ cups milk
1 tablespoon butter, melted
3 large eggs
¾ cup sugar

1 tablespoon molasses
1¼ teaspoons ground cinnamon
½ teaspoon ground ginger
½ teaspoon ground nutmeg
One 9-inch pie shell, unbaked

Preheat the oven to 425°F.

Mix the ingredients for the filling in a large bowl. Pour into the pie shell and bake for 45 to 50 minutes. The center of the pie will be soft, but will set as the pie cools. Serve with whipped cream.   *Serves 8*

Pumpkin Butter

We thought this a novel use for pumpkin, and quite tasty.

4 cups peeled and cubed
   uncooked pumpkin
1 cup sugar
1 tablespoon lemon juice
½ teaspoon ground cinnamon
⅛ teaspoon ground cloves

Place the pumpkin in a saucepan and cover with water. Bring to a boil and cook until the pumpkin is quite soft, about 5 to 8 minutes. Drain well.

   Puree the pumpkin in a blender, food processor, or food mill. Place in a heavy-bottomed saucepan and stir in the sugar and lemon juice. Bring the puree to a boil over medium-high heat, then reduce the heat to a simmer and let the puree cook until quite thick, about 30 to 45 minutes. You'll have to stir the puree frequently, especially as it starts to thicken, because it has a tendency to stick to the pan. If it seems the puree is thick enough, test by taking out a teaspoonful and placing it on a cool plate. If no liquid appears to separate from the puree, the butter is ready. Season with the spices, then pack into sterilized jars. Store in the refrigerator until ready to eat. Eat exactly like apple butter.

Makes about 1½ cups

NOTE: If desired, pack the pumpkin butter in canning jars and process according to manufacturer's instructions.

Pumpkin Chips

The Lions Club of Circleville was selling these good-tasting slivers of pumpkin. They are easy to make. Peel and seed a small pumpkin and then slice the flesh as thinly as possible (if you have a meat slicer, use that) so that you have strips no thicker than ⅛ inch. Heat vegetable oil for deep frying to 375°F and drop in the slivers. Fry for 2 to 3 minutes, then drain quickly on paper towels. Sprinkle with pumpkin pie spice mixed with sugar or sprinkle with coarse salt.

Pumpkin Ice Cream

Add pumpkin pie spice (about 1 tablespoon) to your favorite vanilla ice cream recipe.

THE CIRCLEVILLE PUMPKIN SHOW is held in this Ohio town at pumpkin-harvest time, beginning on the third Wednesday of October. There are events every day for four days, including two parades each day (except Saturday, when there's only one) and a variety of entertainment. Things usually get started just before noon. Rides and games, as well as food stands, are open daily until 9:00 P.M. Everything takes place in a six-block area in the center of town. There are no admission charges; indeed, the Pumpkin Show bills itself as the "Greatest Free Show on

Earth." Parking is on side streets, and it's not too hard to find a spot. A slice of homemade pumpkin pie costs about $1; ice cream runs 50¢; nothing is too expensive, but if you sample enough, it can add up.

Circleville is located about 25 miles south of Columbus, off U.S. 23. For additional information about the Pumpkin Show (and a schedule of events), contact the Circleville Pumpkin Show, P.O. Box 288, Circleville, Ohio 43113.

Late Fall Early Winter

Usquepaugh Johnnycake
<u>Festival</u>

Usquepaugh, Rhode Island

*J*OHNNY CAKE. Journeycake. Shawnee cake. Jonny cake. There are as many ways to spell it as there are stories of its origin. Johnnycakes are cornmeal pancakes that are eaten for breakfast with butter and syrup, as well as plain with lunch or dinner as a substitute for bread or potatoes. It is said that johnnycakes were carried by early travelers who would be passing through sparsely inhabited parts of the country. Others think the name refers to the Indians who first showed settlers how to use corn. Similar cornbread dishes in other parts of the country are called corn pone, hoecakes, mush bread, batter cakes, and ashcakes. In Rhode Island, however, it is the johnnycake, and it is celebrated at the Usquepaugh Johnnycake Festival.

Usquepaugh (pronounced *US-ka-pog*) is a picture-perfect New England village of mid-nineteenth-century houses set alongside the Queen's River, a shaded stream with a small waterfall. In the center of town is the hundred-year-old grist mill, where the owner, Paul Drumm, Jr., grinds and packages stone-ground yellow and white cornmeal, graham and whole wheat flour, rye meal, oat flour, and buckwheat flour. Mr. Drumm began the festival in 1973, as a way of calling attention to this Rhode Island resource, and although the festival has grown over the years, it is still very much a simple country fair. The two-day event features pony and ox-cart rides for children, an antique car show, band concerts, and games for kids, as well as a large crafts show, a parade, and lots of opportunities to learn about johnnycakes.

The festival represents an annual truce among local johnnycake cooks— a break from the friendly dispute that separates them along lines of technique or ingredients. Johnnycakes are to Rhode Islanders what barbecue is to North Carolinians: a matter of fierce pride and controversy. "Everyone will make them different," we were told by Paul Drumm. In

Usquepaugh, near Kingston, most people make South County johnny-cakes, which are small and thick. In nearby Newport County, the john-nycakes are thinner and wider. Some purists feel that the only proper johnnycake is one that is made with flint corn, an early Indian variety that is not cultivated commercially anymore. But all agree that john-nycakes must be made from white cornmeal—preferably stone ground to a fine powder.

On the lawn across from the mill, Dick Donnelly, a local chef, was holding forth in a booth, demonstrating and lecturing to visitors. The johnnycakes he was making were a compromise—a little thinner than South County, but not as big as Newport County style. Dick explained that these cakes today were further modified a bit for newcomers, because it takes a while to get used to eating johnnycakes. Lately, Dick has been experimenting with the basic johnnycake, and has developed ways to serve it as an hors d'oeuvre or a dessert as well.

As a crowd gathered in front of the booth, Dick Donnelly resumed his johnnycake-making demonstration. He spooned portions of batter onto his hot griddle and showed how to tap the batter with the spoon to achieve a uniform size for all the cakes. Then he pointed to the small pucker that developed as the spoon was pulled away after the last tap. This was the "smile," the hole that remains on the bottom of the cake as it cooks and that appears when the johnnycake is turned to brown on the other side. "Always serve johnnycakes with the smile on top," he told us. The finished johnnycakes should be crispy on the outside and soft on the inside. He suggested we try them first plain to appreciate the corn taste, then add butter and syrup as desired. As we ate our john-nycakes, we could hear the steady thumping of the grist mill. When we finished eating, we joined the mill tour to learn how dry corn kernels become fine cornmeal.

Paul Drumm was conducting about twenty people through the mill. He explained how the runner stone turned rapidly a few centimeters above the stationary bedstone. Between them, the corn kernels were ground, then poured through the chute to a barrel below. From above, we could watch the corn drop kernel by kernel from the hopper into the shoe. From there it would go through a hole in the runner stone to the bedstone below. Paul explained to us that only "by keeping his nose to the grindstone," could the miller detect the smell of granite, which would indicate to him that the stones were too close. After watching a few hundred kernels get pulverized, we went into the next room and saw a large sifter sorting through the meal. The cornmeal gets sifted twice, and only the finest goes for making johnnycakes.

While strolling amid the bake sale tables (there are many) and crafts booths, we heard tell that the Richmond Grange was serving johnnycakes, too. We drove up there—the Grange was only about a mile from the festival—to sample some pure South County johnnycakes. As predicted, these were thicker, larger, softer, and not as crisp overall. The corn flavor really dominated these more substantial cakes, and it was easy to see how these could double for bread at a noonday meal.

Back at the festival ground we enjoyed other local specialties, in particular clam chowder and clam fritters. The soup was creamy and had a pleasing clam flavor; the fritters were light and chock-full of clam morsels. We're sure that if you go to Rhode Island the end of October, you'll find, as we did, that the johnnycake festival is worth the journey.

Dick Donnelly's Festival Johnnycakes

The powdered milk in this recipe makes these johnnycakes lighter and crisper than the version that follows. It is reprinted courtesy of Dick Donnelly of Saunderstown, Rhode Island.

1 cup fine white cornmeal	*½ cup dry milk*
1 tablespoon sugar	*1 to 1½ cups boiling water*
1 teaspoon salt	*Corn oil for greasing griddle*

Place the dry ingredients in a bowl and gradually add the boiling water. The batter will be the consistency of thin mush. Mix well with the back of a spoon and set aside.

Heat an oiled griddle until very hot. Spoon out a tablespoonful of batter and plop it gently onto the griddle, tapping the batter off the spoon until the batter spreads to a consistent size. These festival johnnycakes should be about 2 inches in diameter; regular johnnycakes are about 4 inches. Cook on one side until browned around the edges, about 5 to 6 minutes, then dabble a drop or two of corn oil on the top of each and turn the cakes. Pat them down for even thickness. Cook on the other side until somewhat browned, about 2 to 3 minutes. The cakes will be crisp on the outside and somewhat soft in the center. Remove and serve at once with butter, syrup, honey, or a small amount of molasses.

Makes 16 cakes

South County Johnnycakes

This is the Kenyon Grist Mill's recipe for johnnycakes.

1 cup white cornmeal   *1 teaspoon sugar*
1 teaspoon salt   *1½ cups boiling water*

Mix the dry ingredients in a bowl and add the boiling water. The batter will be the consistency of thick oatmeal. Mix well.

Heat a well-oiled griddle until hot (or an electric fry pan to 380°F). Spoon out about 2 tablespoonfuls of batter onto the grill. The johnnycakes should be about 3 inches in diameter. Cook until browned on the underside, about 6 minutes. Turn and cook for an additional 5 minutes on the other side. Remove and serve. The cakes will be crisp on the outside, with a thick, creamy interior.   *Makes 8 cakes*

USQUEPAUGH'S JOHNNYCAKE FESTIVAL is generally held the fourth or last weekend in October. Mr. Drumm bills it as the biggest nonevent in Rhode Island. It's not at all commercial; it's well organized and easy to get around. Parking is $1, and a free shuttle bus runs every half hour, but it's only about a five-minute walk from the parking lot to the middle of town. All the booths and events (except the Grange) are within 100 yards of the mill.

A plate of three johnnycakes costs $1.75; a one-pound bag of johnnycake mix is $2; clam chowder is $1.50. Johnnycakes at the Richmond Grange were $1 a plate (of three). The craft show, tours of the grist mill, and demonstrations of johnnycake cookery are continuous on both days. Johnnycakes are served (both at the festival and at the Grange) from noon to 5:00 P.M. The parade is on Sunday at 1:00 P.M.

Usquepaugh is about 40 miles south of Providence, off Route 138. Arrangements and events are subject to change, of course, so before planning a trip, contact Paul Drumm, Jr., Kenyon Corn Meal Company, Usquepaugh, Rhode Island 02892; (401) 783–4054.

Andouille Festival

LaPlace, Louisiana

*T*HERE ARE A GOOD MANY world capitals in Louisiana. Breaux Bridge boasts crawfish, Gonzales specializes in jambalaya, Bridge City features gumbo, and LaPlace is the Andouille Capital of the World.

Andouille (pronounced *ahn-DEW-ee*) is a hard sausage made from chopped pork that has been marinated in garlic, paprika, and salt and pepper, then smoked until it's dark and chewy. The pork used is Boston butt, a shoulder cut that is sweet and full of flavor. The meat is coarsely chopped (never ground) and marinated twice: first when it is combined with the spices, then again after it is stuffed into beef middlin' casings. The andouille are hung carefully in the smokehouse so that they don't touch one another—if they did, they wouldn't turn to the ruddy brown that characterizes these earthy sausages. They are smoked over pecan wood for eight to ten hours. Old-timers used to smoke them over sugar cane, which imparted a sweet taste; but the sugar cane is scarcer now, and the pecan wood keeps a steady 150-degree heat. Before refrigeration was commonplace, the andouille were stuffed in double and triple casings and kept in a cool place until they were eaten.

Andouille is French-German in origin and, like many good foods, represents a combination of tastes and talents. We mostly think of French and Creole influences on Louisiana food, but in the nineteenth century there was a good-sized German population north and west of New Orleans (between LaPlace and Bayou Manchac). The people refused to listen to warnings, and all perished in the hurricane of 1915. A small graveyard up near Manchac is all that remains of the settlement. That and andouille.

LaPlace is about thirty miles north of New Orleans, along the Mississippi River and the main route to Baton Rouge. Settled by French people who then married the nearby Germans, it became a natural center for andouille. Today, LaPlace is about the only place where real andouille can be bought, making their claim to "world capital" more justified than most. Occasionally some finds its way into a New Orleans supermarket or specialty store, but, say the natives of that city, it's not as good as the andouille from LaPlace.

Cajuns use their andouille as a seasoning for red beans and rice, gumbo, and jambalaya. They also sometimes cook it with greens or simply eat it straight, usually fried. With its strong, smoky flavor and hot spiciness, the andouille makes for a robust brew—the heart and soul of Cajun food.

The air at the Andouille Festival is spicy with cayenne pepper, salt, Tabasco, and onions. In the kitchen tent, cooks (with beer by their sides) are busy chopping up sausage, stirring iron caldrons of red beans and rice, and preparing gumbo to serve to the more than twelve thousand people who eat at the festival each year. Sponsored by the Fire Department, the late October festival has been a big fundraiser since it began in 1977.

Dale Madere, the chief cook at the festival, explained to us that twenty-eight hundred pounds of andouille and fifteen hundred pounds of rice go into the three dishes offered here: a very spicy jambalaya with lots of Louisiana cayenne pepper and large chunks of andouille; an andouille gumbo that was heady with the fragrance of filé; and red beans and rice, which were smoky and mildly spicy. The recipes used are Dale's own, developed over the years and evolved from his Louisiana ancestors. The jambalaya, in particular, is made with Dale's homemade cayenne pepper; and although the food he prepares for the festival is made with a commercial brand of andouille, Dale makes his own andouille when he is cooking for friends or family.

The kitchen tent and the nearby long tables for eating the andouille gumbo and jambalaya occupy a major section of the festival, symbolically as well as literally. There are a minimum of booths that sell other food. Although the customary hamburgers and hot dogs are available, almost everyone congregates at the andouille booth run by the Fire Department. It was unusual to see some booths offering hard liquor; most festivals, expecially in Louisiana, have the usual beer booth and Coke stands, but at LaPlace they were selling mixed drinks. The festival also has a cooking contest, plus rides and games, a five-mile run, and a Miss Andouille pageant. But most come for the andouille.

You can eat it right on the spot, but visitors can also buy some to take home. The Lions Club occupies a small booth with a large refrigerator, in which they keep pounds and pounds of andouille for sale at a very reasonable price. As we approached their booth, a woman came up and asked, "What's in it? Is it true that it's made with armadillo?" After much assurance that it wasn't, she bought several pounds. We bought some of this commercially made andouille also—it's the same brand as is used in the festival foods—but inquired as to whether a more traditional type were sold somewhere. We were directed to Jacob's, a butcher in LaPlace who sold us some of the true, earthy andouille made without preservatives. In contrast to the commercial variety, the sausage at Jacob's was much hotter, coarser, and smokier—a very gutsy sausage, truly representative of the rugged bayou country. If you go to the Andouille Festival, don't miss stopping by Jacob's for a little to take home with you.

Chicken and Andouille Jambalaya

This is best made with real Cajun andouille, available from Jacob's, 505 West Airline, LaPlace, Louisiana 70068. It is available by mail, with a minimum order of five pounds.

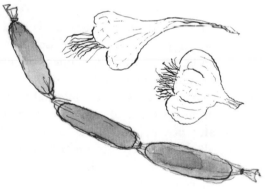

1 chicken (about 3 pounds),
    cut up
3 cups cubed andouille
3 medium onions, chopped
2 stalks celery, chopped
3 cloves garlic, minced
1 cup uncooked medium-grain
    rice
2½ cups water

Brown the chicken in a large casserole or cast-iron pot until the skin is dark brown. Remove and set the chicken aside.

In the chicken fat and browning particles, brown the andouille and add the onions, celery, and garlic. Stir and sauté until lightly browned. Add the rice and coat well with the mixture. Then add the chicken pieces and the water. Cover and bring to a boil, then let simmer for about 30 to 45 minutes, or until all the water is absorbed and the rice is tender.

Serves 4

Red Beans and Rice with Andouille

2 cups (1 pound) red kidney
   beans
7 cups water
3 tablespoons vegetable oil
2 medium onions, coarsely
   chopped

2 cloves garlic, minced
½ pound andouille, sliced and
   then diced
Salt and pepper

Soak the beans in 3 cups of the water overnight. Drain.

In a large saucepan, heat the oil and sauté the onions and garlic until wilted. Add the andouille and stir, then add the beans, the remaining 4 cups water, and salt and pepper to taste. Bring to a boil, then simmer for about 1 to 1½ hours, or until the beans are tender. Adjust the seasonings, then serve over medium-grain rice.   *Serves 4*

THE ANDOUILLE FESTIVAL is held the last weekend in October at the old drag strip in LaPlace, Louisiana. Although there are rides and arts and crafts, eating andouille is the main event. There is continuous music beginning about noon on both Saturday and Sunday; and on Saturday, the party goes on till midnight. Andouille can also be bought to take home. A plate of andouille gumbo costs about $3.50, as do red beans and rice or jambalaya. If you can manage it, we recommend sampling all three! There are no additional charges; parking is in a lot adjacent to the fairgrounds. Eating is done at long tables, standing up. In fact, there is almost no place to sit down.

LaPlace is located just north of New Orleans, off U.S. 61. For additional information, write Andouille Festival, P.O. Box 206, LaPlace, Louisiana 70068; or call (504) 652-2065.

Lexington Barbecue Festival

Lexington, North Carolina

WHEN Sonny Conrad, Joe Cope, Boyd and Roy Dunn, John Little, Wayne Monk, Gene Whitley, and Jimmy Harvey announced they would get together in 1984 to make barbecue, they were making more than just another sandwich: They made history. And it was the chance to witness (and sample) the premier of this culinary milestone that drove us to the first Lexington Barbecue Festival. As any connoisseur knows, Lexington, North Carolina, is the Barbecue Capital of the Piedmont Region of North Carolina. Its barbecue is legendary.

Lexington's first barbecue restaurant opened in 1919—a tent in the middle of town set up by Sid Weaver. Soon after that, Jesse Swicegood opened a stand, too. Business was good, and both men trained other barbecue chefs, including Warner Stamey. Now there are seventeen barbecue restaurants in Lexington (a city of some twenty thousand people), and a majority of the men that run them learned their trade from Warner Stamey. The development of barbecue in Lexington reads like a family tree, with today's chefs using methods only slightly different from the ones Sid Weaver and Jesse Swicegood used over sixty years ago.

What makes Lexington barbecue so special? North Carolina barbecue is pork, almost always chopped (not ground). In Lexington, the pork shoulders are cooked long and slow—about an hour a pound—over hickory wood. They are basted with "dip," a mixture of vinegar, water, salt, and pepper. As the dip and fat drip onto the coals, smoke is created that rises up, surrounds and permeates the meat, and gives it a rich, smoky flavor. Barbecue from Lexington is so famous that Craig Claiborne included it on the menu of the Williamsburg Economic Summit, where the world's leaders got a taste of real American food.

The festival officially begins when the mayor is served a hefty barbecue sandwich. It continues with the Parade of Pigs (people dressed up as pigs, that is). A six-block stretch of Main Street is closed to traffic, and red-and-white banners at either end announce the festival with a logo that shows four dancing pigs. Platforms at each end of the street are stages for the almost nonstop entertainment: gospel singers, square dancers, cloggers, school bands, and the University of North Carolina Theatre for Young People, who perform their puppet version of "The Three Little Pigs." In addition there are a pig-drawing contest for kids, a pie-eating contest, the ever-popular strongest-man- and -woman contest, and other games. Vendors along the street sell arts and crafts (some folksy, some country, some awful), furniture (it's the main industry of the area), raffle tickets to help the school band, cider, fudge, baked goods, and soft drinks (in souvenir cups—with the dancing pig logo on them).

Some unnatural sounds drew us to the front of the courthouse, where the hog-calling contest is held. We watched—and listened—as a series of men approached the mike and let out with hoots, squeals, and shouts. A nine-year-old boy, clearly a master of understatement, got up and said, "Here, hog." But the best (and the winner as well) made noises that we've never imagined possible, prompting a woman near us to remark, "He's been eating the wrong food." Commenting that his call, "ought to bring 'em to the barn," the emcee handed the proud winner his trophy.

Directly following the hog calling were the barbecue cheers. The eleven-girl Lexington Senior High School Varsity Cheerleading Team multiplied the crowd's already high enthusiasm with cheers of "Are you ready/to pig out?/Yes we are/Yes we are" and a very rhythmic "Sliced bar-be-cue"—all done with an amazing variety of leaps and hops. But, "Chopped bar-be-cue/Chopped bar-be-cue/Chopped bar-be-cue/Let's go!" brought rounds of applause. As is fitting, they won the first year's trophy.

Adjacent to the courthouse was a huge tent, the center of the festival. No fewer than thirty-five people were working beneath its red-and-white awning, chopping the barbecue, fixing the slaw, and scooping hush puppies out of the fat. Here from the heart, mission central, came the special festival barbecue, the combined effort of seven masters of the trade.

Festival barbecue is served in two forms: as a sandwich, with or without slaw (it's customary in North Carolina to have slaw on your sandwich, the way you would put ketchup on a hamburger), and as a platter, with hush puppies and slaw on the side. The slaw here is "dip slaw," and it is an essential part of Lexington barbecue. This slaw has no mayonnaise. It's made with cabbage, ketchup, and the same dip that's used to baste the meat.

Though there were many people lined up for the barbecue, service was quick, and very soon we had our platters of smoky barbecue, basted with a thin vinegar-based dip, whose spicy kick came just a few seconds after each bite. Lucky eaters also got some "outside," the prized chewy ends of the meat. The hush puppies were crunchy and light, with a dominating corn flavor; and the dip slaw was tart, the perfect accompaniment to this style of barbecue.

The T-shirts of some festival-goers betrayed their single-mindedness: "Go Hog Wild," from the Lexington Barbecue Center; "Pig Out," from Lexington Barbecue No. 1; the four dancing pigs from the Lexington Barbecue Festival; and "This Little Pig Went to Zimmermans." Everyone was eating barbecue or talking about eating it. This was only the first year of the festival, but we were certain we'd been at the start of a great tradition.

THE LEXINGTON BARBECUE FESTIVAL is held in Lexington, North Carolina, on the last Saturday in October. All events take place on Main Street between Third Street (north of the courthouse) and Third Avenue (south of the courthouse). The immediate area is closed to all traffic, but parking is no problem on the side streets.

The barbecue costs $2.50 for a platter, $1.25 for a sandwich. There are no admission charges. Soft drinks are 50¢ to $1.00. Directly across from the barbecue tent is a large area with picnic tables and benches; many people (ourselves included) chose to sit on the grass in a corner park.

The opening ceremony is at 9:00 A.M., and festivities continue till 8:00 P.M., after which is a concert (tickets are sold at the door or in advance).

Lexington is located in the Piedmont, just 20 miles south of Winston-Salem at the intersection of U.S. 29/50 and U.S. 52. For information, contact Lexington Barbecue Festival, P.O. Box 1642, Lexington, North Carolina 27293; or phone (704) 243-2629.

Yambilee

Opelousas, Louisiana

THE YAMBILEE is one of the oldest harvest festivals in Louisiana, first celebrated in 1946; and it's held in Opelousas, the third-oldest town in the United States. Known in Louisiana as yams, these delicious copper-skinned tubers are sweet potatoes, and they've been something to celebrate since 1690, when European settlers found Native Americans eating them. Already "tested" by the Attakapas, Alabama, Choctaw, and Opelousas tribes, the tasty, nourishing sweet potato became a favorite food of the French and Spanish colonists.

Yambilee has been a part of the lives of the people in this Acadian city for nearly four decades, so folks sort of take it for granted. "I grew up with Yambilee," Bill Bourdier, president of the thirty-eighth annual festival, told us. "My first year I was in the children's parade, and, with eight other kids, we pulled a float. Then there was a torchlight parade and a Yamba parade (all black people). The Yamba parade was always the best one."

Things are different now. There is only one parade, the Grand Louisyam Parade. But there are also a wide variety of events that probably weren't a part of Yambilee's past: a talent show, arts and crafts, a diaper derby, a children's costume contest, and a senior-citizens' dance. Most important are the exhibits, the yam auction, and the coronation of the yam queen and king. Neighboring "royalty," that is, queens from other Louisiana festivals (International Rice, Shrimp, Rayne Frog, Swine, and Orange), are invited to the festivities. They're all there with their crowns and sashes, making the whole event very colorful and glamorous.

The yam auction is a big fundraiser. The Queen of Yambilee auctions off a box of the best (Centennial variety) yams. Bidding is competitive, and the winner usually gets a kiss in addition to a box of beautiful potatoes. The exhibits include agricultural displays, homemade foods, and the fanciful "yam-i-mals." The farmers bring in boxes of beautiful sweet potatoes: Gold Rush, Golden Age, Heart of Gold, Jewel, Centennial, and Travis are the big varieties. Centennial is the most popular, and, to our palates, the best. It is the favorite variety to grow because it has a high sugar content, is disease resistant, and offers a high yield— important considerations to a farmer. It's a mighty good-looking tuber, with a smooth skin and firm orange flesh, that bakes to a sweet intensity that never becomes cloying. The Centennials that we saw on display at the fair (and that we took home with us from the festival) were truly beautiful specimens, making the sweet potatoes that we can get from the supermarket seem like crude rutabagas.

As with most harvest festivals, there are competitions. Cooked yam dishes are a popular entry in the home economics department. Although they sounded good and looked appetizing, they were unavailable for sampling. The most popular competition to enter is the Yam-i-mal, which has five classes—four-year-olds through senior citizens. Yam-i-mals must be made from one odd-shaped sweet potato that resembles an animal, left in its original shape and color. "Add feathers, construction paper, pipe cleaners, playdough, or such to complete the animal appearance; but remember that the least amount of decoration added, the better." Some of the more entertaining cuties included an armadillo, a turkey, a dinosaur, an elephant, and a mouse. The prizewinners are then used as centerpieces for the Royal Luncheon, at which baked Louisiana yams are served.

Unfortunately there weren't too many sweet potato dishes to eat at the Yambilee, other than yam cupcakes and fabulous sweet-potato pies, which were available at several booths. We sampled them all and would be hard-pressed to have a favorite, though we did slightly lean toward the ones at the Ebenezer Baptist Church Matrons' Society booth. Bill Bourdier told us about another Louisiana treat: a yam in a bowl with a rich gumbo poured over. Subsequently, we tried that combination and recommend it highly.

On the midway were many rides, games of skill and chance (an opportunity to win a stuffed animal to impress your girlfriend or boyfriend), and other side-show-type attractions. With over thirty-five years behind it, the Yambilee is good entertainment. We would have preferred more yams, though; and we would have liked to have been able to come circa 1955 (before the Quonset-style Yamatorium was built), when the festival really took over the town.

Old-Fashioned Candied Yams

This is a recipe adapted from one given out at the festival.

*10 medium sweet potatoes,
   peeled*
1 cup sugar
½ cup brown sugar
½ cup dark corn syrup
*½ cup (1 stick) butter or
   margarine, melted*

1 teaspoon ground cinnamon
1 teaspoon ground nutmeg
¼ cup water
1 cup shelled pecans

Preheat the oven to 450°F.

Slice the sweet potatoes like thick French fries, then place in a large casserole. Add the sugar, brown sugar, corn syrup, butter or margarine, spices, and water. Cover and bake for 45 minutes.

Just before serving, remove the cover and sprinkle the pecans on top. Bake for an additional 10 minutes, then serve.   *Serves 6 to 8*

Festival Sweet-Potato Pie

1½ cups all-purpose flour
1 tablespoon baking powder
¼ cup sugar

FILLING

*½ cup mashed cooked sweet
   potato*

*4 tablespoons (½ stick) butter,
   melted*
2 large eggs

1 large egg
¼ cup brown sugar

Combine the flour, baking powder, and sugar in a bowl. Make a well in the center and add the butter and eggs. Gradually incorporate the flour into the eggs and mix well. Knead gently until the dough is firm and no longer sticky; dust with additional flour if necessary. Chill the dough for at least 30 minutes. Preheat the oven to 350°F.

Mix the ingredients for the filling. Roll out the dough to a thickness of ¼ inch. Cut 5-inch circles in the dough (use a bowl with a sharp rim). Fill each circle with 2 tablespoons filling and fold like a half-moon. Seal the edges with the tines of a fork and set on a baking sheet. Reroll the scraps to make a few additional pies. Bake the pies for 20 to 30 minutes, or until they are firm to the touch and only lightly browned. Serve hot or allow to cool.   *Makes about 6 pies*

THE YAMBILEE is held in Opelousas the end of October. Although the festival kicks off with a talent show on Wednesday, most events don't start till Saturday; the exhibits open that day as well. The yam auction and the Louisyam parade are on Sunday. All activities take place on the Yambilee grounds. Sweet-potato pies and other foods are for sale on the grounds; a pie costs about $1. There is plenty of free parking. No admission is charged to the exhibits or grounds, but some events—such as the Royal Luncheon and the Grand Ball—have modest ticket prices. Tickets are for sale on the grounds (at the Yambilee office) or by mail from the Yambilee (see below).

The Yambilee grounds are located just west of town. Opelousas is on U.S. 190, about 60 miles west of Baton Rouge. For information, contact the Louisiana Yambilee, Inc., P.O. Box 444, Opelousas, Louisiana 70570; (318) 948-8848.

Louisiana Pecan Festival

Colfax, Louisiana

*T*HE PECAN is a completely native nut. In fact, the word *pecan* is an American Indian word. According to Waverley Root in *Food*, pre-Columbian Indians used pecans extensively: They cooked with the oil, ground the nuts into meal, and carried roasted pecans as emergency rations on hunting trips. It wasn't long before European settlers learned to appreciate pecans too, and eventually they improved the taste by grafting new varieties onto the stocks of native pecan trees.

There are about a hundred named varieties of *Carya illinoensis*, but only about thirty are grown commercially. In Grant Parish, Louisiana, you can find many of them. This is the center of the natural pecan habitat in Louisiana, and its county seat—Colfax—is the natural site for the Pecan Festival. Held each year since 1969, in early November (harvest time), this festival attracts over seventy thousand people, who come to buy pecans by the sack; to eat homemade pecan pies, cakes, and cookies; and to have fun celebrating the harvest.

Colfax, a somewhat casually paved town, is located on the Red River, halfway between Alexandria and Natchitoches. It's a very small town, with lots of southern charm—not fussed over or gussied up for the tourists. Houses are white clapboard, ranging from well-to-do homes to small bungalows with long porches and sloping roofs. Tall, graceful pecan trees grow along the roads and in most people's yards. Festival activities take place downtown, and "downtown" is about three blocks of stores along the railroad tracks.

Festivities begin each year with the blessing of the pecan crop and the selection and crowning of the Pecan Queen. On Friday of the two-day event, the judges pick the winners of the pecan-cooking contest. All schools in the parish are closed this day so that the children can come to the festival to have their faces painted or fortunes told, or to play with the clowns, Smokey the Bear, or Woodsy Owl. There are also relay races and other games.

On Saturday, a two-hour parade winds from the school grounds through town. It's a calvacade of beauty queens, school bands playing rousing tunes, civic groups, and ever-present politicians. At noon, the Pecanettes, a booster song-and-dance group, provide entertainment. That's also when the carnival opens, with the expected assortment of rides and games. Live country music is heard continuously throughout the day, and the festival concludes with a fireworks display in the evening.

The highlight, for us, is the country store—a small, old-fashioned shop where the homemade pies, cookies, and other goodies are sold during the festival. Some crafts are on display there, and that's also where you can buy sacks of pecans with which to make your own pies. Here, too, other local products are available: cane syrup, sugarcane, sweet potatoes, filé powder, and ground cayenne pepper.

Since this was harvest time, we headed a few miles out of town to the Littlepage farm. There we got close to the trees and saw the husks split open, like an orange cut into sections, revealing the mottled, randomly striped pecans in their shells. We sampled a few varieties: Stuart, the one most favored by shippers and therefore most likely to be found in stores, is dry and tasteless in comparison with more unusual varieties such as Schley, Cape Fear, Sly, and Choctaw. Mr. Littlepage favors the very nutty Schley, but told us that it was susceptible to disease and had to be babied. We also tasted Candy, and that quickly became our favorite—it was so moist and pecany.

Some varieties of pecans have paper-thin inner shells, so removing the nuts from their casing is easy though tedious. It's possible oftentimes to buy pecans shelled, but the freshness quickly fades once the kernels are removed from the shells. A compromise we discovered is to get "cracked" nuts. A clever machine with a small conveyor belt carries each nut, nestled in a little notch of chain, up to a cracker, which gently squeezes the shell and makes a crack around it, making it easy for you then to slip off the tips on either end and remove the pecan halves from the shell. Easily shelled and then quickly frozen to retain their flavor, the pecans can be kept for months without appreciable loss of flavor. We were advised to let the cracked nuts dry for a few days before freezing them. The oil-rich taste of the nuts was too good to let pass by. We bought ten pounds of pecans, had them cracked, and happily munched them all the way home.

Marsha's Pecan Pie

A past winner of the cooking contest, the original recipe was considerably sweeter.

½ cup sugar
3 tablespoons butter or
    margarine, softened
1 cup dark corn syrup
3 large eggs

1 teaspoon vanilla extract
1 tablespoon cornstarch
1 teaspoon vinegar
1 cup chopped pecans
One 9-inch pie shell, unbaked

Preheat the oven to 375°F.

Cream the sugar and butter or margarine. Add the remaining filling ingredients and mix well but do not overbeat. Place the pecans at the bottom of the shell and pour the filling over. Wait approximately 2 to 3 minutes for the pecans to rise to the top of the mixture. Bake for 40 minutes. Let cool before serving.   *Serves 6*

Bourbon-Pecan Pound Cake

This prizewinning recipe was prepared by Mrs. Q. A. Hargis, Jr.

1 pound (4 sticks) margarine, or
    half butter and half margar-
    ine, softened
3 cups sugar
8 large eggs, separated

3 cups all-purpose flour
¼ cup bourbon
2 teaspoons vanilla extract
2 teaspoons almond extract
2 cups chopped pecans

Preheat the oven to 300°F. Line the bottom of a 10-inch tube pan with waxed paper. Grease well.

Cream the margarine or half butter/half margarine and the sugar. Add the egg yolks, one at a time. Alternately add the flour and the liquids. Beat the egg whites until stiff, then fold into the batter.

Sprinkle the bottom of the cake pan with half the pecans, then pour in the batter. Sprinkle the top with the remaining nuts and bake for 1½ hours. Allow the cake to cool, then let it sit for a day or two before serving, unwrapped and at room temperature if possible.

Serves 8 to 10

THE LOUISIANA PECAN FESTIVAL is held in Colfax the first weekend in November. The opening ceremony and blessing of the crop are on Thursday morning; but things really get going on Friday, when the country store opens. Crafts, carnival rides, and live entertainment begin at 9:30 A.M. (the Pecanettes perform around noon) and go on all day. The parade is on Saturday. There's entertainment then, too, of course. All events (except the dance on Friday night) take place in downtown Colfax. On Saturday there is a $1 parking charge, otherwise there are no admission fees. Pecans and pecan goodies are on sale at the country store. A slice of pecan pie costs about $1.25; a five-pound bag of pecans (in the shell) is about $7.

Colfax is on the Red River, on Route 8 about 25 miles northwest of Alexandria. For information about the festival, contact the Louisiana Pecan Festival, Colfax, Louisiana 71417; (318) 627–3711.

Annual Indian Foods Dinner

Salamanca, New York

Cherokee Fall Festival

Cherokee, North Carolina

Feast of San Estéban

Acoma Pueblo, New Mexico

*I*N HER BOOK *Native Harvests*, Barrie Kavasch reminds us that much of what we identify today as classic American cooking came to us from the American Indian. And because their foods are so closely linked with nature, especially with the seasons, it seems natural that Indians have celebrations that could be termed food festivals. We pursued this thought, going to feast days and festivals in parts of the country where Indian tribes were still very active. Events such as the Maple or Cranberry Festivals—once Indian foods—are now everyone's celebration; but there are times when Indians gather to appreciate their traditional foods. We focus here on the Indian Foods Dinner given by the Seneca Indians of upstate New York, then move down south to the Cherokee Indian Fall Festival in North Carolina, and finally go west to the Feast of San Estéban at Acoma Pueblo, New Mexico—all different and all delicious.

ANNUAL INDIAN FOODS DINNER

The ghost bread was the color of a corpse. It was part of a menu that included hulled corn soup, fried salt pork, parched corn mush, roast venison and turkey, mashed potatoes, mashed beans, squash, boiled corn bread, and brine pickles. The blessing before the meal was said in Seneca; *Jesus* was the only word we understood. (We were told later that when there is no Seneca word for something, they use the English word rather than coin a new one.)

This dinner of traditional foods is given each year by the members of the Seneca Indian Jimersontown Presbyterian Church in Salamanca, New York. The dinner was started in 1959 to raise money for the church and also to offer a bit of education for the busloads of tourists coming to visit the new Seneca-Iroquois National Museum nearby. At first the members were skeptical. Who would eat Indian food? they wondered. They very soon found out. Visitors were curious about native foods, especially since so many could be recognized as variations on their own favorites. And the dinners brought together Senecas from neighboring areas, many of whom wanted to find out more about their traditions. Soon the annual dinners became a sell-out event.

Tradition is very much a part of this dinner. The corn that is used in the hulled corn soup, for example, is an ancient variety of white Indian corn, seeds for which are saved each season to be grown the following summer. To prepare the soup, the kernels are boiled in water with hardwood ashes until the hulls float loose; then the plumped corn pieces are rinsed and cooked with salt pork to make a light broth with a dominant corn flavor.

Corn and beans are the basis for a range of Indian foods that can be sampled here—from the almost solid brick of pureed beans studded with chunks of beans; to the parched corn mush, a grainy, nutlike gruel with a hint of sweetness; and the slice of boiled cornbread, intentionally bland to accompany the roasted venison and turkey.

Ghost bread is like a heavy biscuit, permeated with the taste of the fat in which it is deep fried. It marks a tradition, too. Reverend George M. Mighells explained that ghost bread is part of the feast held ten days after a person's death. The Senecas believe that after death, the soul is held earthbound for ten days, allowing time to settle the estate. Since the Senecas have no written language—and therefore no such things as wills—there could be some doubt about the dead person's wishes. On the tenth day, a feast is held and a plate of food—including the ghost bread—is placed in the room of the departed one. If the plate of food remains untouched during the night, the distribution of earthly belongings has been done properly. (If the food has been disturbed, things are not right.)

Things are done right at the Indian Foods Dinner, however, and the ghost bread, along with all the other Seneca specialties, is an unusual taste experience.

༈ CHEROKEE FALL FESTIVAL ༈

On the southern edge of Great Smoky Mountain National Park, the Indians of the Cherokee Reservation hold their annual Fall Festival. Though this fair is not strictly a food festival, there are good opportunities to sample some traditional Cherokee foods while learning about Cherokee culture and buying Indian jewelry and clothing. The week-long event is held on the fairgrounds of the Cherokee Nation Museum. There are demonstrations of ancient rites, archery and blowgun competitions, and a rough game of Indian stickball. Shuffled among the crafts vendors that you can visit between the events are many small booths selling foods such as corn soup, fry bread, and meat pies. The fry bread is really a western Indian food, but it has moved eastward and is very popular here, especially topped with chili, when it is dubbed an Indian taco. Apart from these mild digressions, the food is basically Cherokee, most notably the chestnut bread and the bean bread.

Chestnut bread will fool you. You'll expect something breadlike or a pancake like a johnnycake, but you'll be handed a hot packet with a green cornhusk wrapping. Inside the wrapping is a steamed puree of chestnuts, blended lightly with some cornmeal. The mixture is unsweetened and unseasoned. It's heavy, but truly a chestnut-lovers's dream. The bean bread seems more familiar, somehow, even though it, too, comes wrapped in a green cornhusk. This is a puree of cooked kidney beans, with some whole beans mixed in, blended with yellow cornmeal. The bean puree is steamed, rather like a tamale, and also without salt or other seasoning. The salt supposedly would make the bread crumble into bits, but we have found most Indian foods to be devoid of salt.

A walk across the field to the other end of the fairgrounds leads you to the agricultural tent, where a fascinating display of foods is on hand, much as you'd find at a state or county fair—with white, red, and blue ribbons for the winning displays. Here you can compare the multitude of beans that have sustained the Indian peoples for centuries: red speckled beans, dark maroon beans, butter beans that are violet and dark purple, beans labeled "dry leather britches" and that look as tough as they sound. There are also such oddities, to us, as red okra, as well as herbs intended for medicinal purposes. The displays show foods in Cherokee life, both after the harvest and in their practical applications.

Lest we paint too rosy a picture, remember that the Cherokee Fall Festival is held in a tourist town where things Indian are exploited to their fullest. There are shops in town that sell authentic, high-quality crafts, and there are aspects of this fair that are truly traditional; but in both cases there are also things much better avoided. At the Cherokee Indian Cooperative in town, we picked up a copy of a small booklet, *Cherokee Cooklore*, and read about all the other traditional foods that could have been at this festival—gritted corn bread, yellowjacket soup, deerhorn mushrooms, knee-deeps (early frogs), hickory nut soup, possum grape drink, and slick-go-downs. Perhaps in the years to come, the organizers of this event will focus it more on the traditional foods and crafts of the Cherokees and allow us all to sample more of their rich heritage.

✐ FEAST OF SAN ESTÉBAN ✐

Acoma—Sky City—is the oldest continously inhabited pueblo in the United States. Many people consider Acoma an ideal site for defense against enemies; but for those unaccustomed to the blistering heat of the Southwest (even in September), it is also a blissful seven thousand feet above sea level, where cooling breezes tame the heat of the sun. People have lived at Acoma since about A.D. 1150; today only an average of a hundred residents stay there all year long. Acoma now serves more as a weekend and holiday retreat—a place where Indians who have settled in nearby farming villages and in the larger communities of Anzac, Acomita, and McCartys can return to live briefly in the old style and to celebrate the feast days of their heritage. Acoma hosts many festivals, but the Feast of San Estéban is especially important because it is the harvest festival.

Acoma is a tight cluster of adobe squares, with houses that link together like a child's set of building blocks. Alleyways separate rows of single and double and triple layers of rooms, connected by wooden ladders and doorways that are small and narrow. From the street, the houses look dark inside, but the brightness of the sun against the adobe is deceiving, for when we visited one family's home, we actually found the interior quite light and sunny, decorated with colorful religious objects and pictures.

Inside, furniture was sparse—a wood stove, on which simmered a large pot of red chili; a wide, round table covered with a bright cloth; bunk beds in the back corners; and pots and baskets on the floor. The grandmother and mother are potters; the daughter is now learning the craft. We were urged to share some of their feast-day meal: fiery hot red chili, roast chicken, homemade "oven" bread (as opposed to fry bread), and cans of soda. It was impossible to refuse. It was the Feast of San

Estéban, and sharing food on this day brings luck in the year to come.

The two main alleys of town meet in a broad intersection, almost a plaza, where the traditional Indian dances are held. On feast day there is a lot of dancing, and it can seem long and monotonous, but also riveting, as you watch the costumed men make subtle turns in direction or shifts in position. And while the dances go on, and the chanting and the music, others sell their pottery, for which Acoma is most famous. Many pots have the popular motifs: the storyteller, a woman with lots of children around her; turtles, which mean good fortune; or the best-known geometric patterns done with a yucca brush, called thin-line painting. Some of the pots are made elsewhere and purchased, then painted here, while others are fired in ovens at Acoma. The best of Acoma's pots are collector's items; and you may find some real treasures on this day if you know what to look for.

Also along the streets, on tables in front of their houses or from the windows that front the alleyways, Indian women sell food and drinks. Mostly, offerings are tamales and tamale filling (minus the cornmeal layer and cornhusk wrapper), Indian tacos, fry bread, oven bread (bread baked in the adobe beehive oven), green chili stew, sweet squash breads, pumpkin cookies, and pies and cakes. Of what we were able to sample (the number of stands is vast; almost every house sells food), the foods that were the best were those most carefully prepared: the chili at our host's adobe; tamales with only a thin layer of cornmeal, neatly wrapped in their husks and steamed until the flavors are blended; and fry bread that was simple and light. The food of the American Southwest is largely the food of the Pueblo Indians. At Acoma that food is still being prepared the old-fashioned way, especially at the Feast of San Estéban.

Seneca Hulled Corn Soup

The corn for this soup is usually hulled by boiling it with hardwood ashes for about 1½ hours, then sieved until the skins are separated out. As a shortcut, we found that a similar soup was obtained when we used the dried hulled corn called *posole*, available mainly in the Southwest.

You could also substitute a can of hominy, although you would then cook the beans first and add the hominy at the last minute. The important thing is to have skinless corn kernels that plump up when cooked in the liquid, complementing the simple flavor of the beans.

½ pound red kidney beans　　　　*3 cups dried hulled corn (posole)*
¼ pound salt pork　　　　　　　*6 cups water*

Soak the beans overnight in water to cover, then, when plumped, drain and place in a large saucepan. Rinse the salt pork and cut it into a few pieces so that they fit nicely in the pot. Add the dried corn and then the water. Bring to a boil over high heat, reduce the heat, then cook gently until the corn and beans are tender, about 1½ hours. Add more water if necessary to keep up the level of the broth. The beans and corn will expand in volume and take on the flavor of the salt pork. You may want to remove the salt pork and chop it into small pieces to serve in the soup, or you may prefer to discard it. The soup traditionally has no salt flavoring, but if you find yourself too unaccustomed to that taste, you may want to add some.　　　　　　　　　　　　　　　　*Serves 4 to 6*

NOTE: If substituting canned hominy, cook the beans with the salt pork until tender, then add 1 can (15½ ounces) hominy, drained, just before serving. Heat through and add salt to taste.

Ghost Bread

This recipe, by Mrs. William Bennett, is from *Iroquois Indian Recipes*, published by the Peter Doctor Memorial Indian Scholarship Foundation, Inc. Mrs. Bennett's recipe is for one large bread, but we have adapted it to make four individual breads, since that is the way they are served at the dinner.

2 cups all-purpose flour　　　　*1 cup milk*
3 teaspoons baking powder　　　*Vegetable oil for deep frying*
1 heaping teaspoon salt

Mix the dry ingredients in a bowl and make a well in the center. Add the milk slowly, mixing to a biscuit-dough consistency. Knead a few times on a floured board until the mixture holds together. Divide into 4 equal portions and roll each portion out to a circle about 4 inches in diameter. The dough will be about ½ inch thick. Slash a small opening in the center of each.

Pour enough oil into a small, 6-inch skillet so that it is between ¼ and ½ inch deep. Heat until very hot but not smoking, then place a wheel of dough in the skillet and quickly pierce any bubbles that appear on the surface. Cook until browned on the underside, about 5 minutes, then turn and brown the other side. Remove from the skillet and drain on paper towels while you fry the remaining 3 breads.

Serve quickly, since these are best when hot. They can be cut in half and buttered or just eaten straight. *Serves 4*

Cornmeal Mush

Cornmeal mush is served at the Annual Indian Foods Dinner, but it is a dish that many Indians eat. It is also found in the South, particularly in the Appalachians. This version is slightly sweet, similar to the mush at the dinner.

1 quart water   *1¼ cups yellow cornmeal*
½ cup brown sugar

Bring the water to a boil in a large saucepan, then add the sugar and stir. Keep the liquid boiling over high heat until it returns to a boil, then reduce to a simmer. Holding some of the cornmeal in your hand and cupping it like a funnel, very gently sprinkle the cornmeal on the surface of the water. Stir the mixture and add more cornmeal, continuing to add it very gradually until it is all poured in. This should take you up to 10 or 15 minutes, because if you add it too quickly, the cornmeal won't cook sufficiently and it will swell too quickly. The resulting mush should be the consistency of hot cereal. Turn off the heat. Cover the pot and let stand for about 5 to 8 minutes, then serve. *Serves 4 to 6*

Cherokee Bean Bread

Think of these more as bean dumplings, and you'll come closer to your expectations. The traditional method of preparation is to wrap them in dried corn blades (leaves), but since for many people the leaves are difficult to come by, we suggest another form of bean bread that gets about the same results. Also, we suggest using masa harina in this recipe—a borrowing from the Southwest—because the original version calls for a cornmeal made from hulled dried corn, also difficult to obtain. Masa is essentially that, too, and is available in most supermarkets.

½ cup red kidney beans	*¼ cup masa harina*

Soak the beans in water to cover overnight or until plumped. Drain off the excess water and place the beans in a large saucepan. Cover with water, bring to a boil, then reduce the heat and simmer for about 1 hour, or until tender. Drain the beans and let cool slightly.

Place the beans in a bowl and use a potato masher to crush some but not all of them; your mixture should be a bean mush with large bits of beans remaining. Stir in the masa until the mixture is bound well, then shape into 4 individual balls about 1½ inches in diameter.

Bring a large kettle of water to a boil and drop in the bean breads. Cook for about 30 minutes, or until the balls are soft but not falling apart. Remove from the water with a slotted spoon and serve immediately. *Serves 4*

Indian Tacos

These tacos are a very popular adaptation out West. They combine the spicy Mexican makings for a traditional taco with the chewy crispness of Indian fry bread. Make the fry bread first, then layer your ingredients for the taco.

FRY BREAD

½ cup bread flour	*3 tablespoons water*
½ teaspoon baking powder	*Vegetable oil for deep frying*
Pinch salt	

TACOS

½ medium onion, chopped	*¼ cup water*
1 clove garlic, minced	*½ cup grated iceberg lettuce*
½ pound chopped beef	*1 medium tomato, chopped*
2 tablespoons vegetable oil	*½ cup grated Cheddar or long-*
¼ cup chili powder	*horn cheese*

Combine the bread flour, baking powder, salt, and water in a small bowl and mix well. Knead the dough until soft, then shape it into a ball. Place in a greased bowl and cover. Let the dough sit for 15 minutes.

Pour the oil into a 6-inch skillet until it is about 1 inch deep. Heat to 375°F.

Divide the dough in half and roll each half on a floured surface into a circle about ¼ inch thick. Punch a hole in the center of the circle, then lift the dough up and drop it into the hot oil. Deep fry the bread for 5 minutes, then drain on paper towels. Repeat for the second bread.

While the bread is still warm, make the tacos. Sauté the onion, garlic, and chopped beef in the oil until the meat is no longer pink and the onion is translucent. In small bowl, mix the chili powder with the water, then add the chili mixture to the skillet with the meat.

Place one bread on a plate and top with the meat mixture, the grated lettuce, the chopped tomatoes, and the cheese. Repeat for the second taco. Serve at once. *Serves 2*

THE ANNUAL INDIAN FOODS DINNER is held in Salamanca, New York, the second and third Saturdays of November. You must have advance reservations. There are several seatings, beginning at noon. Tickets (as of this writing) are $7. For information about reservations and tickets, write the Jimersontown Presbyterian Church, 150 Broad Street, Salamanca, New York 14779; or phone (716) 945–1252. Salamanca is at the junction of U.S. 219 and Route 17, about 55 miles south of Buffalo.

The Cherokee Indian Fall Festival is held in Cherokee, North Carolina, in early October. There are a variety of events and competitions every day from Tuesday through Saturday, starting with traditional dancing at 10:30 A.M. All events take place at the fairgrounds, behind the museum. Admission to the festival is $3, which includes parking (museum admission is another $3). Food is sold at individual stands; bean bread costs about 75¢. Cherokee is on the eastern side of Great Smoky Mountain National Park, on U.S. 441, about 50 miles west of Asheville. For information (including a schedule of events), write Cherokee Tribal Travel and Promotion, P.O. Box 465, Cherokee, North Carolina 28719; or phone (704) 497–9195.

The Feast of San Estéban is held September 2 at Acoma Pueblo in New Mexico. Admission to the Pueblo is $3.25, and includes a ride up to the top in a shuttle van. The museum (at the bottom) is free, and parking is in the museum lot. *No cameras are allowed on the feast day.* Food is sold at the top; tamales cost about $1 each. Acoma is off Route 33, about 55 miles west of Albuquerque. For information, contact Pueblo of Acoma Tourism, P.O. Box 309, Pueblo of Acoma, New Mexico 87034; (505) 552–6606.

Bradford Wild Game
Supper

Bradford, Vermont

THE SIGN OUTSIDE the United Church of Christ in Bradford, Vermont, reads, Supper Here Tonight. But the offering inside is no simple covered-dish affair. In November each year, the church raises money by sponsoring its annual Wild Game Supper, featuring such rarities as buffalo, venison sausage, roast boar, and rabbit liver pie. If you've always wondered what 'coon, beaver, or bear taste like, here's your chance. The brochure assures that hunters, too, are welcome—"Come as you are."

Bradford is a picture-book New England town with a wide, tree-lined main street and large clapboard houses that have generous front and side yards. The first Wild Game Supper was held here in 1957, to raise money for a new sidewalk along the south side of the church. Each succeeding year more dishes have been offered, different game ordered, and new recipes prepared. It's grown into a well-run, immensely popular event, with people regularly attending from as far away as New York City and Boston. The supper organizers note that they have had visitors come from at least thirty states and three foreign countries. The first time we attended, we drove six hours from Long Island, ate our dinner, and then drove six hours back home. Before we left, we met a woman who was on her way home to Montreal.

The efficiency with which the supper is run would make a corporate vice-president envious. Reservations must be sent in by the specified date each year, accompanied by a check and your indication as to preferred seating time. Confirmations are sent out, then you need only get yourself to the lovely small town on the third Saturday in November. Usually the roadsides are snowy, and children pull their sleds down the main street. The unmistakable scent of grilling sausages greets you as you get out of your car. When you enter the large white church, you register and are given a number. When your number is called, you go down to eat. To ease the waiting time, Katrina Munn plays tunes on the piano:

"Yes, We Have No Bananas," "I'm Dreaming of a White Christmas," and other old favorites, while the aromas of rich, robust meats get your stomach rolling.

Once downstairs, the serious eating begins. You are handed a heated plate and go on to the buffet line. There the dishes are served in what seem to be infinitesimal portions—till you add them all up! Most meats are prepared in a variety of ways: venison, for example, comes basted, stewed, and in sausages. And there are about eight different meats, not always the same from year to year, but usually including venison, boar, buffalo, bear, 'coon, rabbit, pheasant, and beaver. Sometimes there is Rocky Mountain sheep as well. Each variety of game is identified by a colored toothpick, so that you know what's what. By the time you reach the end of the line, your plate looks like a porcupine. You are handed a card—with a key to the colors and a simple blessing—then ushered to a long table to join others who are already busily under way.

As if you didn't already have a crowded plate, you now must also find room for the cole slaw, squash, and mashed potatoes with gravy. The gravy goes well with the meats, too, since game tends to be rather dry. Cider, milk, and coffee are served; there's no alcohol. Dessert is always gingerbread with real whipped cream.

While you eat family style at the long tables, you'll hear comments like, "This is good; what is it?" Or, "If it's red, it must be the rabbit." Everyone has his or her own technique, as well: Some people dive right in and sample everything all together, whereas others first try the different versions of rabbit, then move on to the boar, then the venison, and so forth. A dining companion from a nearby town summed it up last year: "We don't eat like this every day; it's a little different." Although different it surely is, it is just as surely delicious. We haven't found the meats to be overly gamy or strong-tasting; well, the beaver was a little on the robust side.

As you stagger out, there is one additional temptation—the homemade fudge. We always lay on about a pound of mixed maple nut, chocolate, and chocolate nut to nibble on during the drive home.

The following recipes are adapted from the *Annual Wild Game Supper Cookbook (From Beaver to Buffalo)*, published by the Annual Wild Game Supper, United Church of Christ, Bradford, Vermont 05033.

Wild Boar Sausage

1 pound ground wild boar
1 tablespoon ground sage
2 teaspoons poultry seasoning
1 teaspoon black pepper

2 teaspoons salt
Vegetable oil or other fat for
  frying

Place the meat in a bowl and add the seasonings. Mix well, using your hands to rub the seasonings into the meat. Make into small patties. To fry the sausage, add a little oil or fat to the pan before adding the patties; the meat is very lean and needs the fat to brown properly. Cook the patties on one side for 5 to 8 minutes, then turn and fry on the other side for about 4 or 5 minutes more.   *Serves 4*

Rabbit Pie

The pies at the Game Supper are made in 26-inch pans and serve far more than most cooks are likely to want. Here is a modified version of that recipe, meant for an average family.

2 rabbits (about 1½ pounds each)
1 onion, cut in half
1 stalk celery, chopped

1½ cups biscuit mix
⅓ cup milk

Place the rabbits, the onion, and the celery in a pot and add water to cover. Season with a pinch of salt, then bring the water to a boil. Cover, reduce the heat, and simmer for 1½ hours, or until the meat is tender enough to fall off the bones. Remove the rabbits from the broth; strain the broth, and set aside to cool. Reserve ½ cup of the broth and set aside the remainder for another use.

Preheat the oven to 350°F.

Remove the meat from the bones; you should have about 3 cups rabbit meat. Place the meat in a 1-quart casserole and add the ½ cup broth. In a small bowl, blend together the biscuit mix and the milk. Gather into a ball and roll out on a floured surface with a rolling pin until it is about ½ inch thick. Place the pastry over the rabbit in the pot and seal the edges. Poke a few holes in the top to allow the steam to escape. Bake the pie for 45 minutes to 1 hour, or until the biscuit topping is nicely browned. Serve immediately.   *Serves 4*

Venison Meat Loaf

¾ cup bread crumbs
½ cup milk
1½ pounds ground venison
½ pound ground pork
2 large eggs, lightly beaten
½ cup chopped onion

¼ cup chopped green pepper
1½ teaspoons salt
¾ teaspoon ground sage
¼ teaspoon pepper
½ cup prepared chili sauce
(optional)

Preheat the oven to 350°F.

Soak the bread crumbs in the milk until soft, about 10 minutes. Then add the remaining ingredients and mix well. Pack the mixture into a large loaf pan and bake for 1 hour. If desired, glaze the top with chili sauce during the last 15 minutes   *Serves 4 to 6*

THE BRADFORD WILD GAME SUPPER is held the third Saturday in November. Tickets must be purchased in advance; send your request for information to Mrs. Raymond Green (see below). You will get back a leaflet with instructions for making your reservation, including seating/ serving times and current prices. (In 1985, the dinner was $15 for adults, $7 for children under ten.) The first serving is at 3:00 P.M. The meal is served buffet style in the basement of the Bradford Congregational Church, on Main Street. While you wait to be called, you can sit upstairs in comfortable pews and listen to music. Parking is on the street.

Bradford is off I-91, about midway between White River Junction and St. Johnsbury, Vermont. For information, write to Mrs. Raymond Green, Box 356, Bradford, Vermont 05033.

Bracebridge Dinner

Yosemite National Park, California

*F*OR THE ULTIMATE in food as pageantry, you must go to the Ahwahnee Hotel in Yosemite National Park for their annual Christmas Bracebridge Dinner. Getting here, though, is a matter of chance. There's an elaborate lottery system through which the lucky (one in ten) participants are chosen.

Originally (in 1927, to be exact), a special dinner—"to enhance and dignify the Christmas season for Yosemite guests"—was planned. The following year, a drama director from San Francisco was brought in to produce the first Bracebridge Dinner, a Christmas festival based on *Old Christmas: From the Sketch Book of Washington Irving*. Washington Irving looked at Squire Bracebridge with a humorous eye, in fact a satirical one. But not the San Francisco producer of 1928. As a result, the dinner is played "straight." Since most of the guests don't appear to have read the book, it matters little to them. To us, it was just more fun. For instance, we were called in to dinner by three trumpeters, costumed in bright satin; in the book, Geoffrey Crayon is "in the library, when [he] heard a distant thwacking sound, which . . . was a signal for the serving up of the dinner. The Squire kept up old customs in the kitchen as well as hall; and the rolling-pin, struck upon the dresser by the cook, summoned the servants to carry in the meats."

At the Ahwahnee, the three hundred fifty invited guests gather in the Great Lounge, a room dominated by a gigantic fireplace. Many have celebrated Christmas at Yosemite before; and lots of families consider the Bracebridge Dinner a tradition.

When the trumpets begin, the guests stand, and Squire Bracebridge and his family enter the Lounge, accompanied by a chorus of minstrels. They lead the way into the dining room; the guests follow. The room itself is decorated: banners hang from the rafters, wreaths surround the stained-glass roundels, the tables have centerpieces of red candles encircled with cedar and pine cones. Costumed attendants lead you to your table (previously assigned). The squire and his family sit at a high table set in an alcove at the west end of the dining room. Attendants, servants, waiters, and waitresses sing carols. There are various processions, presentations, music, singing, juggling, and more music throughout the evening.

All of the dishes are first presented to the squire for his approval before being served to the guests. Then—astonishingly—all three hundred fifty guests (at forty-four tables) are served at once.

First is a relish, followed by Hunters Mushroom Soup. Then comes Dover sole. The Peacock Pie is really pheasant pie served in a charming puff pastry made in the shape of a bird. The Boar's Head and Baron of Beef is a roast sirloin cooked perfectly. Luckily all this food is interspersed with singing, dancing bears, and jesters. After the salad comes the Plum Pudding and the Wassail. What Christmas feast would be complete without them? Everyone sings; and then hot mulled wine, cheeses, and coffee are served. It's a meal of many courses and much pageantry—the cast has eighty performers, with lots of work on the part of the staff and lots of fun for the guests. It's formal, but in a comfortable way. The entire production takes nearly four hours. And for that time, one is truly transported.

Peacock Pie

Patterned after the Peacock Pie of the Bracebridge Dinner, this recipe can be made with one pheasant or two game hens.

*3 tablespoons butter or
    margarine
1 pheasant (about 3 pounds),
    quartered; or 2 game hens
    (1½ pounds each), halved
1 medium onion, chopped
1 carrot, chopped*

*1½ cups chopped fresh
    mushrooms
1 tablespoon all-purpose flour
3 cups beef broth or game stock
1 package (17¼ ounces) frozen
    puff pastry
2 tablespoons Cognac*

Melt the butter or margarine in a large Dutch oven and add either half the pheasant or 2 halves of the game hens. Brown the bird over medium-high heat for about 10 minutes, then remove from the pot and add the remaining piece(s). Brown these, then remove and set aside.

Add the onion and carrot to the pot and sauté in the remaining fat until wilted, about 2 minutes. Then add the mushrooms and cook an additional minute or two. Stir in the flour so that it coats the vegetables, then gradually add the broth or stock. Add the pheasant or hens and bring to a boil. Cover and reduce the heat to a simmer. Let cook for 30 minutes, or until the meat is quite tender, almost falling off the bones.

Remove the pheasant or hens from the pot and set aside to cool. Strain the cooking liquid through a sieve, pressing the vegetables to extract as much liquid as possible. Discard the vegetables. Let the puff pastry thaw for 20 minutes. Preheat the oven to 425°F.

Place the cooking liquid in a large saucepan and set over high heat. Bring to a boil, then continue to boil vigorously until the liquid is reduced by about half. This should take about 20 minutes.

When the bird has cooled down, pick the meat off the bones and chop into about ½-inch dice. Add to the pot with the sauce and stir in the Cognac.

When the pastry is soft enough to be worked, roll it out on a hard surface. Cut 8 circles, using a 5-inch cutter (a sharp-edged bowl or wide tumbler), and place 4 of them on a cookie sheet. Cut four 4-inch circles inside the remaining 5-inch circles and use the outer edge to place as rims atop the circles on the cookie sheet. From the remaining scraps, shape tails by making long ½-inch-thick cylinders of dough and cutting them into 1½-inch lengths. Press three or four of these lengths together to make a fan-shaped tail. Roll other portions of the cylinders a little thinner—to about ¼ inch thick—and coil one end like a fiddlehead to make the bird heads. Cut off where the neck would be and shape 3 more coils for the remaining heads. Place the tails and heads on the cookie sheet and bake the pastries for 10 minutes. Watch the baking, because the heads and tails will brown faster than the bodies, and you may have to remove them sooner. When the pastries are done, cut away the inner portion of the bodies to increase the cavity a little more. Save the tops.

Spoon some of the meat mixture into the body of a "peacock," then insert the head and tail, positioning them in the cavity and using the meat mixture to hold them in place. Add a little more meat and sauce and continue for the remining peacocks. Place the tops on the meat mixtures and serve at once.   *Serves 4*

Plum Pudding

Also called Christmas Pudding, this dessert is traditionally served with hard sauce, but at the Bracebridge Dinner a rum sauce is also offered.

*4 tablespoons (½ stick) butter,
    margarine, or suet*
*½ cup each raisins, currants,
    and diced pitted prunes*
¼ cup diced citron
*¼ cup diced candied orange
    rind*
*1 large apple, peeled, cored, and
    diced*
*¼ cup chopped blanched
    almonds*

1 cup bread crumbs
½ cup all-purpose flour
½ cup brown sugar
1 teaspoon ground cinnamon
½ teaspoon ground nutmeg
½ teaspoon ground ginger
1 tablespoon lemon juice
¾ cup orange juice
Dark rum
2 large eggs, lightly beaten

HARD SAUCE

½ cup (1 stick) butter, softened
2 cups confectioners' sugar

1 tablespoon brandy

RUM SAUCE

2 large eggs, separated
½ cup confectioners' sugar

2 tablespoons dark rum

Grate the butter, margarine, or suet into a large mixing bowl. Add the raisins, currants, prunes, citron, orange rind, apple, almonds, bread crumbs, flour, and brown sugar. Stir well, then add the spices and stir again. Moisten the mixture with the lemon and orange juice, then flavor with ½ cup of the rum. Cover the bowl and refrigerate, letting the mixture sit for about 2 weeks. Each day, give the mix a stir, and if it seems a bit dry, add a little more rum—about 1 tablespoonful at a time.

When ready to steam the pudding, mix in the eggs and pour the mixture into 1 large greased pudding basin (3-pound, or 5-cup) or 2 smaller basins (1½-pound, or 2½-cup); we think the 2 smaller ones are easier to deal with. If you don't have pudding basins, use a heatproof bowl that is deeper than it is wide. Cover the basin tightly with foil and set it inside a large pot with water that comes about halfway up the basin. Place over medium heat and bring the water to a boil. When it is boiling, reduce the heat to a steady simmer and let the pudding steam for 6 hours if using 1 large basin, 4 hours for the 2 smaller basins. When the pudding is done, invert it onto a place and cut it into wedges.

To make the hard sauce, cream the butter with the sugar until very smooth and light. Flavor with the brandy and let sit for about 15 minutes before serving. (The hard sauce can be made in advance, but be certain to remove it from the refrigerator about 30 minutes ahead of serving, to allow it to come to room temperature.)

To make the rum sauce, beat the egg yolks with the sugar until they are light and foamy. Separately, beat the egg whites until they form stiff peaks, then fold the yolk mixture into the whites. Flavor with the rum and serve immediately with the pudding. *Serves 8*

Wassail

In his story, Washington Irving describes how the squire's "whole countenance beamed with a serene look of indwelling delight as he stirred this mighty bowl, . . . pronouncing it 'the ancient fountain of good feeling, where all hearts met together.' " Serve this hot drink in a large punch bowl, with the toast slices floating on top.

2 bottles (12 ounces each) English ale
½ teaspoon ground ginger
½ teaspoon ground nutmeg
1 stick cinnamon

1 cup medium-dry sherry
2 tablespoons sugar, or to taste
2 slices plain white bread, crusts removed

Place the ale in a large saucepan and heat until steaming. Add the spices and sherry, then add the sugar to the sweetness desired. Cover the pan and let the mixture simmer very gently for about 30 minutes.

Toast the bread and cut into quarters or sixths. Transfer the punch to a bowl and float the toast on top. *Serves 6*

THE BRACEBRIDGE DINNER is served at the Ahwahnee Hotel in Yosemite National Park, California. There are three sittings: Christmas Eve, Christmas Day, and Christmas Night. Applications for the lottery may be obtained by writing (see below). Directions for entering the lottery are on the application—follow them or you will be disqualified. At the time of this writing the dinner cost $77.50 per person. Wines at dinner are extra; you order them (from a list) when you confirm your reservation and get your table assignment. The wine(s) are at your table when you sit down. No photographs may be taken during the dinner.

You will also need lodging in the park; information about and reservations for rooms accompany the lottery application. There are a variety of accommodations, ranging from $100 a night for a double in the Ahwahnee to $24 for a cabin without bath in Curry Village. A bus takes you from your hotel to the dinner and back. Chains may be required for cars in the park at any time, so phone ahead for information, but be prepared.

Yosemite National Park is about two hundred miles east of San Francisco; in winter your best bet is Route 140 through El Portal. The park itself is so beautiful at that time of year as to vie with the dinner for spectacle. For information about the park, contact Yosemite National Park, California 95389. For a lottery application, write Yosemite Park and Curry Co., Yosemite National Park, California 95389; or phone (209) 373-4171.

Geographical Listing of Festivals

Maps

Recipe Index

Geographical Listing of Festivals

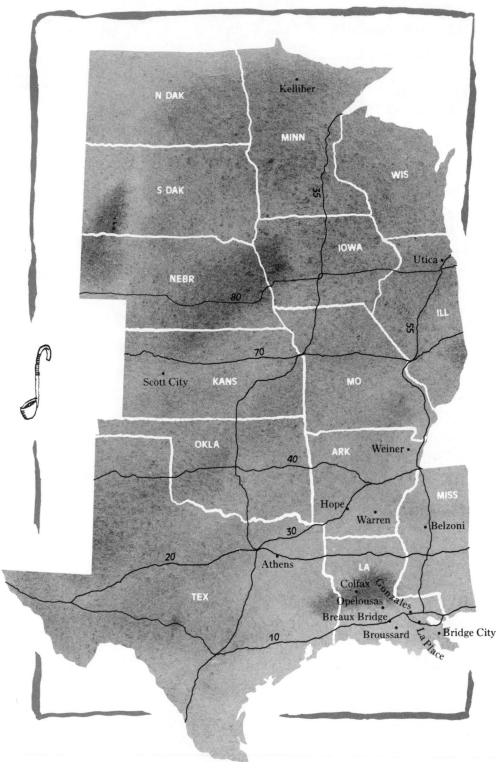

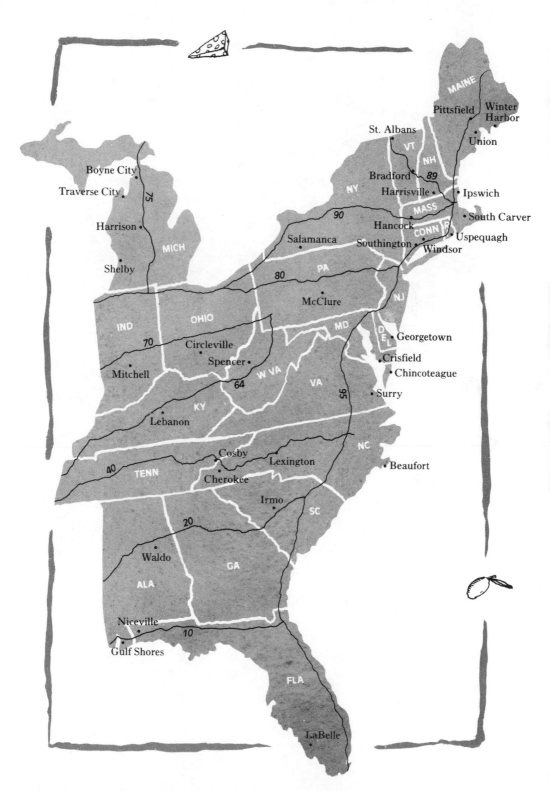

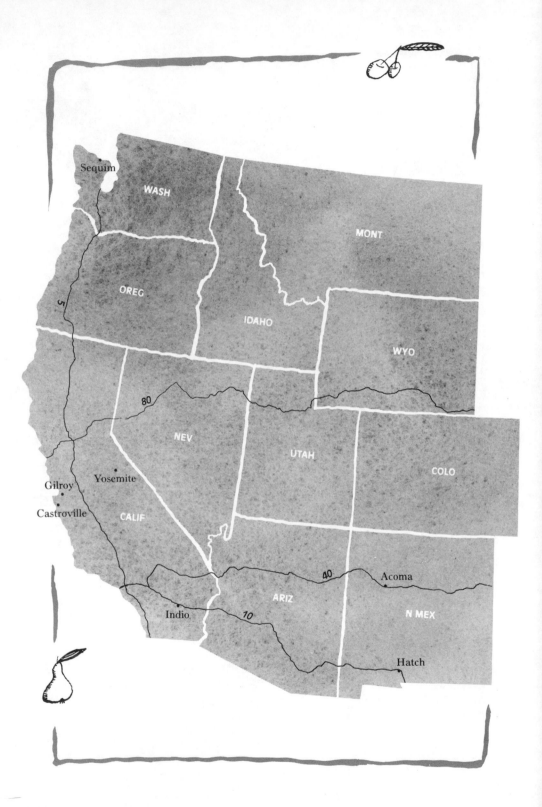

Recipe Index

Andouille: chicken and sausage gumbo, 198; and chicken jambalaya, 229; with red beans and rice, 230

Apple(s): country fried, 170; rings, fried, 174–75; sundae, hot, 174

Artichoke: frittata, 156; hearts, french-fried, 155; soup, cream of, 155–56

Asparagus: quiche, 67; soup, 68; surprise, 69

Bacon and bread crumb sauce, for asparagus, 68

Bean(s): bread, Cherokee, 248–49; Civil War soup, 158–59; green tomato, 57; red, and rice with andouille, 230; maple baked, 20

Beef: burgoo, 206–207; Civil War bean soup, 158–59; garlots, 104–105; green chile con carne, 147–48; green chili burros, 121; home-on-the-range burgers, 120; Indian tacos, 249–50; Kansas barbecue brisket, 120; red chile tamales, 146–47

Black-eyed peas: "Eyes of Texas" salad, 90; and ham, 89

Blueberry: muffins, 134; "pie," 133–34; pie, uncooked, 134–35

Bluefish, pickled, 125

Boudin: blanc, 4–5; hot seafood, 6

Bread: Cherokee bean, 248–49; ghost, 247; Hancock dill, 112; date-nut, 10–11; sweet zucchini, 139–40; two-way wild rice, 84

Burgoo, 206–207

Cake: bourbon-pecan pound, 240; cherry chip Bundt, 80; cranberry sour-cream coffee, 180; date-fudge, 11–12; glazed black walnut ring, 201; heavenly tomato with tomato icing, 59; persimmon upside-down, 167; tart cherry torte, 79

Carrots: Sister Mary's zesty, 113; tomarinated, 58

Catfish fillets, fried, 25

Cheese grits, 214

Cherry: berry pie, fresh, 80–81; chip Bundt cake, 80; torte, tart, with cherry sauce, 79

Chicken: and andouille jambalaya, 229; asparagus surprise, 69; enchiladas with green chile sauce, 145; Gail Tierney's deviled, 52; Harjit Bhatti's chicken korma, 52–53; impossible pie, 53; jambalaya, 63–64; and sausage gumbo, 198

Chile, green: sauce, chicken enchiladas with, 145; con carne, 147–48

Chile, red, tamales, 146–47

Chili burros, green, 121

Chocolate: date-fudge cake, 11–12; heavenly tomato cake with tomato icing, 59

Clams, steamed, 38

Cookies: cranberry, 179; dandy cranberry bars, 178

Corn soup, Seneca hulled, 246–47

Cornbread; jalapeño, 89–90; Tennessee fried, 31; see also Johnnycakes

ABOUT THE AUTHORS

Alice Geffen is the author of many books and has edited and written an introduction to the classic *The American Frugal Housewife*, by Lydia Maria Child.

Carole Berglie is the cookbook editor for Barron's publishing company. She has initiated and overseen the publication of such award-winning cookbooks as *Lenotre's Desserts and Pastries*, *The Joy of Cheesecake*, and *Judith Olney's Entertainments*.